Man with a Lobelia Flute

by the same author
My Travels in Turkey

Man with a Lobelia Flute

A NEW VIEW OF EAST AFRICA

BY

DENIS HILLS

London
GEORGE ALLEN AND UNWIN LTD

PRINTED IN GREAT BRITAIN
in 10 on 12pt Baskerville type
BY THE UNIVERSITY PRESS
ABERDEEN

FOR JOHN RUPERT

GLOSSARY OF SWAHILI WORDS

boma	ring-fence
bure	useless, bad
dawa	medicine, magic
debe	can
duka	shop, store
hapana	no
kali	fierce, cruel, sharp
kanzu	long robe worn by men
kwisha	finished
malaya	whore
maridadi	smart
matoke	steamed mashed plantain
mafuta	fat
mzungu	European
mzuri	good
mzuri sana	very good
polepole	slowly, slowly
posho	maize porridge
rafiki	friend
shamba	farm
uhuru	independence
waragi	distilled alcoholic drink (c.f. *arak*, Arabic)

ACKNOWLEDGMENTS

The author wishes to acknowledge the following for permission to use material:

East African Publishing House Ltd., Nairobi (lines from *Song of Lawino*, by Okot p'Bitek, p. 36); the Editor of *The People*, Kampala (account of Jie raids, pp. 133–4); the Editor of the *Daily Nation*, Nairobi (letter, p. 202); Frank Cass & Co. Ltd. (extracts from *Uganda Memories*, by Sir Albert Cook, pp. 248–9); Macdonald & Co. Ltd. (extracts from *The Desert and the Green*, by the Earl of Lytton, p. 267). I am grateful to my students of the National Teachers' College, Kyambogo, for allowing me to include their writings. The visits paid by Edward Blishen and Veronica Manoukian, of the BBC London, to Kyambogo, greatly encouraged students to go on writing; some of the verse included here has been broadcast on the BBC African Service. Parts of the text of this book originally appeared in *The Times* and *Glasgow Herald*.

PREFACE

A Uganda friend to whom I showed my proof copy of this book told me that some Africans might be offended by the photographs of naked or partly clad people, above all by the apparent preference for out-of-the-way corners of their country. '"Here", they will say, "is another distorted picture of Africa."' (Many Turks, I recall, made a somewhat similar criticism of my book on Turkey. They scanned the material on peasant farmers and Kurds, and said, 'But this is the *old* Turkey!'—as if the old Turkey of small farmers, of mountain herdsmen, and mud walls did not overwhelmingly exist beyond the urban patches of brick and concrete.)

I am tempted to reply that Morukori and Locham are more photogenic than a man in a suit holding a folded newspaper. But the answer to my friend's criticism is that mountain wandering does, in Uganda, take one to the least known and least developed parts of the country, often to its periphery; and that the people I have described—the Teuso with their bare bodies and neck rings, the Suk with their *shuka*-cloths, the Elgon hunter in his skins, the Acholi farmer among his grain bins—were my hosts and travelling companions. How could I ignore them? And why should I? Are not Uganda's magnificent tribal peoples, scattered in their far-away villages and homesteads, worth our praise and attention?

'Very well,' said my African friend, 'but where, in your book, is the modern African without whom your picture is unbalanced? Where are the élite, the educated women, the progressive citizens?' To which I must reply, that this is primarily a travel book. I have not aimed to give an exhaustive picture of African society: rather, a selection of impressions and of tentative conclusions. Nevertheless, it has to be said that the impact on a rural society of a modern town like Kampala (or, in a smaller way, of Mbale) has special and dramatic repercussions. Here large numbers of people from different regions are trying rapidly, in the teeth of economic pressure, to adjust themselves to what for many is an unfamiliar way of life. The anti-social elements that grow out of this situation attract attention and cannot be glossed over.

Finally—the very root, perhaps, of much misunderstanding—there is this frequent nostalgia of Europeans for the countryside. Fugitive from his industrial environment, the expatriate often *prefers* a rural area to work in. People in developing countries, fresh from the rough life of a village, are not likely to share or to sympathise with this attitude. Their bias will be the other way. They will think it woolly sentimentalism (and rightly, too, if it means allowing cattle-owning tribesmen to flout the laws, or conserving a piece of tourist landscape at the expense of some really vital industrial project). The seeds of this problem of outlook are inherent in education at the higher levels. Young Africans ought not to be so drenched with Western syllabuses and with the English language and literature, that they are encouraged to reject their own background—the man with the lobelia flute, the cattle kraal; their own positive traditions and vernacular themes.

Not long ago, on my second visit to Lomwaka, I came to a small cairn of stones on the peak. A soda-water bottle with a scrap of paper in it had

PREFACE

been pushed under the stones. Kalisto and I read the two names written
on it. The late Timothy Bazarrabusa, formerly Uganda's High Commissioner in London, had been there before us. He had looked down at the
same green ridges of the Sudan. He too had enjoyed wandering over the
beautiful hills of his country.

D.C.H.
Kampala
May 1969

CONTENTS

1*

ILLUSTRATIONS

Photographs by the author

PART I

JOURNEYS

CHAPTER 1

Elephants have
right of way

Leaving Turkey

I left Zonguldak, the small Turkish Black Sea coal-mining port
that had been my home for three years, in a wintry drizzle.
The sea, as I drove past a gap in the cliffs, thumped spray
against my windscreen.

On the outskirts of the town I was held up for a few minutes
at a level crossing. A gipsy woman with bare, blackened feet
was picking coals from the railway track. Some old men stared
at me through a tea-house window. No train passed, and when
the crossing-keeper came at last to open the gate, I guessed he
had been prostrated on his prayer mat.

I should probably not see him again; in my overloaded
Volkswagen, and with a yellow fever inoculation certificate in
my pocket, I was off to Africa.

I looked back once towards the violent sea and the cliffs
overgrown with muddy rhododendron thickets. I had usually
left Zonguldak in spring sunshine when black bullocks were
brought out to plough the fields into a brown mat, or in
summer when patches of one-eyed sunflowers waved to me and
the winding dirt road was blocked with farm carts.

Now, as I set off for the last time up the pass that climbs
over the Pontic mountains to the Anatolian plateau, the rain
soon froze into whirling snow flakes. The steep beech forests
were a mass of scabby trunks, and in sheltered places where
winter flowers cluster among moss, the Christmas roses and
pink cyclamen were sealed in a white mantle. Near the top of
the pass a column of lorries was stuck in a snow drift. One of

them had turned over, spilling five tons of groceries into a meadow. The driver and his mate were roasting pieces of meat over a fire.

Ankara had turned livid under its winter pall of lignite smoke, an icy wind blew over the Taurus, and I spent my last night in Turkey under a dingy hotel quilt with my clothes on. I was going to miss the hospitality of these rough Anatolian inns at two shillings a night—and many other things too: the silences and polite arrogance of the Turk, the sour, yellow-crusted yoghourt and innumerable glasses of overbrewed Rize tea, the red gorges, the old temples and forts embedded in sand and wildflowers. But now I had made up my mind to leave, I was impatient to be gone.

It was not until I had entered Syria and dropped down to the Lebanese coast that I left Europe's weather behind. Though snow was sparkling on the ski-runs above Beirut, it was warm enough for me to bathe off the sea front. Beirut had clearly thrived since I had passed through in 1940 when the French were still there. Narrow streets rumbled with ostentatious automobiles. The hotel bars were crowded with Christian Arabs drinking whisky. People had heaped newly manipulated wealth into a small, steep space.

It cost me two offerings of baksheesh to get my car loaded by the Lebanese customs on an Italian ship. We docked at Alexandria after dusk, and with a temporary Egyptian number plate tied with string to my front bumper I set off for the damp, odorous darkness of the Delta. The first Egyptian I spoke to was a respectable looking man in a clean suit of whom I asked the way. He ignored my question, and drew instead a sheaf of pictures—of naked couples copulating behind a flower pot—from his pocket. The encounter was reassuring. It was like meeting again, after long absence, baggage thieves in Naples or Polish labourers drunk on potato vodka at breakfast in Gdynia harbour. I had confirmed a wartime memory—vague, almost unreal—of the touts who used to pester Wavell's soldiers.

I drove towards midnight through Damanhur. A flare showed a man with damaged eyes crouched by a barrow, and there was an overpowering smell of rotting oranges and scorched horse dung. Several times I tried to doze by the wayside but was roused by fingers rapping the car windows and faces that peered hideously at my belongings. Dawn—an enormous flamingo-coloured flush—revealed fields of emerald clover, children defecating in a ditch, men scurrying along canal paths on strong white donkeys.

Soon the sun was shining on the pale sands of Qassassin and Tel-el-Kebir. They were unfamiliar to me, now, without their wartime clouds of tentage. By midday I was searching the quays of Port Said for a ship.

'Nasser's Egypt', an official assured me, 'is a much better country than it was in your time.' Nevertheless I had to part with a lot more baksheesh before the customs police would permit me, at the last moment, to be rowed out after dark to *La Bourdonnais*, a French passenger ship bound for Mauritius. I was shown into a cabin with a whirring fan. At last, after the austerities of provincial Turkey, and a glimpse of the old nightmare quality of Egypt, I could relax (at British government expense) in a comfortable hotel steering towards the equator.

La Bourdonnais

The Indian Ocean was steel-blue, the sun rode high, sharks like torpedoes glided about the ship. I had Karen Blixen's *Out of Africa* to read, and—a curious find in a Beirut shop—Martin Green's *A Mirror for Anglo-Saxons* with its doleful opening words ('All England has an unfortunate air of being preserved—a mild green gherkin in cloudy spirits . . .'), its gibes at the English gentleman ('he has outlived his usefulness'), and its unforgettable description of the new type of 'essential Englishman' ('He is small, neat, quick-moving, with a fresh-coloured, neat-featured, unemphatic face, without physical stateliness, wheeling a bicycle, carelessly dressed, open-necked, plain-mannered, shrewd, sceptical, friendly-jeering in tone . . .').

I scanned the adjectives with disquiet. None of them, I hoped, fitted *me*. Mr Green evidently had someone else in mind; some youth hosteller, perhaps, some Peace Corps type, or accountant's clerk. And yet—there was that reference to a bicycle, and to the inelegant shirt . . .[1]

There was one inconvenience to the drowsy days: the coolest part of the boat deck was occupied by a dozen incontinent dogs in kennels which they were slowly battering to pieces. When their owners, with cries of affection, came to lead the dogs out for exercise, they fouled the space round my deck chair. I cuffed them behind their masters' backs. In Turkey, where dogs are considered unclean, I had got out of the habit of thinking of them as pets.

Christmas—and the Equator—were only a week ahead. I dreaded having to face those burning spears of heat and light with a hangover thumping behind my ears. But I needn't have worried. The mainly French Catholic and Indian passengers celebrated quietly. There was midnight mass conducted by a Belgian White Father in a creased soutane, a vast spread of cold meats and ice cream, soft music and paper hats—but no false noses and no Anglo-Saxon horseplay. The only casualty was an elderly businessman from Lancashire, who woke on Boxing Day tormented by gout. 'I must have sprained it,' he lied, looking miserably at his swollen foot.

I was gathering scraps of curious advice. 'Among Africans,' a young Ismaili student from Dar-es-Salaam told me, 'say "Jambo" frequently. Make jokes. Don't show anger. When in doubt buy them a beer.'

'Don't get stuck on the road at night. Carry a gun,' said a Frenchman from Madagascar.

'Keep away from water,' warned the Belgian White Father, 'otherwise you may catch bilharzia and pass blood for the rest of your life.'

'Beware of car thieves,' everyone said. 'Luckily, with a left-

---

[1] The passage reminded me, vaguely, of something I had once read by Gerald Brenan. I have looked it up (*The Face of Spain*) but find that what Brenan wrote on returning to England after long residence in Spain was 'I see all about us a throng of plain, rounded faces that lack the distinction of real ugliness. Faces like puddings . . . smooth vegetable faces . . . placid cow-like faces. . . . Yet there is kindness and good humour in their little bird-like eyes. . . . My Spanish-conditioned faculties tell me that this is a sensible, fair-minded, humorous people. But not a beautiful or a dynamic one.' There is of course a reference to the weather. 'A thin rain is falling, there is a smell of macintoshes . . . the stars came out faintly, as if wrapped in overcoats.'

hand drive your car will be less attractive to them. Sooner or later, though, you're bound to have the wheels stolen.'

'In that get-up,' said the Lancashire businessman, looking at my white shorts and stockings, 'the natives will take you for a policeman or a white settler. You're asking for trouble.'

I watched the tawny hills and the faint, feathery palms of the coast slip by, and felt impatient to touch one.

Mombasa

We came to Mombasa at night: a few winking lights, a bright orange flare from the oil refinery, pale stars in strong moonshine.

I had already, at Djibouti, set foot on the African shore. I had walked, in fact, the eight long, unshaded miles to Djibouti town centre and back. I had seen a crow on a garbage heap, a pale, overweight Frenchman wearing a leather belt, and some Somalis with stick-like legs. All I had gained from the experience were the jeers of taxi drivers, a sweaty shirt, and a gaudy picture postcard of a Somali warrior.

Mombasa, after Djibouti, was large and splendid. But there is lethargy in its soft, warm air. The new Kilindini dock installations are magnificent. No one, however, during the New Year hiatus seemed willing to operate them. It took me three days to clear my car through a hierarchy of British, Indian and African officials, which seems to show that baksheesh works quicker than honest red tape.

Mombasa strikes one as almost more Asian than African. Indians and Arabs control most of its business, own the shops, and stock everything from Japanese cameras to waste-paper baskets made from an elephant's foot.

Muslim Africans throng the poorer quarters. Their women are muffled and plain. The dingy shrouds they have to wear do not—and are presumably not meant to—suit them. Those black sheets are the crow-like garb of an oriental discipline. The beauty of African women lies in their bold, smiling faces, in bare and gleaming limbs set off by the brightest colours. (How drab, too, they look in a grey London street, with the dark, preoccupied face and stockinged legs sticking out of a winter coat.)

After work, Indians with their handsome wives in saris and their dark-eyed children inundate streets and gardens, trailing a sweet odour of hair grease. At nightfall, like the cockroaches, slim chocolate-brown half-caste girls come out, followed by pimps in white shirts, and dishevelled seamen roam the bars.

My hotel was full of British families regretfully quitting Kenya for ever. One tough old Englishman of eighty, who had lived for fifty years in a lonely place far to the north of Nairobi, told me sadly that he had been bought out, as a 'security risk', by the government. He wore khaki shorts and had immensely thick arms and legs. He had soldiered against von Lettow-Vorbeck. He made jokes but was grieving. 'I'm being sent back to England to die,' he said.

He had booked a cheap passage home on a British cargo boat, whose captain he introduced me to. The captain, as we drank beer under a flamboyant tree, made one outrageous remark 'All Indian men', he pronounced, 'are impotent when they are forty.'

I asked him to explain himself. 'Well,' he said, 'how would you feel if you had poked your wife twice a day for over twenty years?'

I spent much of my time at nearby Nyali. Here, in a lagoon formed by a coral reef, the Indian Ocean lies sluggish, warm and grey against a bolster of coconut palms. The beach for over a mile was monopolised by Kenya Europeans and British servicemen with blistered backs. A cool sea breeze blew over soft coral sand as white and fine as chalk dust.

But there were flaws. One could swim only at high water, and then, in the late afternoon when the tidal broth came streaming over the reef, it turned temporarily black—as if tea leaves had been emptied into it—with gouts of swirling seaweed trapped within the lagoon. At low tide visitors unscrupulously scoured reef and rocks for shells.

Europeans learned early to appreciate this still beautiful coast. Sir Frederick Jackson has described his hunting trips there in the 1880s, the stench of old Lamu, the strange dugong, the lonely orange creeks, the shore birds and dhows.[1]

Today many parts of the seventy mile coast line running north of Mombasa to Malindi are planted with military rows of

[1] For a note on Jackson's memoirs, see Annotated Book List.

sisal. But along coves and sandy beaches Europeans have built delightful hideouts for retirement, holidays and sport. Their bungalows peer behind casuarinas, coconut palms and frangipani. The package tourists from Switzerland and Germany pass them by. From sun-whitened verandas you can watch the sea leap over the reef, look across a creek mouth crowded with herons and with mangrove trees whose claw-like roots, sparkling with tiny shells, are washed purple by the tide. In moonlight the white beaches pulsate with sandcrabs with little eyes on stalks, and clustered seaweed scuffles in the wind like scraps of burnt paper. With very little effort you can catch your own speckled parrot- or crawfish for lunch. A Giryama houseboy wearing a length of striped cloth will cook it for you.

I did not know this then. I was feeling a little depressed by my warm bath in seaweed, and by the shell hunters.

Nairobi

I had come to East Africa with an open mind. My impressions, however, would for a time be coloured by my eight years in Turkey. I would notice at first what was different: the Englishness of hotel food (no bitter sheep-cheese for breakfast, no pine kernels in the rice), the cheerfulness of Africans, their love of beer, the absence of prudery among their women (the Turk is grave, he will brood for an hour over a glass of water, and the vast majority of his women—their forbidden flesh still wrapped and bloomered—are inhibited by a Puritanical discipline).

I would notice too the splendid municipal golf courses (Turks would have grazed cows on them), the absence of horses and carts (the poorer African uses a bicycle, which, like an Arab his donkey, he loads with wife, bags of cotton, *matoke* plantains), stout white men wearing shorts (anathema to Turkish male dignity).

So with two dozen sweet bananas and a warning from the A.A. that elephants had right of way, I started for Kampala over 700 miles to the north-west.

The country at first is dotted with huts and plantations shaded by mangoes. There are rows of coconut palms and fiery patches of tulip tree. Bare-breasted women were plodding homeward, wearing skirts made of lengths of coloured cotton, the buttocks bolstered by wads of twisted cloth.

Then, after twenty five miles, interminable thorn bush set in, festooned with black galls. Palms gave way to baobob trees— obese, gigantic, hung with big woody fruits and sometimes with a beehive made from a hollowed log, or a rough shelter like a stork's nest for boys herding cattle. The road soon lost its tarmac and turned into a ribbon of hard *murram* clay, rutted and knobbly after recent rain.

This was the sort of wild and empty country which the nineteenth-century explorers and early foot travellers would still have recognised, a dry, discouraging moonscape of shimmering scrub rolling towards ochre escarpments and silent black hills.

From the scrub pricking the red road, troops of baboons grimaced at me before diving like dogs into cover. I drove past an elephant, a mud-stained hulk with tiny eyes, ripping a tree. A warthog ran out of a thicket, and there was a clamour of birds—clumsy looking hornbills and squawking guinea fowl, francolins and gaudy starlings. I was passing through the fringe of Tsavo game park.

I stopped to make an early morning round of part of the park, but my excursion was unprofessional and brief. Zebra and giraffe peered at me through tall grass. From a cabin beside a pool I looked at a family of hippopotami, and a crocodile inert under a warning notice. Some Germans who had parked nearby were feeding small monkeys with scraps of *Schinkenbrot*. Then at a look-out post I joined an Italian honeymoon couple. They were staring at an elephant that had been focused, half a mile away, in the lens of a fixed telescope operated by an African ranger in a fez. The elephant in its reddish coat of mud was so still and nicely placed, it might have been a dummy. Dominating the western horizon, Kilimanjaro stuck its snow cap into a thundery sky.

By the time I was back at the park entrance near Mac's Inn, I already suspected that organised staring at animals was not going to suit me. The atmosphere struck me as not quite right. One was car-bound—a ticket holder viewing wild life from a seat. Too many others were doing exactly the same thing. At the end, instead of a camp fire under Orion's dagger, there was a hotel lounge where one read the overseas edition of the *Daily Mirror*.

I bumbled slowly along the Nairobi road, for I wanted to enjoy, alone, the detail that escapes the motorist in a hurry: a giraffe, its patterned neck stretched like a great rubber spout, tugging at acacia leaves; pied kingfishers diving into a pool. It was delightful to recognise the trumpeting hornbills, a giant monitor lizard, and bush buck, from memories of old picture books.

I stopped frequently, and sometimes from the apparently deserted bush a naked boy would emerge and stare silently till I had gone, hoping I would leave behind something of value— an empty bottle, a tin, some scraps of bread. Then, not far from Hunter's Lodge, the thick scrub began to dwindle to open country dotted with thorn trees. Near Nairobi the corrugated dirt road merged again into tarmac.

It was Sunday afternoon. Nairobi in its garish jacket of bougainvillea had a drowsy air. The parking bays, crammed to exasperation on work days, were empty. Along side streets a few patient Indian faces were framed in the doorways of grocers' shops. Motorists seemed irritable, ignoring traffic signs and charging the roundabouts.

Above this garden city, which straggles into waste ground, the roadside becomes a track for stocky Kikuyu women humping loads secured to a headstrap. Then suddenly—for I had quite forgotten about the Rift—I was braking at the edge of an escarpment, and found myself looking down into a great gap in the earth's surface, a vast arena smoking with haze and dust. A startling sight to come across round a bend in a suburban road!

But, when I stopped, boys ran up with raffia ware. So I spiralled down into this huge geological fault which splits East Africa in two, and turned off the highway to Lake Naivasha.

The lakeside hotel was run by an elderly British couple who complained they had just been violently robbed. An English

23

customs official from Mombasa told me gloomily, 'The axe is falling. I shall be on my way home in a fortnight.'

'African governments,' he went on, 'want new men—the type who will say "Yes, sir."' He gave me a look. Was I one of the new weaklings? By his standards I probably was. At any rate I was not wearing tight trousers or winklepickers.

I put up my camp bed under some trees near the flooded lake side and was roused early by the splashing and crying of hundreds of water birds. I took out my bird book. Those long-legged fowl ferreting among the papyrus beds were purple gallinules. The bird with the big yellow bill and bare red face was a painted ibis. There were pelicans, white-breasted cormorants, and dabchicks. A fish eagle threw up its great white head like a bugler to utter a penetrating cry. Fat humpless cattle herded by an African with torn ears were coming out to graze the dewy grass. Weavers' nests swung like Christmas decorations on the acacias.

From here through the mauve jacaranda shadows of Nakuru, up and over the western edge of the Rift and into the White Highlands, I drove across wide cattle-ranching country sprinkled with plantations of imported trees—Monterey pine, cypress, eucalyptus. The night air at Molo, where I slept at the edge of a copse, was so chilly that I had to wrap myself in my old Turkish quilt. Standing on the Equator—it is marked by a painted signboard giving the altitude (9,109 feet)—I was buffetted by a cold wind. In Eldoret Europeans wore pullovers.

No wonder British settlers seized on these cool, delightful highlands for their Arcadia. They have created an astonishingly homely atmosphere with their British beef and dairy herds, their brick and timber farmsteads with a gate and the owner's name on a board, their beautiful gardens, golf links, and shopping centres with flower and newspaper shops. In the big brick fireplaces, logs are lit at night, and there is bacon and eggs for breakfast.

Along the roads, between the eucalyptus and the pines, drive pink, beefy men and British wives with shopping bags (though not often in British cars, for the Volkswagen and Peugeot are preferred). I felt there was something incongruous about it all. I realised that I had not expected to find so many tubby

Europeans leading familiar, workaday lives on the Equator. My image of tropical Africa was temporarily shattered by this oddly feudalised extension of the British countryside. I resented the shopping bags, the sausage rolls and buns, the James Bond paperbacks and books on rose-growing stacked among the London newspapers.

It was obvious, too, that immense labour, skill and capital have been expended in transforming this wild grassland into profitable farms. Where the European farmer has big tractor-ploughed fields, and produces milk enough to feed much of Uganda as well as Kenya, the local African villager is generally still scratching at a plot which grows barely enough maize for his porridge and beer.

From Eldoret the last eighty miles of road through Kenya to the Uganda border petered out in *murram*. I drove in a spray of brick-red dust and small flying stones, with the long misty ridge of Elgon darkening the northern skyline.

At the Uganda border there was no control post—a relief, after those morose policemen who for years had scowled at me across the barriers of Eastern Europe and the Middle East. The tarmac recommenced, and at the Rock Hotel, Tororo, where a waiter in a purple fez was playing darts with an English schoolboy, the portions of food were enormous. A Muganda official at the bar assured me I should be happy in Uganda. 'The atmosphere,' he said, 'is more relaxed than in Kenya. We like Europeans. You are our guests, not settlers. As for the game parks, you can drive right up to crocodiles—almost touch them!'

Kampala

Now that I had left the high Kenya plateau with its northern conifers standing black in the sharp air against open farm-land, the sun struck fiercely through purple thunder clouds on the dark skins of Basoga villagers, and banana groves waved ragged fronds over fiery red earth.

Beyond the sugar plantations of Jinja, where the Nile is squeezed at its source through a concrete trap, plantain eaters were landing with cackling cries on tall evergreens. The plump

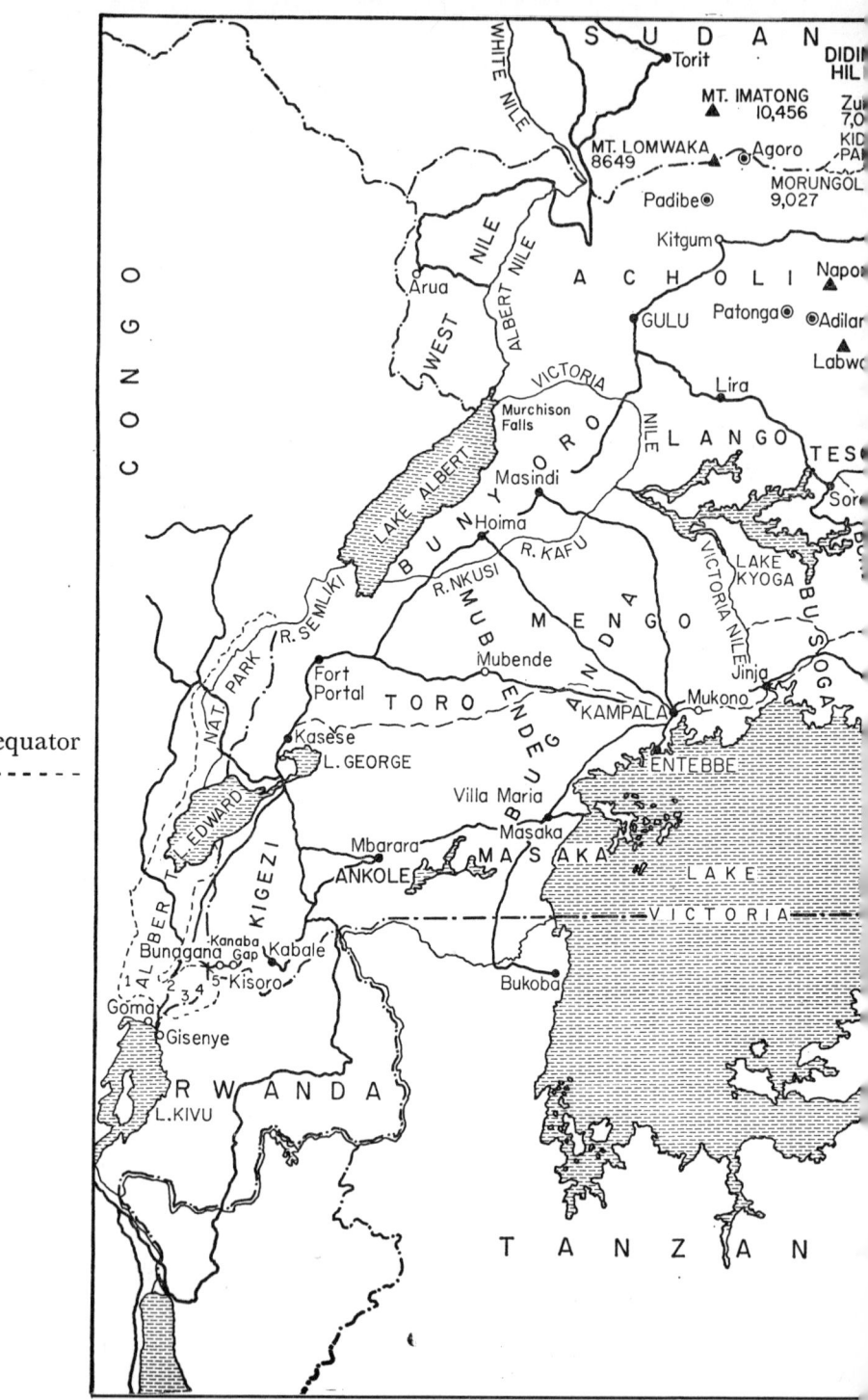

The numbers refer to the Virunga (Mufumbiro) range of mountains on the Co...

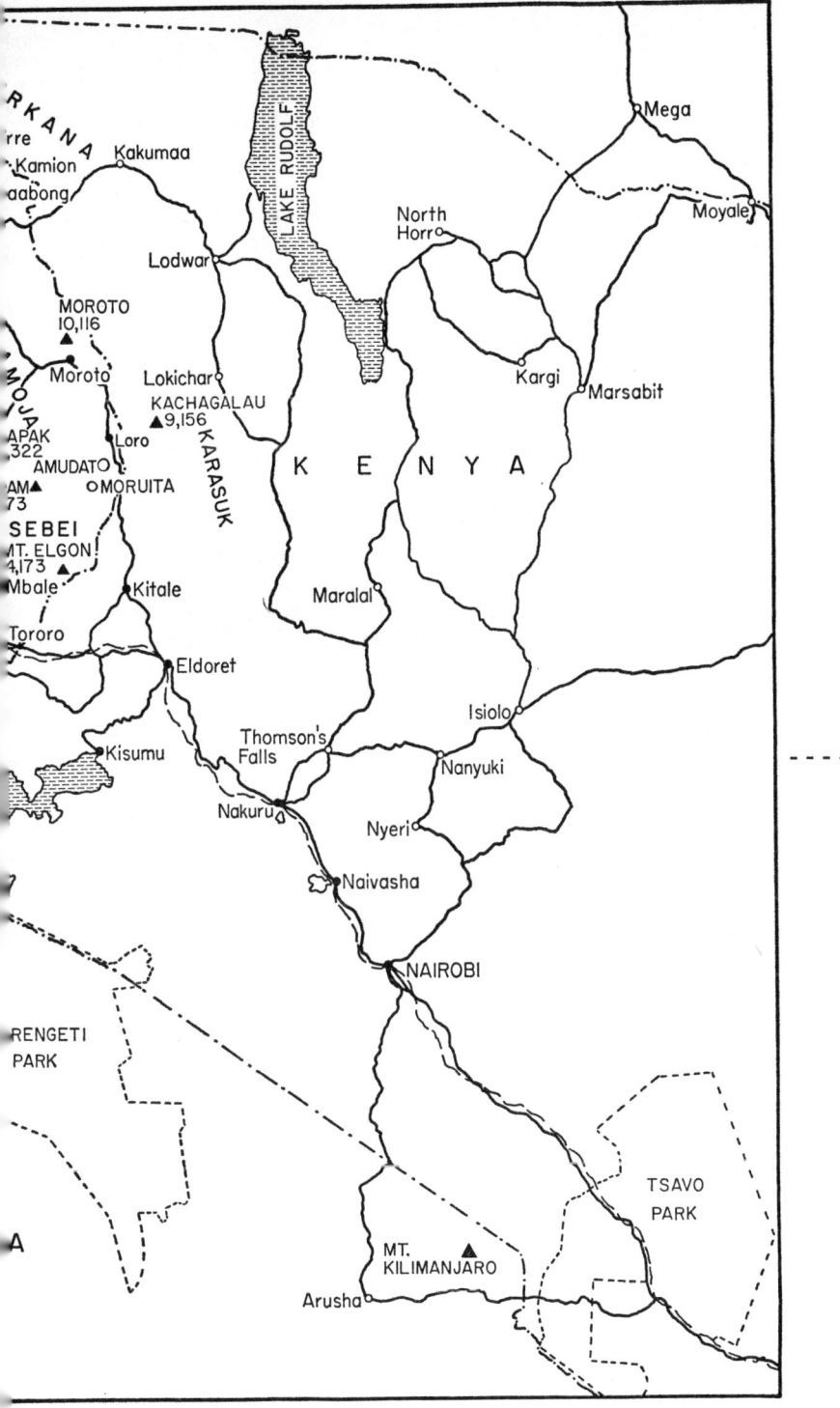

anda border 1. Nyamuragira, 2. Nyiragongo, 3 Karisimbi, 4 Sabinio, 5 Muhavura

and smiling women gliding under head loads like sleep-walkers, hands outstretched for balance, looked magnificent in their trailing robes of vivid primary colours. I recalled the haggard Kikuyu women trudging with bent backs near Nairobi. Was it the banana diet or the soft, humid air that gave these Baganda women their glossy skin and plump, rolling bodies?

When I came to Kampala, thunder was growling round its grassy hills and gusts of wind were scattering the cassia blossom. I went into a café. I had stains of sweat on my shirt. The Greek next to me was picking his teeth with a fork. No one took any notice of me.

I had been ten days in Africa and had seen an elephant at close quarters and some giraffes. I had driven eighty miles through a downpour that I thought would bog me down in a stream of red mud. I had glimpsed the snow cap of Kilimanjaro. I had crossed the source of the Nile on a concrete bridge with a small rainbow in its spray, and I had seen vast fields of sugar-cane shining like bushels of burnished spears. I had eaten two dozen bananas at one farthing each. And I had spent five days over a journey that most people did in two days in a rush of flying stones and dust.

The sky began to flush. Suddenly I noticed the fruit bats, thousands of them, drifting like smuts from a smoking chimney across the dying radiance of the sun.

When I drove next morning to Makerere College I saw the bats again, hanging now like bunches of blackened bananas in a line of eucalyptus trees, quarrelling, screeching, blindly fluttering among the fouled leaves. Some American tourists were photographing them through the roof of a zebra-striped safari van.

CHAPTER 2

Kampala (1)

Settling In

I had been appointed to Kampala as an Education Officer after interview at the old Colonial Office.

An undignified moment had preceded the interview. I had gone to an underground lavatory at Marble Arch to change my shirt, lost my way in the hideous tiled labyrinth that led me there, and when at last I arrived, had found the toilet occupied by two Liverpool Irishmen, both drunk, waiting for a victim.

'Give us that shirt, mate,' they said as soon as I opened my travelling bag. One of them held up a beer bottle, the other an open razor.

I decided to play it cool. 'Look,' I said, 'I need this shirt. I've got a date with the Government.'

The fellow with the razor stepped closer. ''and it over,' he repeated.

We stood looking at each other. This was no time for me to be gashed.

'Your hand's shaking,' I said, 'you'll cut yourself.'

He lifted the razor.

'Piss off,' I said.

The razor-man hesitated. Then his friend with the bottle sniggered. 'Leave 'im alone, Ted,' he said.

'You're all right, mate,' they added grudgingly. We all began to laugh.

The two retired civil servants from the Gold Coast, who interviewed me half an hour later in a cubicle, asked me a few gentle questions. Why had I chosen Uganda in preference to Kenya? Was I prepared to work under an African principal? What were my hobbies?

'You are', one of the interviewers suggested towards the end, 'rather old. Most of our applicants for a first job in the tropics are young graduates.'

There followed a silence.

'Still,' the other put in helpfully, 'an older man often knows how to take care of himself better than the young fellows.'

I hoped, silently, this was true, and left. Whatever the outcome of this gentle confrontation I had done my best: a fresh shirt, hair cut, and conventional shoes. Perhaps the fading aura of a 1930s degree in ethics and monetary theory would still count in competition with Hull and Stafford.

Now, arrived six months later in Kampala with no exact knowledge of what I had to do, I found I was to help run an emergency teacher-training scheme for African students who had not done well enough at school to enter Makerere University College, but were urgently needed to fill gaps in African secondary schools. The course had just begun and was temporarily using the Institute of Education's buildings at Makerere, where, inevitably, some of the permanent staff made it clear they considered us to be poor relations.

I was introduced to my colleagues, warned against burglars and car thieves, advised never to address servants as 'boy', and given an advance of pay with which to open a bank account.

While search was made for a government flat, I was put up at the Speke Hotel. I soon got to know its few permanent residents, among them an alcoholic half-Greek lady whose job—for her a maddening one—was to count freshly minted coins in a locked bank room, and a young sewage expert from Padua who wore highly polished mosquito boots (he once leaned over and stroked my arm. 'Very rough skin,' he said. 'Just put your hand on an African lady. Very smooth and cool. Like snake.')

Sitting near the bar were usually two or three African girls with straightened hair and tight skirts that revealed knees burnished with oil. They ate hearty breakfasts of pawpaw, cereals, and ham. They looked healthy and clean. Their profession was love-making.

They were not the only women haunting the hotel, with its attractive odour of rich food, its two bars and moneyed guests. An inferior sort of tart paced the pavements outside while their pimps watched at a distance. Whoever you might be—American Ambassador or clergyman in mufti—their white teeth flashed an invitation out of the frangipani shadows.

Kampala View

I explored Kampala, whose heart is a long shopping street lined with buildings of haphazard growth. The Indian-dominated commercial centre spreads outwards along a jumble of side roads to the surrounding hills where the suburbs are pitched. These hills split the city into semi-separate sections that diversify the residential pattern and give a skyline whose landmarks embody much of Uganda's recent history and her mixed racial character.

To orientate oneself one should stand on a high point, on the green grass of Old Kampala hill, for instance. The puzzle then takes shape, with the new industrial area seen to be tucked away at one end of the urban axis, Makerere College at the other. To the west on Rubaga hill rise the twin towers of the Roman Catholic cathedral founded by the French Algerian Mission of the White Fathers. Its altar painting, of Africans being burned alive on faggots, commemorates an episode which the Catholic Church especially never tires of recalling—the martyrdom of the first native converts, who rather than recant, submitted to being put to death horribly by Mwanga, Kabaka of Buganda, in 1886.[1]

Namirembe hill, nearby, which was allotted to the CMS—they reached Buganda in 1877, a year before the White Fathers—supports a squat, domed Anglican cathedral. An earlier thatched building was struck by lightning and burned down in 1910.

In its burial ground are the graves of men well known in their time: Bishop Hannington, murdered on his way into Buganda in 1885, Alexander Mackay, leader of the first Protestant Mission (died of fever 1890), Captain Raymond

[1] See Faupel in Annotated Book List.

Portal (died of fever 1893), and Sir Albert Cook, pioneer doctor of the CMS hospital (died 1951).[1]

Old Kampala hill overlooks the trough where the commercial centre is concentrated. This is the green knoll where Captain Lugard, in 1890, built a fort (since dismantled) on behalf of the British East Africa Company, and where Sir Gerald Portal, in 1893, hoisted for the first time the Union Jack.

Facing Old Kampala hill, east of the commercial centre, Nakasero and Kololo hills have been set aside as a retreat for Europeans, prospering Indians who have built their own houses, and—especially since Uhuru—the rapidly growing number of African civil servants.

The red roofs of their bungalows peep through hedged gardens and flowering trees that are noisy with crows and starlings. The town centre immediately below is seen to be a medley of cubes and rectangles with shoddy roofs, dazzling white when the sun is on it, the uncompleted nucleus of what is still, despite encroaching tentacles of congestion and slums, a garden city embedded in a countryside of banana groves and coffee blossom.

Muslim mosques, Sikh and Hindu temples, churches of different Christian orders, and Baganda tombs, symbolise the variety of peoples who live in Kampala. They reflect their rivalries and their tensions, their different Gods, codes and colour. They represent too what has been so far a surprisingly successful experiment in multi-racialism.

Entebbe

I had been moved meanwhile into a government flat on Kololo hill. Looking for somewhere cool, I tried Makerere College swimming club. The first member I spoke to was a bald, very brown man from Birmingham, who was lying on a bank eating hard-boiled eggs. He had a bluish, cone-shaped eruption on top of his head. Sweat had collected in trickles on his back. 'This', he said, cracking a small and rather dirty native egg, 'is my idea of gracious living.'

---

[1] For notes on these men see Annotated Book List.

The tropics are not generally kind to sunbathers. I soon found that to sit for long in the sun is more enervating than moving about in it. Here in the city, when the sun shines through moist haze, the white man's skin turns red, then yellow. When the sun bursts through afternoon thunder cloud it strikes like a hot iron, as though the very sky were boiling. On a bright, clear day glare frays the temper. Yet in the shade it is always delightfully cool.

Africans sensibly avoid the fierce heat of the sun unless they have very pressing work to do. At home, in gardens and villages, they like to sit outside their dwellings in the early morning, while the women dress their hair, and again as dusk comes on, when men gather round their beer pots and the women fetch water to sluice down their children and cook the evening meal.

The Indian covets a fair skin and sees no point in darkening it by exposure. It is the white man, conscious of his pallor in this penetrating equatorial light, who wants to be brown.

The swimming pool was popular with mem-sahibs. Their teenage children on holiday from schools in Kenya or England smoked cigarettes, used four-letter words, and littered the changing room with elastic-sided winklepickers. Peeping through the walls surrounding this chlorinated tub, African housemaids and their children gaped when English tots jumped off the diving board and swam about with the ease of tadpoles.

At Entebbe, twenty miles away on the edge of the vast Victoria lake, one swims at the risk (a few Europeans and many Indians ignore it) of getting bilharzia. A pity, for on a hot day the blue water lapping against a green shore is tantalising. A cool lake breeze regularly disperses the fierce midday heat, and the splash of tiny waves gives one the impression of being by the sea.

On a strip of silvery sand I read Speke's *Journal* and Canon Roscoe on the fat wives of Ankole who, he says, were so obese (they were kept on a milk diet and forbidden to work) that they could scarcely stand and had to be moved about on litters. I

2

read too about the lions that used to eat railwaymen, and of Mackay's troubled life at the Kabaka's court.[1]

I still go to the lakeside to read. No one disturbs me on my patch of sand. Only the scream of the fish eagle rings at intervals, like a shrew scolding, out of the sky. Gulls and egrets scatter as the great chestnut-tinted bird sails by. Even the drowsy hammerkop is put to flight.

Sometimes an air-liner comes low over the airport fence, a screaming silvery juke-box, chasing birds from the runway— the grey herons suddenly transformed from snake-necked silhouettes into flying hunchbacks, crested cranes disappearing with their legs trailing and heads haloed by a straw-coloured crown of bristles.

Then, as the sun begins its steep fall, some village women come to fill petrol cans with water. As they stoop they point their buttocks sharply upward, in the African way. They carry the cans on their heads, gliding away over the tussocks with their wet legs gleaming like polished sticks. About this time, an Englishman, released from an office, trots by throwing stones for his dog.

At week-ends the lake-shore peace is shattered, for scores of mainly Indian families drive out from Kampala with bottles of Pepsi-Cola and transistor sets tuned in to wailing music from Nairobi.

African boys bathe naked in the lake. Indians are more prudish. The waist-deep immersion has the nature of ritual. The Sikh, having placed his turban on the sand, floats gravely in baggy underpants and a biblical tangle of hair that streams from his top-knot. Girls are made to keep their skirts on in the water, women their robes. When the bath is over there is an embarrassed scramble into the back of a van.

The outward modesty of Indian women is part of their charm. Their inhibitions, though, make them sly as well as shy.

When the week-end crowd is away, there are many birds about, egrets stepping delicately among the breaking wavelets, pale-breasted cormorants, pelicans that sail in line like a squadron of paper boats and come circling home like toy bombers, anvil-headed hammerkops feeding silently in sedge.

[1] For notes on these writings see Annotated Book List. For the lions, see Patterson.

Pied kingfishers, with big beaks stuck like bayonets on their small, sturdy bodies, flutter and dive constantly over the water's edge. A sharp-eyed kite banks and then circles me with its shadow, hoping to snatch a cheese sandwich from my hand.

The lake shore slopes upward in green banks to red-roofed bungalows hidden among mangoes and hibiscus. In the botanical gardens, among labelled trees, black ayahs are wheeling pink children in prams. Below the hotel there is a fragment of Surrey: a cricket field with weathered sight-screen, a golf course to prepare members for their first sundowner.

Crocodiles and sleeping sickness (which almost depopulated the northern shore of the lake at the turn of the century) have long disappeared.[1] Now a tamed lake-side, merging hazily into cumulus cloud and wooded blue islands through which the equator runs, gives air-travellers to Uganda their first glimpse of 'Darkest Africa'.

Bars

The City Bar, I was told, used to be an exclusively European meeting place where Englishmen drank, bawled out insular songs and jokes, and stumbled against the snooker table. Now, like any other café-bar in Kampala, Africans frequent it as much as Europeans. Here gather Mill Hill Fathers without their dog collars, African officials, a Japanese expert in the manufacture of fish nets, schoolmasters, and painted tarts whose thighs, squeezed into skin-tight skirts, broaden immensely from the slender legs.

I met here a Scottish veterinary officer employed at the slaughter-house. 'Africans', he told me, 'may look strong but they've no guts, no stamina. It's the poor diet and worms. . . .' Was this truth or prejudice?

Another Scotsman—with a ragged beard and wide khaki shorts—introduced me to his 'little Nandi wife'. She had no conversation but knew her duty, which was to get him home when the bar closed. He was slowly killing himself with bouts of drinking that left him trembling and speechless.

[1] See Sir Hesketh Bell in Annotated Book List.

35

I have met since then a dozen Europeans with African 'wives'. It would not be fair to say they drink more heavily than others. Perhaps, though, they do more of their drinking in public bars. Certainly they seem a little scruffier, more good natured, than the rest. Like truant schoolboys they tend to club together.

The White Nile Club was my first experience of a honky-tonk. I found it to be a big gymnasium-like room in a quarter notorious for thieves. It had a lively Congolese High Life band and a great many cheerful girls with prominent, raised buttocks. Their complexions, treated with bleaching creams, were often much lighter than the men's. The men, since it was hot, wore no jackets, and to make sure no one got at their beer, they carried the bottles about with them.

Africans, as everyone knows, dance beautifully, naturally, with verve, grace and stamina. Here they swayed and shuffled in faultless rhythm, rarely holding. Their style of dancing, with the moving of belly muscles, can be sensuous. Yet it looks oddly respectable compared with some Europeans' compulsion to rub, hug and embrace in public. I could see only one representative of this school. He was a young schoolmaster with a reddish beard and a sharp nose. The African girl with whom he was violently necking must have felt that her face was being attacked by a tin-opener. I thought his approach wrong, for Africans, I had been told, do not like kissing on the mouth.

In Okot p'Bitek's *Song of Lawino* an Acholi village woman laments her educated husband's defection to Western ways as follows:

> You kiss her open-sore lips
> As white people do,
> You suck slimy saliva
> From each other's mouths
> As white people do . . .
>
> I do not like it,
> Holding each other
> Tightly, tightly,
> In public,
> I cannot.
> I am ashamed.
> Dancing without a song.
> Dancing silently like wizards . . .

Staying On

I had come to Kampala with no special attachment to Uganda or indeed to any part of Africa. I had liked the Middle Eastern countries with their simple codes based on a religious discipline, their comforting emphasis on the male prerogative, and the opportunities—in Turkey and Persia—for wandering over wide tracts of relatively unspoilt country.

But it had seemed to me, as I scanned the advertisement columns of *The Times Educational Supplement*, that the most attractive teaching jobs in the Middle East and neighbouring areas were becoming a near-monopoly of the British Council whose selection board, after prying into my record some thirty years earlier at Oxford ('Why, Mr Hills, were you rusticated?'), had turned me down. I came to Uganda on the spur of the moment.

Now, before six months was over, I had made up my mind to stay; and with good reason.

After many years of living in the mercenary, the Slavonic, and the war-stricken countries of Europe, among chauvinists and marching men, among religious bigots, among people obsessed with work, with rheumatism, insurance policies and tinned peas, I was now enjoying a winter-free life among a cheerful and tolerant race who would rather drink a bottle (or calabash) of beer than worry too much about tomorrow.

There were other, profounder reasons. Africa, for me, was a new and immensely exciting dimension with an incalculable future. In its strange, misunderstood environment one could reassess oneself. I was beginning to identify myself with the personalities and hopes of my students. And there were those mountains with enticing names—Virunga, Kadam, Morungole . . .

CHAPTER 3

Kampala (2)

Street View

After long drought the rains had set in again. The gorgeous
dresses of Baganda shopping wives flapped in the streets and
muddy lanes, like wet sails. On Kololo hill elephant grass had
invaded the flower beds. At night swarms of pale termite ants,
roused by the drumming of the rain, left their conical mounds
and, drawn towards the house light, deposited their wings in a
papery mass on my doorstep.

Now, the clouds that had been rolling in from the lake since
midday began to darken and then, to a series of detonations
that went growling round the hills, a torrent of rain fell on the
corrugated iron roofs and bungalows.

I ducked into the City Bar. The usual sort of people were
there: a White Father from the Congo, his soutane stained with
red *murram* mud, drinking Tusker beer with an American lady
who was doing the round of game parks; some Italians playing
snooker—they run a driving school, and make ornamental tiles
and road material; two or three African girls—hair straightened
and oiled—in too-tight skirts, and, along the bar, a row of
thirsty Europeans in shorts. Their white calves were bared
above small socks, their hands rough with straw-coloured hairs.

I recognise the large, silver-haired Dutchman who not long
before, in a bar, had smashed a picture of the then Prime
Minister, but had been forgiven. 'It slipped,' he told the
magistrate.

The drunken Hindu compositor is also present, slopping his
beer on a stranger's table. He has reached the stage of maudlin
indignation. 'Look at them,' I hear him saying, as he points to
some Indian businessmen who may be cotton merchants from
Soroti. 'Scum! I tell you, scum! They landed at Mombasa with

nothing but a spare dhoti, and now they're in the money. Cheats! Swillings of Bombay!'

He has no shoes on, from which I deduce he has left them with some bar keeper to cover his drink bill. I don't want to catch his eye, for he will come over and dribble into my glass. Worse, he may follow me to my office one day, embarrass me with authority.

The owner is an Ismaili from the Gujarat, and there is a picture of the youthful Aga Khan on the wall. His followers put up their leader's portrait wherever they have an office, shop or bar. He gives them directives and advice. He has a modern, clean-shaven face, the face of a Western business executive who knows about investments, and not, as in times gone by, of the shaggy leader of an Oriental sect descended from those fierce Old Men of the Mountains, who, from their fortified eyrie at Alumat, sent assassins reputed to be crazed with hashish to murder a caliph, a prince, or a Crusader king.[1]

Meanwhile, traffic lights in the empty, drenched street were winking uselessly outside the British Information Office, whose window display of scenes from Shakespeare—gaped at, every day, by scores of uncomprehending country families—had not been changed for weeks. Its reading room would be crowded with young Africans in thin white shirts, some of them asleep with *The Times* draped over their faces. A lorry load of police went by, in steel helmets and capes.

When the rain stopped offices were disgorging their employees, and while the Europeans streamed in a long column of cars to Kololo, Nakasero and Mbuya, groups of African workers began padding homeward to the beer bars and banana-fringed shanties beyond the city boundaries.

The sun was already low over Makerere. There, among dung-stained eucalyptus trees, the fruit bats, pestered by hornbills, would be fluttering and quarrelling before taking off in a long sky-train for a meal of wild figs and pawpaw. Day after

---

[1] The term 'Assassin' comes from the Arabic *hashish* Indian hemp (*cannabis sativa*). Bernard Lewis (*The Assassins*, 1967) has argued, however, that the Ismaili sectarian Assassins' old reputation for having been drug addicts has no proven basis in fact.

day, against the glow of sunset, the sky is thick with their silent, blind procession. Scarcely anyone notices them. They are often mistaken for crows.

Then suddenly the street was alive with promenading Indians, scores of them, emerging raven-haired from cubby-holes behind shops and little offices, filling the parks and squares, saluting, gossiping: loose-jointed women in sandals and bright saris, large-eyed children with slender limbs, ear-rings and pigtails, the men—Sikh artisans in turbans, Hindus, Goan Christians, Ismaili Muslims—walking gravely and a little apart.

I observe that rare exposure of flesh—the belt of naked skin above the hips—which Indian custom permits its women. Bodice and sari are drawn so tight that the amber flesh, revealed in the gap between them, is constricted, on either side of the spine, into a groove shadowed by tiny silken hairs.

When I catch their eye I get a sly—never direct—look in return. The women have fine eyes and handsome profiles, but a little coarsened, and often with a predatory expression that shows their peasant origin, for the Indians settled in Uganda are not of high caste or class.

The men look shrewd, thoughtful, tired. I recognise the bank official who deals so kindly with my overdraft. He is dapper, and wears polished shoes that are too tight. He is accompanied by his wife (who also works in the bank) and two babies. The Indians' love of many children—and of the honour they confer on their parents—is a problem. Is it not a little short-sighted to go on unloading these countless offspring on a country that is poor, that does not belong to them, and may one day reject them?

At this moment, a mile or two away, Englishmen will be pounding the golf links, clipping rose bushes behind a cypress hedge, savouring the first sundowner in government apart-ments decorated with a graduated row of wooden elephants and with waxed cement floors the colour of tomato sauce.

Mist rises from the golf course, the kites fly home, and red lights twinkling on the television mast above Kololo usher in the Southern Cross and what little night life there is within the limits of the city proper: cinema going for Europeans and

Indians, a few dinner parties in restaurants, a round of the bars
—not many stay open late, and soon after pay-day they are
generally hard up for custom.

By midnight a small army of watchmen with staves and old
army greatcoats has curled up to sleep in doorways of shops and
offices, and it is so quiet—though not in the African bars and
honky-tonks of outlying Mengo—that black-headed herons
stalk the traffic roundabouts and hairy shadows of mongooses
creep along the grass verges of suburban roads.

Now is the time to lock and put away your car. Car thieves
are a menace: prising out windows, running off with the
wheels, spiriting away your new Peugeot to be cannibalised
under a mango tree.

People had told me that by the standards of some West
African towns Kampala was a little dull. Certainly most of its
architecture is muddled and provisional (though a fresh start
has lately been made with a large hotel and business blocks
that tower above the tin roofs and the cassia trees); and
its unexciting shops, like those of any English suburb, are full
of boring commodities for the mem-sahib—breakfast cereals,
linoleum and antiseptic soap. The Indians who dominate so
much of the city's life are generally abstemious, wrapped up
in business and family affairs. The European community,
increasingly diluted by a new generation of recruits, seems
to harbour few genuine eccentrics (no one wants to lose his
job).

Much of the African population is in government employ
and covets (at least in the public eye) white collar respectability. The colourful, cheerful mass of it lives its own chaotic life
outside the municipal area, in cheap huts and shanties beyond
the poor Indian belt and along muddy red tracks obstructed
by piles of rotting *matoke* peel.

Nevertheless I was finding Kampala, in its setting of round
green hills, pretty and pleasant. Multi-racialism smoothed by
African good manners and humour was a most striking
attribute—even though integration is not perfect (for one thing,
the residential pattern that has grown up over the years results

2*   41

in considerable *de facto* segregation of the three main communities; for another, the preponderance of Indian traders obstructs the growth of a native middle class).

Green *shambas* and evergreen trees bring the countryside right into the city's environs. Lake Victoria is a pale blue splash only a few miles away. There are tarmac roads, and, in Makerere College, a cultural centre to offset most people's uninhibited preoccupation with money.

Gardens

Every garden has its birds: long-tailed mouse-birds with aggressive, ruffled crests, scarlet-breasted shrikes and purple starlings. The blackbirds that hop about English grass are replaced here by the dark hadada ibis which lands with a wail and a shimmer of green-tinted wings, to dig its scimitar-like beak into your lawn. Cattle egrets, like scraps of white cloth, dot the golf course. Vultures watch over the slums.

There is blossom (though not all of it indigenous) all the year round: hibiscus, jacaranda and frangipani, yellow-flowering cassias, the flaming trusses of the tulip tree, walls of thevetia and copper leaf. Yet the brightest flowers can scarcely rival the gorgeous colours of the *busuti* gown.

Draped ankle-length, in folds of saffron and magenta, round plump, gay women, it is perfectly matched to the chocolate-dark skin of the Baganda, to the red earth and fiery sky. The hips roll beneath it; the sculpted neck, bearing above it the glossy head, is a polished stem. The *busuti* isn't practical, but it is showy and beautiful.

My day had started with bird song—the staccato 'Quick, doctor, quick!' of the bulbul and a mad cackling of yellow-billed plantain-eaters. It ended now at midnight with the barking of innumerable overfed watchdogs set to guard garages and barred windows. ('It's a polefisher's dream,' warns a regular police announcement in the *Weekly News*, 'if you leave clothes near a window.')

Behind my apartment block the house servants would have fallen heavily asleep among pots, beer bottles and children, in their tiny, stuffy cells—which by subletting to friends and hangers-on they have turned into a small tribal camp.

Along the storm drains by the pawpaw trees I watched a mongoose steal. The Southern Cross was shining in one corner of the sky, the Plough in another. It was 22 degrees Centigrade and the air smelt of damp mango blossom. As I banged and bolted my door I startled a gecko, and swifts twittered under the tiles.

CHAPTER 4

Kilimanjaro

Mountain Walking

When Sir Hesketh Bell, Governor of Uganda 1906–9, first arrived in the country, he travelled for much of the way from Mombasa to Kampala on the 'cow-catcher' of a railway engine. He had a thrilling view of huge quantities of game.

Europeans these days are generally catapulted into Uganda by air at over 500 miles an hour. Wan, too warmly dressed, and slightly bilious, they plummet out of the sky, together with the London morning newspapers, on to Entebbe airport and are hurried past rows of banana groves and red termite mounds to Kampala.

There they may live and work for a year or two with scarcely more than a conventional glimpse of Africa. For unless one is posted up-country, the white family's travel experience is likely to be limited to the game parks, a visit to Nairobi, or holidays by the sea at Mombasa or Malindi—for which accommodation must be booked many months ahead.

Even government service regulations discourage the expatriate from exploring. When, at the end of two years, he gets long leave he is required for reasons of health and morale to spend it outside the tropics. So back he goes, whether he wants to or not, to his 'place of recruitment' to await, in rented rooms, or on the charity of relatives, the start of another tour.

Then again, without his car the European in East Africa is a snail without its shell. Walking in town heat is no pleasure. You arrive at the office with a wet shirt and trousers like a crumpled paper bag. Even the poor African has a bicycle.

Since the white man walks so little (and bush too can be travelled by Land Rover) he has a problem of physical exercise. Some play golf, or squash in a cemented cellar splashed with sweat; a few weed their flower beds, though Africans consider this sort of manual work undignified and an encroachment on the rights of a paid native gardener. My own solution, I decided, would be to look for bumps on the map and climb them. I had done so in eastern Anatolia and Persia, why not in East Africa?

Mountain walking attracted me for several reasons. It would cost little. I should be out of sight. There would be clean water, and no mosquitoes. And a mountain was a definite goal. For you cannot, in Uganda, simply dump your car anywhere and start rambling alone through the adjacent bush or *shamba*-country with a stick and a smile. Villagers, children, country police will pursue you. You will lose your way in tall grass, and be scratched by thorns. You won't know where to find water. At night hyenas will frighten you. You may even be robbed. If you take to the roads, motorists will insist on giving you a lift.

A mountain, though, is private, its top a specific objective; to get there involves a safari—a march with rules of its own which the local African understands. He may think it queer of you, without a gun and for no apparent material gain, to plod up a steep hill. Yet he will, I have found, guide you faithfully and well through his tribal territory (not, though, into anyone else's), locate water holes and wild honey, make a shelter out of a thorn trees when it rains, get a fire going out of nothing, and see that you come to no harm. For a little money, some *posho* and tobacco he will do all this and sleep naked too.

Kilimanjaro was an obvious first objective: a well-trodden mountain, said to have good shelters and reliable guides, and, of course, the highest point in Africa.

There is a harmless *snobisme* about having been to the top of a high mountain. Demavend tempts in Teheran. Turkey has Ararat, with wolves thrown in.

Here in Kampala, I gathered it was almost a point of honour with some expatriates to tackle Kilimanjaro. Even their wives pushed them into the adventure. It made a good story to tell the folks back home in Boston or Düsseldorf. It confirmed virility in the middle-aged. One could take colour pictures of Masai and giraffes on the way.

But not many people, it seemed, set out to enjoy Kilimanjaro for its own sake. Kilimanjaro is too well known. It is a freak, an icy monster in a roasting equatorial plain. Kibo ice-cap has become a tourist prize.

Marangu

I bought a length of hard salami sausage at an Indian grocer's in Nairobi, then drove off south on a bumpy road that runs through a hundred miles of straw-coloured grassland and scrub. Here game is as common a sight to motorists as chimney-pots along an English highway. Giraffes browse close to the road, their forelegs splayed and their elastic necks wrapped round a thorn tree. Within half an hour I had seen bustard, ostriches and secretary birds stalking through the brown grass. From the shade of scrub, wrinkled old Masai and a few ochre-painted youths waved their sticks.

When I stopped for a snack at an Indian *duka* (the usual hard-boiled eggs with pepper), a group of them followed me in. Flies were buzzing round the eyes of these somewhat decrepit representatives of a cattle-herding, warrior tribe petted and beloved by the British. They had large, uneven teeth, and high, thin shoulders. They smelt of sweat and beer. They were scroungers.

I was of course on a much used tourist route that leads both to Kilimanjaro and to the Serengeti game reserve that has been brilliantly popularised, especially among the Germans, by Professor Grzimek. I watched a party of them—stiff and dusty after a bone-shaking journey but with appetites heroically undiminished—get out of a striped van at Namanga River Hotel. '*Es gibt Kuchen!*' cried the first woman to reach the tea room, 'There's cake!'

The package-tourists now being brought in thousands to East Africa attract some not always good-natured criticism.[1] Their money is welcome. But they intrude in what retired settlers and residents used to consider private places. Their cameras are obtrusive. They are caricatures of oneself—of the inquisitive, impatient and perspiring European self.

[1] Kenya had 117,138 visitors in 1967, of whom 40,319 were British, 20,392 Americans, and 10,504 from West Germany.

It is good, though, that people should prefer a fortnight's glimpse of East Africa to a few yards of expensive raked sand at Rimini lido. The tourist deserves to see a lion, and to capture that snapshot of a man posing with a spear.

It was near Arusha that I got my first clear view of Kilimanjaro. Through a tangle of weavers' nests hung on a thorn bush, I saw a cloud roll away to reveal, more than fifty miles off, a huge ice-cap glittering above the long smudge of its pedestal, as though airborne. For the next eight days its presence was going to dominate me.

Marangu village, start point of the popular climbing route, stands among coffee and banana plots in the fertile *shamba* zone of Kilimanjaro's lower southern slopes.

Between 1886 and 1919 the mountain belonged to Germany (it was Queen Victoria's birthday present to the Kaiser). A German geographer, Professor Hans Meyer of Leipzig, and his guide Purtscheller, were the first, in 1889, to reach its highest point. They named it Kaiser Wilhelm Spitze.

Traces of the old German connection linger on. Lutheran churches, neatly signposted, are scattered throughout the neighbourhood, and Marangu's Kibo Hotel, which has stayed in German hands, reminds one of a Black Forest *Kurhaus* with its *deutsche Küche*, its damp, tree-shaded mountain air, and its numerous German guests, some of them—elderly residents of East Africa—still in the knickerbockers that used to be favoured by pre-war Prussian school masters. And there is, of course, a coming and going of restless tourists flown from Frankfurt to Nairobi.

Both hotels in Marangu, I soon realised, have a proprietary attitude towards 'their' mountain, and make a good profit out of it. They have a virtual monopoly of local Wachagga guides and porters. They undertake to get you up and down the peak, or as far as your legs will carry you, in five days for £20. And they will supply you with everything from a floppy brimmed sun-hat to hot porridge at 15,000 feet.

But the fireplace in Kibo Hotel was already surrounded by Italian Alpinists from Milan, and as I never (unless I am travelling at government expense) pay money for a bed, I went into the Lutheran church and, with the rain rattling on its corrugated roof, slept among the pews. I was roused by a smiling African clanging the church bell, which was hung in a tree.

Two shy Hindu schoolmasters, who had already hired a guide and porters, now invited me to join them. Virjee, a sports teacher, confessed to me that climbing Kilimanjaro would be a recommendation for a better paid job in Nigeria. His companion Nirad taught botany. Neither was confident of the outcome. I noticed that in addition to iron-pointed canes, they carried a quantity of pills, toilet paper, and curry powder. I had my ice axe and sausage.

The porters stuffed our gear into sacks, lifted everything on to their heads, and we set off in a drizzle. Children were going to school under banana-leaf umbrellas; hornbills hooted mournfully. I envied my companions the plastic Japanese raincoats they had bought in a village *duka*—until one after the other the buttons dropped off and the coats flapped about their shoulders like paper sheets. At first, while we were still interested, the botanist pointed out castor trees, maize and podocarpus. Then, soaked and silent, we entered thick forest. A turaco bird, like a brilliant butterfly, flashed red and blue in a high tree.

Kibo Hut

Bismarck Hut (recently, to conform with national sentiment, renamed Mandara Hut after a former Moshi chief) stands about five hours' walk from Marangu at the edge of a steep stand of tree heathers whose serried and twisted trunks are draped in streamers of lugubrious grey lichen.

We were lighting the stove when an exhausted Austrian doctor and then a young German in muddy baseball boots came in. They had that very day walked twenty miles down the mountain.

A fresh fall of snow, they announced sadly, had made it impossible for them to go on to the top. The doctor had heart pains. He masticated a home-made bolus of treacly meat essence then fell asleep snoring with his clothes on. The young

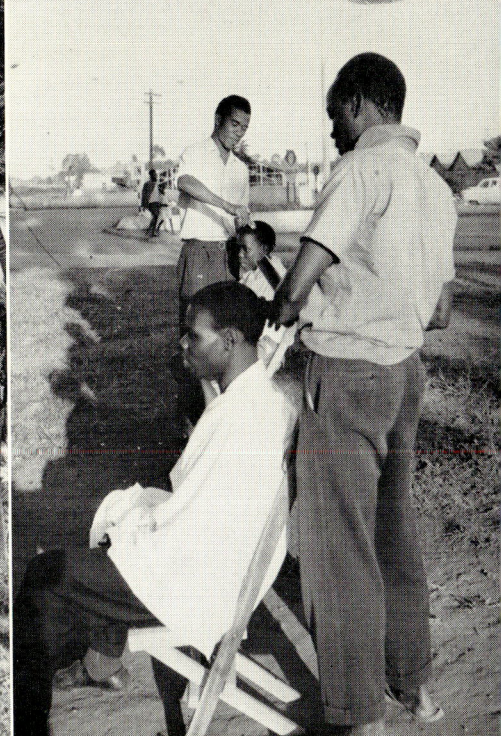

Palm trees, E. African Coast, near Malindi, Kenya

b. Open air barbers, Kampala

Edge of Lake Victoria, Entebbe

d. Muganda woman, Kampala

2a. Kilimanjaro from the plain near Arusha

b. Crater walls at Kilimanjaro summit

a. Author at Gillman's Point, Kilimanjaro

b. African guide on Kilimanjaro

c. Mawenzi peak seen from Kibo Hut

4a. Giant groundsels and everlastings at foot of Wagagai in crater of Mt Elgon

b. Carrying through bamboo forest, Mt Elgon   c. Poacher on Mt Elgon, forest zone

German, with his nosegay of mountain flowers, disappeared into the twilight.

In the morning our porters, with 50-lb. loads on their heads, skipped nimbly up the forest track; we straggled behind. We had been joined by three other climbers—two Englishmen from Tabora and an Israeli dentist. The dentist immediately made himself useful by excising, with his penknife, a jigger and its little black nest of pus from my foot. I had carried the flea about with me for some weeks and grown attached to it—but it had begun to itch.

Above the heather forest we trudged through coarse, open tussock grass sprinkled with golden everlastings. Here we met the rear party of Italian Alpinists hurrying downhill in red stocking caps. We learned that the snow fall had prevented even these enthusiasts from going beyond Gillman's Point.

A little later I saw for the first time the weird high-altitude vegetation of equatorial East Africa: the solitary obelisk shapes of giant lobelias, and scattered tree groundsels with heavy crowns of cabbage-like leaves. Then came fire-swept ground strewn with the charred remains of countless bushy proteas, whose discoloured flower-heads, where they had survived, protruded like an egg out of the eggcup.

We found Peters (now Horombo) Hut at the edge of a pretty glen watered by a brook. Cloud still obscured the summit of Kilimanjaro, but far below to the south a flash of lake water was dancing in the plain. We were in good shape. The two Hindus dined off curried rice, mineral water, and aspirins. My three other companions sat over a pail of stew prepared by their cook. I ate some of my sausage. Outside the hut ravens waited greedily for scraps.

The first trial of endurance came next day when we plodded at over 14,000 feet across the seven-mile saddle of yellow gravel and lava stones that, like a fragment of the cold Mongolian wasteland, separates Mawenzi peak from the main Kibo cone. Headaches and nausea soon struck everyone silent. Kilimanjaro was no longer a botanist's joy. It had become a physical fitness test for middle-aged foreigners who, having paid their money, still hoped to get value for it. At Kibo hut—another cheerless metal shed—the tinned curries were left untouched, the cook's

49

stew was rejected with groans, and the sight of my mutilated sausage brought bile into the throats of my companions.

Not until late afternoon did the sky clear. First to the east Mawenzi appeared, its black towers sprinkled white. Then immediately above us Kibo unfolded an immense flank shining with fresh snow that tapered down in patches to our feet. The crater lip, battlemented by ice walls, glittered bluish against the sky. Across it puffs of cloud scurried like smoke.

Until then I had caught only distant picture postcard views of Kilimanjaro—a remote sky mass, part ice, part cloud, floating high in space above a pedestal of haze. Close at hand, its crest was now revealed as huge, cold, but accessible.

The Ice Cap

We were roused grumbling and short of breath at the traditional hour of 1 a.m. An early start, says the guide book, gives climbers the benefit of frozen scree, adding that one probably cannot sleep in any case, and 'it is quite a good thing not to be able to see the stretch of slope ahead'.

Our guide went first, *polepole*, at snail's pace, swinging my lantern in the moonlight as though shepherding a file of convalescents. For an hour or so there was a funereal scuffle of borrowed boots on crusted snow and iron-hard lava scree. Then when I looked back I saw that our party had straggled and shrunk. At the arched rock overhang known as Meyer's Cave I found I was alone with the guide. Only the two Englishmen followed. The Israeli dentist, the Hindus, and two other climbers who had set off with us had stolen silently back to bed.

The guide book told us to look out at this stage for the dawn rising over Mawenzi. There it was, spreading like a bush fire along the dark pinnacles. One of the Englishmen got up and crouched bent and desperate in the cave's mouth. He was retching.

In greying light we started to plough a slow, zig-zag furrow up the ice slope. The snow was firm, the sun soon warm on our backs. The guide, transformed now from a respectful servant into a tyrant, began to bully us. Far below I glimpsed one of the Hindu school masters. He had lost his cane and was sliding home on his back. I found my rhythm and left the others behind.

I was nearing the crater now. The sun had mounted brilliantly into the sky, the pitch was steepening. Just below the knoll of Gillman's Point I began to count my steps. I was elated, scooped snow into my mouth, and chewed a handful of groundnuts. Then came the moment of deflation.

Two English ladies appeared from behind the knoll. 'Good morning to you,' they said, tripping past me as I leaned panting on my ice-axe. They looked cool and relaxed, their cheeks were rosy. Mine were dirty with stubble, and I could feel dried scum on my lips. I scowled at their neat, descending figures.

A few more heaves through waist-deep snow, and from the glorious height of 18,640 feet I was looking down into Kilimanjaro's magnificent crater.

I forgot the two intrusive ladies, and my thumping heart, in that moment of personal discovery.

Like a frozen, forgotten lake the crater lay sterile and dazzling white within its steep cliffs of ice, tier on tier of them buttressing the immense sunken mouth. I felt the sudden elation of having escaped from the burning tropics into a silent Arctic world. The great plains to the south, with their heat and thorns, their irritating flies and spindly, humped cattle, had merged into the blue haze of Africa. A little below me, my two companions were still battling on. The dark zigzag of our footsteps stretched, a ladder that stained the snow, down and out of sight.

We were spared further effort for the fresh snow made it impracticable to walk west along the crater rim to the highest point, Uhuru Peak (formerly Kaiser Wilhelm Spitze), another one and a half hours' walk away. So we photographed the crater, shared some dates with the guide, who looked bored— he had, he claimed, made the ascent 'hundreds of times'— then turned back on the rapidly melting crust to flounder homeward.

It was dusk on the following day when I descended through the maize and banana plots to Marangu. I was not wearing the crown of pink and yellow everlastings which a boy, who wanted a shilling for it, had tried to put on my head. My feet were swollen, and I could feel by the looseness of my trousers that I had lost weight.

I was the last to return. A new lot of climbers, spruce and enthusiastic, was in occupation of the hotel fire. Our porters had drunk their beer and gone. When a waiter in a fez beat the dinner drum, I went off to sleep in the church.

As I spread my quilt among the pews I reflected that I had not entirely enjoyed my walk. On a mountain I prefer to be alone, to dawdle, boil tea, and sleep by a camp fire. Here I had been chivvied relentlessly by professional guides in gum boots over sixty miles of forest, bog, and scree. To them I was just another client. But I had got Kilimanjaro out of my system. I would go now and climb something else—privately, and at my own pace.

I have since learned that Kilimanjaro is often climbed by parties of schoolboys whose instructors rush them up and down as though it were an assault course; and that hundreds of people make the ascent every year.

Such a trampling of feet does of course put the great mountain into the category of a tamed wonder. But there are other and bolder ways to the top besides the tourist *piste*; and one is not compelled to engage a hotel guide and porters with a chop box at £20 a time.

I had my last glimpse of Kilimanjaro from a patch of Masai country, where guinea fowl were squawking behind the shaggy termite mounds and slim, ochred youths with spears begged me for bread.

Soon there was nothing to see of the mountain but its bonnet of cloud. Some giraffes wandered on to the red *murram* road, blocking my path, like dazzle-painted pylons. When I got started again my car was full of flies.

CHAPTER 5

Elgon

Bumagabula

The nearest high mountain to Kampala is Elgon (local name Masaba). It has for centuries been a meeting point of migrant tribes. It has been associated with border fighting, flight, refuge and massacre, long surviving cults; and nowadays with thriving foothill agriculture.[1]

Elgon's long misty ridges are visible for miles along the Tororo-Eldoret road. The changing silhouette of its escarpments, banded grey and green with rocks and trees, and splashed with falling water, dominate the drive through Mbale. Along its north side, facing the open scrub country of Karamoja, a rough mountain road winds through coffee *shambas* and then high wooded spurs where bearded maize stalks crackle, to a ford on the Kenya river-boundary at Suam.

I had been told that Elgon has extensive layers of fascinating high-altitude vegetation as well as a magnificent crater. I had spent the night sleeping in a steep meadow under a tulip tree. Now an askari in a smart red fez and puttees, but without boots, was guiding me over the last three miles of track to Bumagabula, a Bugisu village on Elgon's lower western slopes.

We found the headman squatting yellow-eyed in the shade of his hut, baking sweet potatoes in a heap of embers. The food looked unappetising, like stumps of charred wood. He had spat in a circle round his feet. A little boy whose navel sagged snout-like over his stomach was waiting to eat.

[1] The expert on Elgon, its lore, languages and tribal history, and especially on the Sebei, is John Weatherby, an Englishman from Kampala who has spent many years exploring the mountain and its caves. Weatherby is the sort of elusive, independent traveller who, according to what I have been told by up-country missionaries, is liable to appear suddenly out of the blue with a donkey, or in an old Land Rover. When asked where he is going, he points into the distance and says 'Over there.'

I had scarcely told the headman the purpose of my visit—which was to walk up Wagagai, Elgon's highest point (14,178 feet)—when three men with broad-bladed pangas came running up and offered to accompany me. They must have been eager to earn my money. It took them only a few minutes to divide my gear into three head loads—to which they added a bunch of green *matoke* plantains—and without more ado we were off.

To the crater

We walked at first up a path that twisted through tiers of maize, bananas, and plots of coffee whose white, star-shaped blossom hung over the beautiful shrubs like a wedding dress. 'Arabica coffee,' said Damiano, leader of the three Bagisu. The berries would be sold to the local co-operative society at 1.60 cents a pound. He grinned. 'There'll be plenty of money for *pombe*.' He already smelt of it.

As the escarpment began to tower above us and the plots petered out in rough grass tussocks, Damiano, who like the rest of us was sweating heavily, asked me for two shillings and ran off with my two-gallon plastic water can to the last of the huts. He brought it back half-full of a thick yellow sludge.

'*Pombe*,' he said happily, licking some of the sour-smelling maize brew—it reminded me of coarse Turkish *boza*—from his fingers, '*mzuri sana*'.

The escarpment is a massive wall of steep rock. We came to it through a last tall cluster of *euphorbia neglecta*, and climbed up crude steps worn smooth by the hard bare feet of generations of hunters and woodcutters. At the top, trees in melancholy lichen streamers closed in on us, then dense bamboo forest, trembling, feathery, silent. In its green twilight big flies settled on the thin shorts and bare legs of my companions. Our feet, treading the black humus, made no sound.

We had been going for over six hours before we came to our night refuge—two shelters in a clearing by a brook. They were in poor shape. The porters' shed had been stripped of most of its corrugated iron sheets, the Bwana's rondavel had lost its bunks and stove. Its walls, though, had been enlivened by a startling fresco of fat, naked women reclining within a circle of male genitalia. '*Muhindi* (Indian) pictures,' said the porters. They were not interested in them.

It was a cold night. I shared my bedding with the porters and we made an early start over a carpet of rime. Soon the bamboo labyrinth gave way to twisted tree heathers mingling with the first giant groundsels and vast thickets of bushy everlastings whose papery white flowers lay over the bracken like snow drifts.

I know now that there is an almost mathematical precision about the occurrence of vegetation zones on the mountains of East Africa. One can roughly, with adjustment for local weather conditions, calculate one's altitude by them. The sad lichen streamers on trees are one of the signs that one is getting high; the twisted shapes of tree heathers are another. As we neared the cleft of the gorge which gives access to the crater rim, the tall heathers dwindled to scrub and before us stretched mile after mile of coarse tussock grass sprinkled with tree groundsels and the spikes of giant lobelias whose shaggy mantles of green bracts obscured tiny blue flowers.

We passed a file of Bagisu hunters in old skins and rags trotting downhill with bows and spears, small sharp-faced dogs, and lumps of meat wrapped in bloody sacking. Damiano got from one of them a large rat, already skinned and roasted.

Jackson's Summit is the peak usually climbed by visitors. But it gives no view of the crater and is not Elgon's highest point: so we left it alone and in a hailstorm went straight down into the bowl.

According to my guide notes there should have been another mountain hut here. But, said the porters, 'rogues from Kenya' had carried it off for their own private use. The Sebei, they added, were to blame. With the Sebei, their neighbours on the northern spurs of Elgon, the Bagisu have a long tradition of tribal enmity. They quarrel over land, kill, and burn each other's crops.

My companions knew exactly where to camp. Not far from a prominent fissure (Suam gorge) in the crater's north-east wall that overlooks the Kenya side of the mountain—whose top the frontier roughly bisects—we crowded into a shallow cave with a floor of ashes strewn with bones.

55

After a time the sour fumes of the cooking fire drove me out. The three men heated water to mix with the *pombe* gruel, ate the rat, and sat coughing over the burning groundsel wood.

Damiano (his name is a common corruption of Damien, the Belgian leprophile) was a Catholic. Politics, he told me, was for him a matter of coffee price and Bagisu tribal interest. The phrase 'Uganda nation' meant little to him—it wasn't local enough; and he disliked Kampala—a place, he said, 'where you have to pay money even for a drink of water, and sleep in the bus park.' He was going to spend his porter's wage of twenty shillings on *pombe*.

I had by now learned enough common Swahili to talk to my companions, though I had not found it easy to practise in Kampala. The Baganda consider Swahili 'kitchen or barmaid's talk' and if they speak it at all, they do so very badly.

But I had bought Le Breton's *Up-country Swahili* ('for the use', writes the author in his preface, 'of soldier, settler, miner, merchant, and their wives'), and memorised words.

Mzungu, I learned, means both 'European' and 'strange and wonderful'. *Malaya*, 'whore', is also the word for a 'barren woman' (in African eyes a valueless creature).[1] A good many terms (*kiberiti*, 'matches', *kitab*, 'book', *bandera*, 'flag') were already known to me in Urdu or Turkish.

Yet the more correctly I tried to speak, the less I was understood.

Wagagai

I woke up stiff and cold. The white everlastings that hung over the cave had closed their flowers into tiny silver bells. In the frosty morning light I looked down at the crater floor, and saw what appeared to be a forest of suburban chimneys with mops stuck through them.

These were groundsels with their squat trunks and heavy rosettes of cabbage-like leaves. There were hundreds of them, bent into antlers and thick lyres, attenuated, or simply stubby plinths stained with bog water. The old leaves do not fall off.

---

[1] It is the man who has no children, not the beggar with empty pockets, who is considered truly poor.

They stay on the stems, creaking and rattling dismally, burdening them with decay and adding two foot or more to their girth. I found them grotesque, a botanical curiosity, primeval, rather than beautiful.[1] The groundsels were not in flower; and many were so rotten that like the giant lobelia poles they could be felled with a blow.

We recrossed the crater bed through a swamp, and with Damiano I walked up Wagagai, highest of the knolls that encircle Elgon's dented crown. The top was bleak, and littered like an old Muslim burial place with lichenous stones.

From it we could see only a fragment of the great rambling mountain which we had climbed. But we had a vast view of the slopes immediately below, chequered black by fire—a favourite though cruel and wasteful method for driving game; of Mbale town to the west, a blur in a patchwork of crops; of Kenya simmering in a blue haze. To the north the Napak hills lay like a dinosaur across the entrance to the Karamoja plain.

Karamoja! The name was beginning to haunt me. Some people joked about its naked men. Others found them awesome. An American lecturer told me he had swopped his jacket for permission to take photographs of an old man. So there was chicanery too. I must go and see it for myself before it was too late.

We slept again in the rondavel, among the disturbing frescoes, and early in the morning my companions, now hungry and impatient—they had stalked, without success, a duiker among the groundsels—hurried me back through the heathers and swaying bamboo. They had come to regard me as a dawdler, for ever fussing with camera and field-glasses, peering tediously about me at the trees, the small brown hill chats, and the patches of blue distance, stumbling over roots embedded in the black trails that furrow the ridges.

But I wanted to prolong the last hours. I liked the solitude of Elgon. It was a more private mountain than Kilimanjaro. There were no paper wrappings or red marker flags along the track, no other wan gentlemen being urged uphill; only the

[1] The persistent dead leaves serve the purpose, however, of forming a thick insulating cover round the senecio stem that protects it from intense cold at night.

ashes of a few hunters' fires under blackened boles, and clay-coloured droppings of leopards on which gaudy butterflies settled with quivering wings.

Back at the escarpment edge I looked forward to a short halt. My companions would not hear of it. They accelerated down the cliff face and made straight for a large thatched hut that stood alone.

I saw when I got there why they had spurted. For Damiano it was the journey's end. We had stepped into Cockaigne land.

A pombe party

There must have been at least a hundred Bagisu grouped on the grass round big communal pots of *pombe*. They were sucking it through long tubes that joined them like umbilical cords to the nourishment. They were sucking in silence (for it was still early) and with such concentration that they scarcely noticed our arrival. It was ritual. They reminded me of Turks at their hubble-bubbles.

They were mostly men, in a medley of village clothes—white *kanzu* gowns, old battledress jackets, animal skins, a few beautiful colobus capes. Someone gave me a green tea pot to drink from. A youth sprang up and jingled a string of bells strapped to his leg. An old woman came up with a jug and waggled her hips at me. Her job was to top up the *pombe* with hot water till its strength failed and the dregs were tipped on the ground for dogs to devour.

I hid my cigarettes and sat on a bank with Damiano. He was gulping the stuff out of a kettle. I asked him if a wedding was being celebrated. 'No,' he said, 'it's just that the Bagisu like drinking. It is the custom.'

I found the *pombe* sour and refreshing; and there was food value in its thickness. But I knew that for long afterwards it would go on fermenting in my stomach. It would act as a purge, and I would break wind for hours. After a time when I looked at my companions I saw that their eyes, with the liverish whites, were beginning to glaze. It was time to leave.

'*Safari bado kwisha*,' I said in my bad Swahili, 'we're not home yet, *kwenda*.' But it was midday before I could persuade them to dump my gear at the bottom of the valley.

Kitale

I had not quite finished with Elgon. My immediate destination was Kitale, which meant motoring round the northern spurs of the mountain along a rough switchback road.

The winding seventy-mile track constantly unfolds fresh angles of entrancing landscape. It traverses, against the mountain wall, great spurs and ridges clothed in forest that radiate towards escarpments swimming in mist. To the north, on the open side beyond the foothills, it looks over the Karamoja plain, dotted with scrub and rocky outcrops and dominated by the huge Kadam massif.

There are glimpses of lovely places: Sipi, on Sebei territory, with its waterfall streaming over a cliff, like a rabbi's beard; village greens with donkeys and little African-owned *dukas* (there are no Indian traders here) that sell Coca-Cola and worm powders; deserted copses brightened by the flaming torches of the coral tree. The maize fields are braided with purple ipomoea. Sebei women with dark Ethiopian features stand by their water pots, as straight and still as figurines.

Then, near Suam village, the colobus monkey leaps and flies like a trapeze artist along the quivering branches of tall trees. But the river that tumbles down from Elgon's crater has been stocked with rainbow trout, and oh! what did those notice boards say? NO FISHING. TRESPASSERS KEEP OUT.

My countrymen were here. I had reached the Kenya frontier.

Now come the wide ploughed fields of white-owned farmland: rows of eucalyptus, and heavy humpless cattle; tractors, petrol pumps, and land skilfully turned to profit by hard-working men with British and Dutch names, who live in thatched farm-houses which they have filled with easy chairs, shelves and Persian rugs. A good tarmac road runs swiftly over the last lap to Kitale.

But Kitale, when I got there, was dismal and dark. Everything had closed except for the run-down European hotel and an African bar or two. Even the marabou storks had gone for the night.

I had coffee in the hotel lounge. It was filled with settlers. They reminded me, with their open shirts, their thick forearms and healthy brown faces, of a crowd of greying army majors. Seeing I was alone a big red-faced farmer asked me to his table for a drink. He had a young Goan with him.

I didn't realise he was drunk until, after a few conventional inquiries (my home, war-time regiment, and job), he suddenly looked very fierce and thrust his face into mine.

'You're a Communist,' he said, 'a bloody Communist.'

I let it go. I knew that, to many old-timers, a connection with Makerere College was anathema. They imagine it to be a nest of turncoat Englishmen, bearded and sloppily dressed, who fraternise with black men and teach them sedition.

But when, a little later, he rose to his feet and put his fists up, I felt challenged. 'You're yellow,' he bawled. 'You've no guts.'

I would have knocked him down, but the Goan intervened. 'Go,' he whispered to me urgently. 'For God's sake, go!'

Disgraced, and with many eyes upon me, I backed away to the door with the farmer breathing over my face. My car was outside, and—when I reached it—so was the farmer. He came at me like a bull, so I threw him on his back. He toppled over like an old chimney pot. I did not help to pick him up—the Goan would see to that. 'Go away,' he was saying to me. 'We want no more trouble from *you*.'

Outside the town I put up my camp bed in a field. It was a clear night, filled with the rustle of leaves and grass and the piping of crickets. I watched a satellite dribble across the sky— like a small travelling lamp that seemed to be dodging the stars.

It was cold now that the day's heat had flown swiftly starward, but I had my old Turkish quilt. Somewhere a house dog was barking, and I thought of the angry farmer. I bore him no grudge. He would be tucked up by now in a four-poster bed. In the morning he would complain of a sore back, and his wife would have to rub Sloan's liniment on it.

CHAPTER 6

Kadam

Moruita

From the slopes of Elgon I had seen, some fifty miles to the north, the wooded mass of Mount Kadam gradually disengage itself from the plain, then towards evening sink back into shadow: a giant horned rock overlooking the scrub and cattle country of Karamoja.

Now, two months later, I was driving to it from Mbale. Close to the roadside giraffes were browsing acacias, stretching their painted necks to get at the high branches, tugging with sinuous black tongues at the small thorn-protected leaves. Ostriches paced gravely away. Herds of fat roan antelope turned to watch the dust of my car. A man in a loose cloth ran across the road. His naked buttocks looked sleek with health.

I found Moruita Rest Camp, at the foot of Kadam, occupied by a detachment of special police. A sentry, in the African way, challenged fiercely, pointing his rifle at me. But the O.C., a stout good-natured Assistant Police Superintendent from Lango, welcomed me with a mug of scalding tea from his thermos, and let me set up my camp bed under a thorn tree.

The thatched settlement of Moruita is a potentially explosive meeting point of several tribes: tall Karamojong whose greased and naked bodies glisten among the drab huts where they lounge with sticks (spears are forbidden) and tiny wooden stools; their rivals, the local Suk, who graze adjacent territory towards Amudat and the Kenya frontier; a few sharp-nosed Somali shopkeepers; more than 2,000 recently settled Didinga refugees from southern Sudan; and Tepeth, a tribal pocket, shrewd, wiry and poor, and looked down on by all the others.

The police detachment had been detailed to check cattle-raiding and violence in this troublesome border area. During

61

the night the O.C. asked me to drive him on an errand among the dim-lit huts of the plain. 'The Karamojong,' he said as we passed their dark shadows on the road, 'consider me a "bad man," for I have recovered hundreds of head of stolen cattle from them and arrested the thieves. But we shall be safe with this,' and he touched his sub-machine gun which was resting on my food box.

'There are often lions about,' he added as we swerved below the moon-lit escarpment of the mountain. But all we saw were rabbits scuttling in the headlights, and night-jars which at the last moment rose moth-like out of our path with a whirr of speckled wings. When I braked to avoid the rabbits, my companion smiled. 'My drivers,' he remarked, 'would enjoy running them down.'

I have encountered, since this early meeting, a good many special police units: in the Moroto foothills and at Kaabong, both centred in cattle-raiding areas; in the Toro and Kitgum frontier districts; on the Uganda border with Rwanda and the Congo; and picketing the boundaries of Buganda.

To me these armed policemen have always been helpful and efficient. Many are northerners. They are taught English and educated to a standard well above that of the rough Uganda rifleman. They do not interfere with *bona fide* travel.

Their presence throughout the country, though, is proof that Uganda has her share of Africa's tribal and frontier problems. Nor, as the sharp end of a government policy that has to be enforced in unruly districts, can they expect everyone to like them. When they make an arrest, they are tough.

Tepeth

I was awakened by the cries of a cock having its throat cut by the cook. Three battered men in vests and shorts that had disintegrated into mere shreds of rotting fibre were squatting on the ground with their muddy eyes upon me.

'We will take you up the mountain,' they announced. 'We are Tepeth—hill people.' One of them held out an empty Coleman's mustard tin. 'But first, give us some sugar.'

The store where I went to buy *posho* and cheap Kali cigarettes was crowded with stocky young women who were fingering groceries and bolts of cloth and carried their money in bits of knotted rag. They were loaded with beads and metal hoops. They had greased and twisted their hair into mops of strings like candle wicks. Their skin was scarified, they smelt strongly of sweat and cow hides, and, when they jostled me, they showed great mouths of teeth.

It was like being caught up in a rugby scrum of warm, sleek antelopes. Among the bare bodies the Somali store-keeper's Muslim wife, in a shawl and bulky skirts, seemed comically overdressed. Remembering the porters' request, I bought plenty of sugar.

Then, with the three Tepeth—we were shortly joined by a fourth—I set out along the foot of Kadam. I followed them blindly at first, through a dense thatch of soft, eight-foot high grass, studded with thorny acacias and protea scrub. It was like wading through hair. Some of the proteas were in flower, the cool white conical heads set on their pink saucers reminding me of beautiful cream confections. When three hours later we entered thick woodland, my companions promptly sat down to chew leaves, swallowing the green juice with pinches of sugar from the mustard tin.

We made slow progress over the soft forest floor. Halts for leaf-nibbling and doses of sugar were made at half-hour intervals. I had time to study my companions.

Gwido was leader. He was small, wrinkled, and had badly bloodshot eyes. He ate more leaves than anyone else, carried the broad-bladed panga, and doled out, with reluctance, the day's ration of Kali cigarettes.

Korkoi wore a heavy metal plug which thrust forward his lower lip and collected spittle that made him drool. Above one ear grew two big warts like brown gooseberries.

Loupon had a deep sore above his ankle, and to prevent his trousers rubbing against it, walked with one trouser-leg rolled to the knee. Gwido's son, Lorikit, the youngest of our party, was carrying the heaviest load and did most of the leaf foraging for the others.

They all looked scruffy, underfed, dissipated, and unwell. But I knew they were far tougher than I was, and would see me up the mountain and down again.

It was, I found, the pale and slender-boled *catha edulis* tree whose young shoots they were plucking so ravenously. I asked Gwido about the leaf.

'We call it *muirungi*,' he said, '*usingizi hapana*, it keeps you awake. Good for the head,' he went on, 'but bad to taste'— hence the sugar. To emphasise the effect of the leaf, he jumped to his feet and skipped a few yards up the path.[1]

Camp

But the Tepeth did not march far that day. Well before the sun was down they camped on a rocky terrace at the fringe of the forest, and here for the first time I had a clear view of my surroundings.

The Kadam massif, an isolated lump in an open plain, runs for fifteen miles along a bent axis. Its steep tiers of bare brown escarpment, stained by falling water, are edged by forest below and by sparsely covered rock slopes above. Moving south along the lower face, we had so far traversed only a small part of the extensive forest belt. But we had climbed above the plain, and an augur buzzard with chestnut tail, floating over the green gulf at our feet, aided the illusion of height. Obda peak, our objective, stood somewhere to the south-west at the farther end of Kadam.

My companions were already grumbling about the sugar ration. But at dusk the following day, when we halted by a cascade, they spotted a faraway wisp of smoke. 'Tepeth,' said Gwido. He went out to find them, and came back with some sticky scraps of honey in the comb. Everyone was now happy. My companions still had plenty of *muirungi* and they tore and sucked the delicate skin off the thin red shoots as though it were asparagus. It seemed to make them too talkative to sleep. They

[1] According to *The Medicinal and Poisonous Plants of Southern and Eastern Africa* (J. M. Watt and M. G. Breyer-Brandwijk, 1962), the leaf, which is widely known as *khat*, has a marked sustaining effect with release from fatigue and hunger feelings, as well as euphoria. Taken in excess it produces inebriant effects which simulate those of alcohol and ultimately a deep stupor; and excess may result in insanity and have a toxic effect. *Khat* is used as a stimulant especially in Arabia and Somalia by Arabs, and in Abyssinia. The Muslim may chew it without breaking Mohammed's proscription on alcohol. In Kenya (where it is also called *miraa*), *khat* is commercially cultivated in the Meru area. It is retailed in Mombasa.

sang and spat, and stirred the fire into a blaze that scorched their feet, startled the birds in the trees, and threw sparks on the little pile of kit where I lay. I looked up at the sky. Over Obda hung the Southern Cross. Behind us, oddly inverted, the Plough.

During the day I had been haunted by the cries of unseen turaco birds—a single scream like a call for help swelling into a chorus of penetrating brays: hysterical, prolonged, abruptly stifled.

Now, a little after dawn, I was roused by the roaring of colobus monkeys. I could see them sitting in a grove of trees with their bushy black and silver tails swishing and their white faces turned ghost-like towards our smouldering fire. They capered and jumped and roared still louder when we stirred so that the damp gorge reverberated as though invaded by mighty frogs.

Obda

Gwido and his son took the panga and my two light blankets, and leaving the others behind we entered the last strip of woodland. Soon tree groundsels and spindly dracaenas—like the slender type of groundsel, they sprout their rosette of strap-like leaves at the top of a thin stem—began to tower up in sunlit glades.

I watched Gwido fell a brittle giant lobelia spike and set about puncturing the hollow stem with glowing splinters of wood. Within a few minutes he had made a four-foot lobelia flute on which he blew a range of mournful notes.

The rocky slopes above the forest were bristling with burnt protea scrub whose tough charred skeletons tore and blackened our clothes. A family of baboons ran off barking like dogs.

I don't care much for baboons. Their hairy, melancholy faces, the craven way they scuttle off to a safe distance, their shiny red bottoms, their quick, furtive onslaughts on the poor man's maize crop, make it hard for me to like them. Unseen, cowardly, they cough and grimace as one passes by.

As we trudged uphill to the long exposed ridge of Obda, a mass of rain clouds gathered overhead, then hail and a sharp

3

wind began to sting us. Gwido and his son wanted to turn back for they hated the cold. 'Europeans never climb farther than this,' said Gwido untruthfully. He squeezed himself into a crack in a rock wall, shivered and sulked. It seemed I would have to go on alone.

But I had not gone far when the sun showed itself again, my companions came running up, and we hurried through the last patches of tree heather. A little later, wrapped like a Moor in my blanket, Gwido was playing his lobelia pipe on the 10,073 foot summit of Obda.

From there I could see the whole massif—a curved and knobbly spine ribbed with innumerable spurs and wild valleys that rose again, several miles northward, to a peak whose turrets shone red in the sun. My map showed it to be only a few feet lower than the point where we stood.

Around us were four bulky silhouettes: Elgon to the south, Moroto mountain to the north, the Napak hills to the west, and, to the east, the Karasuk range marking the frontier with Kenya. They gave the impression, as they lay sleeping on the bed of the plain, of great age and of torpid, smouldering distances in which men and animals are ants.

I know something now of those shrouded and mysterious ranges. None of them has the spectacular symmetry of the Mufumbiro volcanoes. They are rambling and shapeless.

But they have well marked and even partially humanised personalities: Elgon, still roamed by skin-clad poachers carrying bows, arrows and spears, and nourishing water-fed valleys rich in cash crops; Moroto, a green mountain in a drought-wrinkled scrub land; Napak, a cultural boundary stone between the glistening Karamojong and the trousers and white shirts, the bicycles and neat village greens of Teso; the Karasuk range, overlooking cattle camps of Suk in feathered carapaces.

Elgon I had visited. The others were still to be explored. What walking country it looked, with its high views and cold nights!

On top of Obda there was a small cairn, and instead of a sophisticated summit book in a metal case, two old gin bottles. They contained faded messages on scraps of paper. 'Arrived very tired,' someone had written irritably. 'I carried John's blasted kit.' Who was John? A bearded schoolmaster in unsuitable sandals? A missionary weakened by stomach-ache? Some government officer who had sprained his ankle?

We descended warily through the sooty mass of protea skeletons. Nightfall caught us still far from camp in a liana-tangled forest only faintly flecked with our morning panga marks.

This was Gwido's chance to show his skill. With scarcely a moment's hesitation he led us on the long, scuffling trek through black walls of creepers and undergrowth. It was nearing midnight when we spotted our companions' fire. I was lacerated and grey with dirt, and Lorikit's shorts had split between the buttocks. The terrace was unpleasantly spattered with phlegm. Loupon, I noticed, had taken my dressing off his sore and reverted to spittle and ash.

Didinga

Next day at the foot of Kadam we turned aside from the tall grass and plodded through several miles of maize and rusty-headed sorghum. All this treasure of ripening food had been planted by Didinga refugees—tall, very black Nilotics who had stuck little wooden crosses (they are Roman Catholics) on their huts, and when they smiled showed mouths crammed with large, uneven, dazzling teeth. Naked boys set to guard the fields shouted fiercely at Gwido. I asked him why he was so ill at ease. 'Didinga,' he said, 'are our enemies.'

Back at the police camp the O.C. was sitting in his vest looking depressed. One of his drivers, he told me, had just driven a new Land Rover transport vehicle into a tree; and that very day he had been inspected by a senior official. He longed to be posted to Kampala, to an office job and a flat.

My companions took up their bundles of *muirungi* leaf and padded off into the dusk. 'What did you pay them?' asked the O.C. 'Twenty shillings each,' I said. He grinned. 'Far too much. They'll get drunk for a week and thrash their wives into the bargain.'

I drove slowly south next day, past Namalu prison farm where the hundreds of convicts swinging hoes looked at a

67

distance, in their snow-white caps and uniforms, like a great flock of restless egrets, and through Namalu village, last outpost of the Karamojong.

Then skirting Elgon I came to Mbale. A loud noise of Beatle music was coming from Jimmy's Bar. I bought a currant loaf at the Indian baker's. Mbale has a pretty residential area centred on a good hotel. But the gaudy South American bougainvillea, and odour of Oriental frangipani by the European golf course, seemed alien and artificial after the thorn scrub, the sausage trees, and those scorched protea slopes where green-lipped Gwido had played his lobelia flute.

CHAPTER 7
Sogoloman

Moroto

Not far from Jinja I passed some silent villagers gaping at a smashed bicycle and the body of a youth half-covered by a bloody sheet. There was no sign of the vehicle that had run him down from behind. Perhaps its driver, scared of a beating, had hastened on to report the accident at a police station. Perhaps he had simply fled.

Then beyond Tororo on a straight road I passed another small crowd staring at an overturned Peugeot. Earlier that morning I had seen an army lorry standing on its roof at the edge of Kampala golf course. One of its wheels had rolled into a bunker.

With all this fresh in mind I drove carefully along the new Soroti highway. I hooted at lorries pounding towards me on the crown of the road and crawled past the sleepy cow-man with his half-dozen lurching bulls.

The landscape had been very gradually changing from village greens and fields to scattered scrub. Now, when I drove through the Napak gap, I saw that it had become quite different. There were no more leafy *mvule* trees, cotton fields or green grass. I was entering a vast tract of black soil, cracked by drought and bristling with thorn trees which glistened, as though rime-sprayed, with a pale armature of three-inch spikes. It all looked dead and empty. But when I got out of my car I realised, suddenly, that the stunted thorn bush with its ugly, plum-like galls was full of bird song, and the burnt plain seemed less desolate.

Towards Moroto tall men, quite naked, were idling with their cattle in shady patches of scrub. Their skins were dusty and did not shine. Some government sheds looked ugly among the thatched beehive huts.

Moroto town is grouped round a handful of Indian-owned shops, a petrol station and bar. A cluster of heights, wooded and cool-looking, overhangs it. I asked the African petrol-pump attendant if he knew anything about the mountain, as I wanted to climb it. 'Don't go,' he said, 'unless you have askaris with you. Bad men live on the mountain. They will kill you.'

So I called at the Rest House and, while I was browsing among its shelf of obsolete fiction (Galsworthy and Gilbert Frankau spotted by tropical rain and mould), a party of Swiss came in. They were being driven by a tourist organisation from one game park to another. They looked bruised.

'*Wir müssen sofort baden*,' intoned the women. 'We must have a bath—immediately.'

The men wore new mosquito boots. One of them went outside and, after careful thought, photographed an aloe. Another, when he had finished, did the same thing. The aloe was not attractive. It bore no flowers, it was tattered, and it was stuck against a gate for dogs to urinate on.

Moroto has a large permanent garrison and was crammed with soldiers and police whose lorries, speeding along the dirt roads, throw up stones that cause havoc among windscreens. Behind the trading centre are a geological survey camp and a cluster of government bungalows. Here I met an Englishman trundling his baby in a pram. Moroto, he told me, was no longer the pleasant up-country place it had been. Its garrison was attracting droves of women, burglaries (hitherto almost unknown) were on the increase; worse, bilharzia worms had recently invaded the swimming pool. Several members had been infected and were very ill.

I slept in a garden and was woken by an enormous, naked old man begging for cents. When I had done with him he stalked off to sit down with a policeman's family who were breakfasting outside their hut. They accepted him without embarrassment. The policeman's wife gave him a piece of bread while her husband went on cleaning his teeth with a stick.

Katikekile

To approach the main peaks of the Moroto range I had to motor eastward along its southern flank for another twenty miles. There, at a fork on a stony track that dipped through lonely scrub, I came to Katikekile village. A professional hunter was encamped nearby with a five-ton lorry, a Land Rover, refrigerator, and tents.

He was a Dane from Kampala, a big blond man in unpressed khaki, unshaven, with a pale sun tan, and in good spirits. 'My client', he announced, 'has just shot a leopard. It was shitting on a rock.' She came, he added, from Texas; the safari was costing her £60 a day. He gave me some tinned beer, and I went off to find porters.

The headman took me to the village. Its beehive huts stood in a clearing within a circular fence of thorns, like a Victorian explorer's sketch. From the outside the village looked dead. The next moment, like an exploding anthill, it was erupting people. Within a minute I was surrounded by a hundred Tepeth.

In Moroto town I had found it a little odd to stand next to a naked man in a grocer's shop. Here, in clothes, it was my turn to feel conspicuous. I stared back at the Tepeth: at the shaven-headed children with their spidery bodies, their bright eyes and gleaming teeth; at the women in their beads and rancid-smelling leather aprons. What an array of breasts! Breasts like pumpkins, like small pawpaws, like tubers or yams, like black pears. Breasts with scarification marks. Breasts dried up with age into flaps of skin above stomachs deeply furrowed by pregnancies. Since there was no obesity among them, there was no real ugliness.

I looked at the jostling men: at their lip-plugs lodged like loose dental plates in the gap where incisor teeth had been rooted out; at their feathered coiffures, their lean, scarified bodies, their hairless bellies and dusty buttocks. They carried sticks and spears. Some had glazed and damaged eyes, one or two were blind. They brought with them a swarm of small, irritating flies. They wanted cigarettes.

This, my first confrontation with naked tribesmen, was an unforgettable moment. I have had 500 Italian prisoners-of-war stripped for delousing in the Western Desert: they were merely white men whose pallor was stained with dark patches of hair; without dignity, bawling out in their high voices the names of

71

their friends, grinning and scratching themselves. This sort of nakedness, though, had style. The Tepeth were not, in fact, naked at all, but they had subtly refashioned their nakedness in a decorative way. In the virtual absence of clothes it was their *bodies* they had cut, coloured, disguised, and pierced with bits of finery. The dark pigment was a varnish, the beaded necklaces and flashing armlets the skin's mosaic.

Sogoloman

The headman chose two active-looking men wearing only their brown *shuka* cloths flapping round the shoulders, and as an afterthought a youth fresh from school, in a fancy shirt (it had a pattern of champagne glasses), to interpret. Within twenty minutes we were off, carrying very light loads, for I should be back, said the headman, before noon next day.

We turned north into the bush, which at first was very hot and dry. Even the weird *euphorbia candelabrum* trees with their prickly, spreadeagled arms had a grey, dessicated look. Then after two hours we started to climb; the spindly acacias began to thin out, a slight palpitation of the air stirred across our faces, and we passed into a zone of protea trees with fresh green leaves and white flowers bursting like spun sugar out of the calyx. By late afternoon we had reached a plateau at about 8,000 feet.

Here an extensive plantation of young pines was springing bravely out of rough soil. Observing my interest in them, my escort, who had been puzzled about the object of my journey, decided that I was an agricultural expert. Having thus identified me, they felt happier. A dikdik ran out of a thicket. Liman—the one who carried a minute wooden comb in his hair, and a chewing stick—stalked it with a stone but missed.

The headman had extolled the forest station hut nearby as a comfortable place, as good as a rest house. It turned out to be a flimsy shed fouled with cattle dung and guarded by a dozen whistling kites which swooped on our food box. My companions lit a fire, boiled the maize meal, and chain-smoked my cigarettes. In the night they coughed miserably. I was a little more comfortable. The ground was cold and greasy against my back, but I wore clothes.

In the morning my companions led me, at first, downhill instead of up towards the crest which ran green and lumpy along the northern horizon. Only Lokitari was willing to turn back with me to the top.

Lokitari was the most elegant of our party. He had plastered his hair into a blue-painted mud cap, and I noticed how careful he was to wipe the mucous from his fingers (he had a cold) on the soles of his feet. He walked with such grace that, while I had to hurry to keep up with him, he simply floated along.

Three hours later we had climbed along a cliff buzzing with swifts, and emerged on a delightful grassy ridge that led up to the summit we had seen from the forest hut. This knoll, which I now climbed, is called Sogoloman (9,632 feet). Sokdek, the main peak, 500 feet higher, stood a little ahead beyond a thick growth of forest.

I decided to leave Sokdek alone and to rest with Lokitari on the ridge. It was soft to sit on, and there was a small herd of cattle grazing its edge, with a timid herdsboy whom we had to flush from behind a bush. The grass, recently burnt, was shooting fresh and green from the charred soil. It was speckled with the silvery everlastings that, on the higher slopes of East Africa's mountains, take the place of Alpine edelweiss.

Sogoloman was not very high; but it had got me away from the hot, wrinkled plain—I could see it stretched out below, peppered with tumuli and small cloud shadows—and the flies that plagued the eyes of children and animals. It had also enabled me to be with Lokitari. To intrude successfully, to communicate—that is the European traveller's problem in Africa, where his methods of transport, his status, and his impatience are generally a barrier to enjoying common ground with simple men.

My point of contact with Lokitari was, of course, a very tiny one, the experience we were sharing minute. The specialist in such relationships works on an altogether different plane. He selects his community with care and lives with it for a year or more, sharing its squalor and some of its joys. Its life, its language, its genealogies and clan patterns absorb him. He must pry on people and yet appear not to, subtly interrogate, play the role of Good Samaritan. But even the anthropologist

3*   73

cannot stick it indefinitely. Sickening at length of porridge, ticks, and the small sores that refuse to heal, he collects his notebooks and escapes for a breather to his library and to proper meals. I, on the other hand, was merely taking a walk.

Water hole

We returned next day down a trail that at the bottom of the valley took us through a mile-long stretch of rough millet and sorghum cultivation. Trees felled by fire littered the stony plots like white bones of animals. All the termite mounds had been broken up for food.

At a muddy water hole my companions splashed themselves with water from the cooking pot and rubbed their bodies till the skin that had been dulled by grime shone like polished metal. Women with goats watched us, and when we had finished, borrowed our pot to bathe their babies in.

Another five hours' march through arid scrub faced us—the worst because they were the last and the most impatient ones. The sun was overhead, and the sandy track imprinted with big splayed feet seemed endless. It meandered over pebbly stream beds, across cattle-trampled grass, round termite mounds and along ridges bared by erosion. We disturbed guinea fowl, baboons, and braying hornbills. The go-away bird called insolently from the crown of an acacia tree. There was a harsh crying of shrikes. My companions seemed to glide along, chewing sticks and using their short cloths as shoulder pads for the empty loads.

Now the scrub was thinning. A cloud of flies flew to meet us. Then I saw my car, a white beetle surrounded by gentle bulls, with a man guarding it.

Soroti

The headman came up to collect his presents, my companions knotted their twenty-shilling notes into the folds of their *shukas*, and we saluted each other—the Tepeth throwing an arm upward in their unmistakable way. With a raging thirst I began to bump along the stones to Moroto.

74

When I got there only a single store was open. But the two Patel Hindus who ran it from behind a formidably high counter sold beer. A Sikh with his arm round a fat girl in a short skirt winked at me.

Now I was on the dirt road running south-west through the nail-sprayed thorn trees to Soroti. Army lorries were trailing dust, naked men beckoned me from the roadside to stop—they have learned that European motorists will pay them money to pose for a photograph.

Beyond the Napak hills, in Teso, it was green again and villagers in white shirts were shaving grassy lawns with pangas.

'What sort of country is Karamoja?' I asked a Teso store-keeper, ingenuously.

'Too many thorns,' he replied. 'Very bad for bicycles.'

'Are the Karamojong a good people?'

'Yes,' said another man, 'very good—at stealing cattle.'

Just beyond Soroti I stopped at a lake swamp to cool off. The constant splash of pied kingfishers diving into the water was like the plop of stones. A little later I overtook the first wobbling cyclists with big bunches of green plantains on the carriers. Then the sun dropped behind black storm clouds. In Busoga and Buganda it was the time of rain. It would be lashing the bay near the Irish nuns' leper hospital at Buluba and drumming on the corrugated iron roofs of Kampala. I was nearly home.

CHAPTER 8

Kachagalau

Amudat

I had seen the Karasuk range of hills from the top of Kadam.
They pointed in the direction of Turkanaland, and I wanted to
walk there. So I had come to Amudat in the Suk country of
north-eastern Uganda.

Amudat has the usual handful of Indian and Somali owned
stores lining a dusty road, a police post, an ADC's office, and
rival mission stations of the Verona Fathers and Bible Churchmen's Missionary Society. The Verona Fathers run a school
next to some shacks on a hill stripped by goats. The BCMS has
a small hospital. The Rest House is a clean corrugated iron
shed with two cubicles surrounded by scrub and noisy starlings.

I had reached the Rest House after dark, to find it already
occupied by a stout man in a vest whom I could see shaving by
the light of a pressure lamp. He was well equipped. He had a
servant, a folding chair, a table (laid for supper), and a radio.
Hoping it would not rain I put up my camp bed under a tree
and scowled at him.

Unjustly, though, for soon, having observed perhaps that
I was brewing tea in an old tin, he called me over to share his
supper of Mulligatawny soup and fried sausages.

He told me, in a pleasant Dorset brogue, that he was a
marketing officer travelling from Moroto to auction native
cattle. After supper he invited me to hear the test match score
on his radio, and then debate his considered opinion—common
among old timers—that 'Africans are nice fellows but not yet
ready to run their own affairs'.

On Rhodesia we could not agree. A white teacher in East
Africa is almost bound to have liberal views. It is one thing for
European officials and businessmen to scoff, in private places,

at African 'inefficiency' and to retail with *Schadenfreude* the latest gaffes of their African colleagues. But a teacher not only has daily confirmation of the ability and potential of his students: he is morally bound to believe in that potential— what otherwise would be the point of teaching? With some natural conceit, and the image of his brightest pupils in mind, he firmly believes in the future.

'The British government lost its nerve,' was my host's summing up of African politics. 'It dished out *uhuru* right, left, and centre, and now there'll be hell to pay.'

Morukori

A little farther along the red *murram* road, at Loro, I saw in bright morning light the 9,156-foot Kachagalau peak rising twenty miles away above flat thorn scrub. It looked cool and green, it was higher than any other point in the range, and from the top I would have a view of the Turkwell river running behind. So I asked the headman for someone to accompany me there.

Volunteers ran up ready as usual to start that very moment. My gear—four 5 lb. bags of maize meal were the heaviest item—was quickly tied into small loads, and we set off across the dessicated plain at a sharp pace.

When I told my four Suk companions to go slower, Morukori, the leader, looked at me with some contempt. He was even more disgusted to learn that I was unarmed. There were, he said, dangers. We were passing through country often raided by rival Karamojong.

'We have no cattle. What would they want with us?' I asked.

'They like to kill someone', replied Mario, who was attending the Verona Fathers' Mission school near Moroto, and spoke English, 'in order to be a gentleman.'

Morukori was tall and grave, not black but dark brown. He wore his loose cloth knotted like a toga at the shoulder, green ear-rings and a metal armlet; and with his hair plastered into a painted mud carapace surmounted by feathers, he was as magnificent as an early American Indian. Mario, in shirt and shorts, looked by comparison like an office boy. The two other

77

Suk had folded their capes round their necks and were plodding silently along, chewing sticks to keep the saliva running.

The trail wound through the sort of landscape that was becoming familiar to me: thorn bush, *euphorbia candelabrum*, whose upstretched bare arms end in blunt and prickly stubs, and spiny aloes with swords of small rusty flowers. Among this monotonous growth, hornbills dipped and trumpeted and shrikes flickered black and white. Our first halt was at a dry stream bed with a tiny water hole scooped under a kigelia tree. Strings of big sausage-shaped fruits were dangling from its branches like the outsize *Wurstwaren* that festoon a Munich butcher's shop—uneatable as plastic imitations but used when sliced to ferment and flavour native beer.

Walking, mile after mile, through thorn bush can be dull—a mere means to an end. To break the monotony I like to stop and watch a woodpecker, or the tiny ants scurrying from a punctured acacia gall, or the changing silhouette of a hill.

I am in fact a slow walker, and I break the rules. It is recommended on foot safari to start early and to camp (those Victorian fears of sunstroke!) before noon.

I prefer to bumble along all day, stopping when I feel like it for a mouthful of water and a smoke. Each morning I fill my old Vermouth bottle with boiled water and it lasts me till we camp at night. I eat scarcely anything until the first stars come out and a fire is lit. After a day or two I find, when I shave, that my face has sagged. But I feel very well.

Now, to distract me, there were warthogs running off with their tufted tails in the air, tiny dikdik antelopes, and baboons. By dusk, when we made camp at a bore hole and the Suk boiled their maize meal into a snow-white paste, we had come only twelve miles. The high interwoven crown of the copse where we were resting trapped the firelight and became an illuminated dome bright enough to read by.

Kachagalau

Next morning, at the foot of the mountain, we came to a Suk village. Around it naked men with spears and elaborate coiffures were grazing cattle on scraps of grass. Their women, with the tails of their leather aprons tucked beneath them, sat dressing each other's mops of hair. They were loaded with rings and scarred with ornamental cuts and keloids. Their small worn bodies had lost the lines of youth. But their faces, with the flawed eyes—spoilt since childhood by flies, smoke and con-junctivitis—broke readily into delightful smiles. The solitary trader among them was a recent Somali refugee from the Congo, and all he had in his dark little hut was some salt, a pan of milk, and a wrapped-up wife in *purdah*.

As soon as I saw the *catha edulis* shrubs lining the track up Kachagalau, I knew we should be slowed down. From now on my companions plucked and chewed incessantly the bright green *muirungi* leaves, till their eyes turned muddy and we made an early camp under the main mountain wall. Only Morukori disdained the leaf. He preferred my Norwegian sardines, and snuff which he prepared by grinding a lump of native tobacco and mixing the powder with salt.

He affected to have a better opinion of me now. He had, he confided, four wives and 'dozens of children' ('divide by three' remarked Mario). As he finished off my packet of Mombasa cashew nuts and got ready to sleep with his head propped on his tiny neck-stool, he called me *dumee*, warrior-like, then *simba*, lion.

I watched the night breeze lick the fire, and I knew that I could drop off to sleep at will.

In Kampala, fidgeting on a government spring mattress, I start when a dog barks (a thief after my car, or a man with a hooked pole trying the windows?). The narrow burglar-proofed openings do not let in enough air. There is a smell of drains blocked by old shoe-polish tins.

When I hear the muezzin's faraway call and then a little later a bugler sounding reveille in the police barracks, I know I have had a poor night.

I looked at my companions. Using their *shuka*-cloths as blankets they were lying perfectly still. The night was a harp, with a twang of insects and the rustle of leaves. The fire was dwindling to a nest of embers. I could hear an animal moving near at hand in the bush. Perhaps it was bent on mischief. But I didn't care.

In the morning we left the sunlight behind and climbed abruptly into a dark forest—scabby, lichenous, and smothered in rope-like lianas, with a floor of sodden black humus. Some of the tallest trees had been felled and their trunks hacked in sections to be hollowed out for bee hives.

Then, above the forest, we found the crest barbed with thorns which pierced the thinning soles of my plimsolls. I had to duck through the spines and brambles, but my companions marched straight on. The thorns which drew blood from me left on their bare bodies only a pattern of light grey marks.

The crest

Swifts swooped over our heads as we rested among patches of tree heather on the summit. I saw, though from a different angle, a landscape that I was getting to know. The plain lay in a haze that thickened with distance. Eastward, running parallel to the range on which we stood, the Turkwell river was heading darkly into the ochre spaces of Turkanaland for Lake Rudolf. Loro was diminished to a twinkle of tin.

One could of course have climbed Kachagalau in half the time. A mountaineering club would have hurried to the top and back in a day, or, more likely, ignored Kachagalau completely, for it has no steep pitches, no challenge to rope work. It was just a big bushy hill, almost waterless, sheltering a few poor cattle camps and some rotting beehives slung in trees.

I liked sitting there. I opened my tin of Tanzanian bully and leaned against a rock varnished with lichen. The knoll was everywhere strewn with immortelles. The swifts were swishing back and forth like darts. Even my companions seemed to be enjoying themselves. They had been studying landmarks through my binoculars. Now they had fallen asleep with the sun on their bare genitals.

I wondered where to go next. South, along the continuing range of mountains towards the settler country approaching Kitale? West, to the Acholi hills where the old men meander from one calabash of millet beer to another? Or to those Congo frontier volcanoes where, I had been told, mountain gorillas make their hammocks in the giant heather trees?

-d. Making and playing the Lobelia flute, Mt Kadam

6a. *Protea*, Mt Kadam

b. *Dracaena*, Mt Kadam

c. *Khat* leaf, Mt Kadam

d. Walking through scrub below Sogoloman

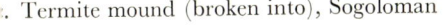

a. Termite mound (broken into), Sogoloman   b. Walking past *Euphorbia candelabrum*, Sogoloman

c. Morukori (guide) on Kachagalau

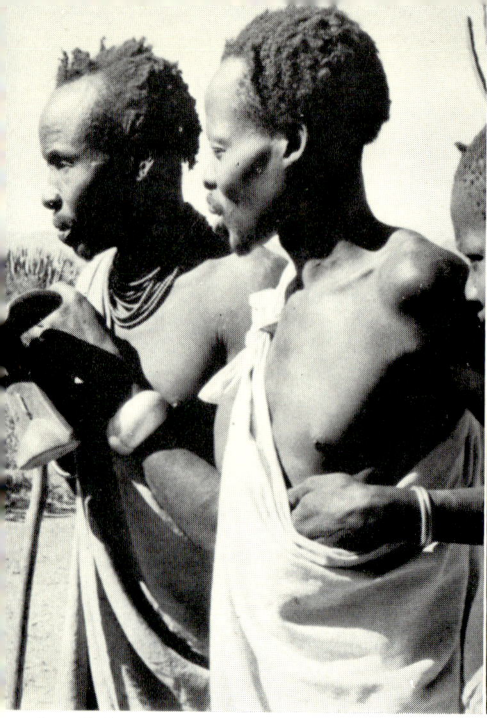

8a. Suk men

b. Suk women

c. Suk women

CHAPTER 9

Sabinio

Two inns and a school

The three Mufumbiro volcanoes stand at the edge of Kigezi district along the Congo-Rwanda border. I had already—not long after my arrival in Kampala—travelled through part of Kigezi, to observe some of my students on teaching practice. It had been (to use that debased word) my first 'safari'. The striped hills, the green-blue distances smouldering above the papyrus swamps and curved horns of cattle, had left a sharp memory. Here are some of those early impressions.

Since the government was going to pay my bills, I had broken my journey at the Ankole Inn, Mbarara. I had heard people sneer at this hotel. They said the food brought on stomach-ache, that the baths were rusty and the mosquito curtains had holes in them.

'Dysentery Hall', however, had attracted me. Its walls were painted a sickly pink. Scruffy vultures were waiting outside the infamous kitchen for scraps. The owner, an Englishman of an earlier generation, now old and deaf, but a redoubtable traveller in his day, evidently had a soft heart for Africans— which, I assumed, was the root cause of all the prejudice against his hotel. I saw them trooping in with pots and totos (small children) to fetch water from his taps. He did not mind who entered his bar, with the result that a prim Anglican clergyman might find himself being jostled by some brazen local tart with a beaded waist band jingling under her skirt.[1]

After dinner, when I walked through the garden to my room, two of these girls came towards me out of the shadows. The moon shone on their cheap finery, their white teeth and oiled

---

[1] Mr Hall has since sold his hotel to Indians, and it has lost business to a new motel with a chromium-plated bar. But he has stayed on in one of the rooms, and he appears silently for meals.

legs, and they were giggling; hoping for an emolument that I would take one of them into my bed beneath the yellowing mosquito curtain. I told them to try the next bungalow, which was occupied by a silent Dutchman from South Africa.

The White Horse Inn at Kabale was quite different. Two English ladies ran it—quietly, efficiently, hygienically. We had to dress for dinner. The cook prepared shepherd's pie, puddings and custard. No one shouted or fell down in the bar. The lounge with its hunting trophies, its elephant-foot rubbish baskets and pale log fire filled up in the evening with elderly Americans who were touring the game parks. They were taking no risks with their health. They had clean, grey complexions, and went early to bed with little bottles of soda water.

Local Africans and improperly dressed Europeans used a side bar with separate entrance. Here I met an African headmaster who, in return for a double whisky, sent me, next morning, a box of small, strong-tasting eggs.

A golf course screened by imported trees runs past the inn. Even the rose bushes, the dripping cypress hedges, the red earth worms and the cold early morning mist that made me cough, reminded me of England.

Not till the mist cleared did the rusty roofs of the town emerge at the foot of a hill. Like any other provincial town in Uganda, Kabale spreads outwards from a row of Indian *dukas*, with the residential area for officials on high ground at a proper distance away. All about lie the rounded Kigezi hills striped with green and straw-coloured contour plots.

The three students whom I had come to visit were teaching at a secondary boys' boarding school a mile away, along a side valley crowded with papyrus swamp that was rotting the building foundations. It was an almost entirely African school—Indian children rarely board, for among other things they miss their customary food—and it had a European staff.

The staff room was a happy, muddled place. A man with an extraordinary beard—for a moment, I took him for Trollope—was marking essays among old cricket bats and tea cups. No one minded me prowling about.

I soon saw—what everyone had told me would be the case—

that a great weakness of the young African teacher is his limited background knowledge—which is inevitable, for he is required to struggle with a vast range of subjects, from Babylonia and the ancient African civilisation of Meroë ('distressingly little is known about it', say even the specialist historians) to coffee growing in Brazil. This, for him, encyclopaedic task enslaves him at first to the few elementary facts given in a class textbook, so that each lesson tends for a while to be a set-piece, small, thin and rigid.

The pupils in African schools, on the other hand, are extraordinarily teachable. They come to learn. Their parents have sacrificed to scrape together the school fees. To pass exams is vital. Success will revolutionise their lives, lift them out of the village hut into an entirely different, twentieth-century dimension.

Here at Butobere not all the boys wore shoes. Their white cotton shirts were fraying. Their long legs and heavily muscled bodies seemed too big for the desks. They carried pens stuck in their hair. In class they were shy and soft-spoken.

There was dust and noise, for building was still going on under supervision of an old Sikh foreman. Crested cranes were strolling about the football pitch. The staff were young Englishmen serving two-year contracts which the Ministry of Education hoped they would renew. They had brick houses to live in, game parks and hill climbing for recreation. They had been able to buy cars on government loans, they could dress as they liked, grow beards, save a little money. They were said to be good teachers, and they were enthusiasts.

When I left Kabale, many small smouldering fires—they are often lit to keep flies from grazing cattle—were filling the valleys with smoke plumes. I stopped to boil tea at the top of a pass. A small herd of muddy Ankole cattle came up swishing their enormous horns like scythes. The man with them said, 'Jambo', his women giggled at me behind their hands. Then they turned off the road, and treading softly as gipsies disappeared uphill among elephant grass and stubble.

In another hour of driving I had left the pepper-pot hills and the blue mist behind. I had already made up my mind to come again.

To Kisoro

Now, eighteen months later (November 1965), I was free at last to visit the Mufumbiro volcanoes.

But there was still political tension between Uganda and the Congo. There had been reports of violence on the frontier, and the area where the three peaks stand had been declared a restricted zone. I needed a police pass to get there.

The lift which took me up to the pass office in Kampala had a pencilled drawing of a vagina glaring like a distorted eye from its white wall. 'An Indian did it', said the African lift man.

A small Welshman with a boxer's broken nose was in charge of the pass office. 'You can go as far as the Uganda customs post at Kisoro,' he said, 'but no farther.'

I told him this wasn't good enough. The peaks I wanted to visit lay beyond Kisoro.

'Impossible, and dangerous,' he replied. 'You don't want to get shot as a white mercenary, do you?'

So without a permit, but trusting that officials in the field would (as they generally are) be broader minded than those at the controls, I set off.

Long drought had been causing havoc to agriculture in the northern districts and in Kenya. But the banana zone of Uganda remained green, and, in uncultivated patches of scrub, thorn trees carried furry scented balls of blossom.

Beyond Masaka, however, not far from where the equator crosses the road, grass was being burnt off the dry land, revealing through smoke and crackling flames a vast rash of termite mounds spotting the charred soil like black warts. In this temporary wasteland the only cheerful colours were the scorched trusses of a few coral trees and the cream-tipped fingers of the *euphorbia candelabrum* which now reared starkly from the bald termite mounds as if on plinths. Kites were circling over the holocaust, devouring insects and small scurrying rodents. The sun and the hills were hidden.

At the Ankole Inn the vultures were still squatting by the dustbins. The owner's wife had arrived to ginger things up.

She was a large, freckled, handsome woman in a heavy skirt. She joined me for tea, spoke sharply to a servant, and began to grumble.

'I'm constantly having to chase these boys,' she said. 'Straight off trees. Know nothing. Yet I have to start them off at a hundred shillings a month.'

She was born in Kenya—'a much better country than this. The Europeans here', she went on, 'are a poor lot. Officials mostly, scared of losing their jobs. Scarcely a real *man* amongst them.'

'And how do you get on with Africans?' she asked.

'Fine', I said tactlessly.

Yet it must have been dull for her, used to the tough, hearty society and common memories of Kenya settlers, to be stranded in this up-country hotel whose guests were a few harassed tourists and tired government employees in transit.

As I was leaving, a hired car came up the drive. It was filled with men carrying plastic leather briefcases. They wore thick Central European suits, tight shoes, and they looked pale and sweaty. They were Poles and probably belonged to a trade delegation buying Uganda coffee.

Spotting immediately something to photograph, two of them approached the vultures dozing by the dustbins. Slowly, at first, so that the photographers were encouraged to pound after them, the vultures staggered off a few paces; and then, of course, as soon as the cameras were about to click, they opened their wings and flapped quickly out of range to go on with their vigil in a tree.

The Poles look dejected. The fine red dust had turned to a smear round their collars. They would have been more comfortable in the shorts and open shirt of a discredited colonialist.

The dirt road running west of Mbarara to Kabale was being remade. For thirty miles, enormous machines had gouged up the surface, so that it was already dark before I crossed the Ankole border into Kigezi.

On the Ankole side, among the rough grazing and open scrub, hills were still aflame with grass fires that, at a distance, looked in the night like strings of lighted villages, then turned, nearer at hand, into red writhing snakes. Dust had stained hedges a sickly yellow. The winding road was sometimes blocked with small droves of cattle whose eyes glittered like marbles in my head lamps. There were no stars, and nothing to lighten the black Kigezi serpentines but the rare glimmer of a wick.

Kigezi was dead, the last drunks quarrelling in torn shirts outside a bar. I put up my camp bed on the golf course and was almost asleep when someone's house dog got wind of me, and set up such a barking that the owner, fearing thieves, came out with a stick.

I woke early to find a man waiting to sell me three eggs. I drove off in an English mist. All about lay the rounded Kigezi hills—row upon row of them, like striped mushrooms, their domes and sides banded with dense contour cultivation. The sly brown hammerkop was feeding among papyrus bog and gusts of soft air ruffled the head feathers of the black-crested eagles that watched over looping valleys.

Ascending the pass to Kisoro I stopped at the Kanaba gap and had my first sight of the three Mufumbiro peaks. They stand, lapped in watery haze, exactly on the Uganda-Rwanda border (it bisects them), at a point where the two territories converge on the Congo. Their symmetry is startling. Over the side I had ascended I had an airman's view of black lake-water and huts like haycocks.

This—like the great sunken shaft of the eastern Rift near Nairobi—is one of the unforgettable views of East Africa. The Rift, in the Naivasha area, used to be Masai country; the Kanaba gap is getting very near its western limb, towards the heart of Bantu Africa. The eastern arm had been roamed by a cattle-keeping people; along the arm I was approaching, countless thatched villages were embedded among dense undergrowth.

A crested eagle mewed suddenly over my head. The white patches on its black wings were shining like snow flakes on coal.

The Travellers' Rest

Kisoro has the usual double row of mainly Indian stores that sell everything from Japanese cloth to Hong Kong torches, white man's toilet paper and Dutch tinned milk. The exit road was barred by tall soldiers in floppy hats. They were not prepared to argue. I could carry my luggage, they said, through the barrier to the Travellers' Rest hotel 200 yards away, but I would have to leave my car with them.

I found Walter Baumgaertel, the German-born hotel proprietor, tossing beer-bottle caps to a magnificent Alsatian bitch. 'A guest,' he cried. 'Bravo!'

I had hoped to creep quietly into his hotel, spy out the land, then slip away unobtrusively in the direction of the mountains. I did not want to attract attention.

But Mr Baumgaertel was evidently bored, sad, and irritable; and he welcomed me with such a harangue that I feared immediate trouble with an army major who was sitting in the lounge over a bottle of stout.

'All these nonsensical police restrictions', he declaimed, 'are ruining my business. I've had to sack my servants, hump my provisions from the shop like a porter, give credit to soldiers— *Ich hab' es bis zum Hals heraus*, I'm fed up, broke!'

I looked furtively at the major, but his face, bent over the stout bottle, stayed expressionless.

The only effect of closing the Rwanda and Congo borders, Mr Baumgaertel went on, was to enrich smugglers. Everyone was drinking Rwanda Primus beer (cheaper and stronger than the Uganda brand), which of course he dared not sell.

What was worse, even the gorillas that used to be the hotel's main attraction had not been seen for a long time in their old mountain haunts. It was thought they had been driven off by leopards, and had taken refuge on the Rwanda side of the Mufumbiro range.

'If I could collect the money people owe me,' said Mr Baumgaertel, looking at the major, 'and find some Indian to buy this place, I'd be off tomorrow.'

Mr Baumgaertel is sixty or more, with a kind, old-maidish face and the soft hands of a music teacher. A romantic (I think) with intellectual interests, coping alone with the daily frustrations of trying to run a small business in a part of Africa that had been temporarily disorganised by neighbouring chaos. In happier times he had written a gay autobiographical book called *König in Gorillaland*. He now took me into his garden and looked sadly past the drooping moonflowers to the three conical silhouettes in no man's land from which even the gorillas had fled.

'*Schön, nicht wahr?*' he said. 'I have a hut on Mgahinga saddle —probably wrecked by now.'

I was impatient to mention my own business. But some government clerks had gone into the bar, and Mr Baumgaertel went back to serve them. He began to voice his grievances again.

'Any sort of hooligan can come in here these days,' he said loudly, 'swill beer, break my furniture, and expect credit. *Scheissdreck!*'

This was going too far. I looked warily at the major and at the inoffensive clerks. I had listened without protest to Mr Baumgaertel's tirades. My cause was surely lost.

But to my astonishment the major winked at me, and I saw that everyone had started to grin. So Mr Baumgaertel's rantings were a joke. He was a privileged person, a *rafiki*, a man without a wife to shout at. He could grumble as much as he liked, and no one would take offence.

The major, when he had finished his stout, came across to me. 'You can go and fetch your car,' he said. 'You won't, I regret, be able to use it—but you are free to go for walks.'

That was all I wanted.

Sabinio

I set off early for Sabinio, most westerly of the three peaks, on what turned out to be the first stage of a six-day trek.

I walked at first through fields planted with copper-headed sorghum, sweet potatoes and peas. Bahutu women were breaking the black soil with long-handled hoes. Their babies, strapped to the back in a cloth pulled tight across the top of the breasts, were lurching and bobbing their little cannon-ball heads to the rhythm of the hoe.

The African village baby in its snug pack on the mother's back must have a fine feeling of security. It accompanies her in whatever she does, is never left alone, is given the breast immediately it starts to cry, and peeping sideways or, when she stoops, over her shoulder, sees the world as an exciting place full of people and of movement.

The cloth in which the child is slung must surely distort the mother's breasts. These—roughly handled, dangling un-supported—are a functional apparatus that rapidly lose their early beautiful shape. But there is more honour in the worn mother-breast than in the smooth, horned gourd-shapes of a pretty girl.

Boys with shiny black goats offered to carry my lantern and water bottle. The only soldier I saw was asleep on a grassy bank with his hat tipped over his face. I walked softly past him.

Outside his hut I was joined by Reuben, the guide, and a wiry little porter with a thick neck, a sickle-shaped panga, and wooden club. I had already heard of Reuben. When tourists and gorillas were more plentiful, he had a great many customers. They have taken innumerable photographs of him as he parts the bush with his stick or examines a piece of gorilla dung.

Reuben is getting old, his brown equine face is furrowing, he dislikes being hurried. But he still looked business-like in his worn kepi with the game guard's badge, his puttees and plastic yellow sandals. He carried a spear and a ten-foot bamboo pole. His water bottle contained beer and grains of maize.

We walked that day as far as Sabinio hut. The *shambas* petered out in coarse grass where we trod among yellow ever-lastings. The rounded hills smouldered with haze. As we tramped through fields of peas, friends greeted Reuben with an exchange of grunts, musical and expressive, that sounded like the noises carters used to make to their horses. We filled our pockets with the peas.

A Munyankole builder's foreman was working near the hut, and I asked him about the fat women of Ankole who used to be fed on milk and forbidden work, so that they swelled to an enormous size. What, I asked, had become of them?

'It's no longer the fashion,' he said.

Did Ankole husbands like making love to such colossal pumpkins?

He laughed. 'The more fat,' he said, 'the more honour. A fat wife showed that the husband was a wealthy man.'

'Like today's owner of a Mercedes-Benz?'.

Soon after we had begun to ascend the lower bamboo forest above the hut, we had our first encounter with smugglers. There were at least a score of them, sturdy Bahutu from Rwanda in old raincoats and cast-off city jackets, shouldering rolls of hides along a stream bed.

Reuben, with a show of official rage, ran at them with his spear. They skipped off, mocking him, with their loads. We passed other groups of smugglers, about a hundred men in all, trotting silently in single file with sacks and bundles. When they had gone the forest was still again except for the buzz of flies and the sigh of a small wind tickling the bamboo tops. Gaudy butterflies sucked the juice of leopard droppings. We trod among elephant dung.

Above the bamboo we entered a belt of tree heathers braided with moss and lichens. Sabinio, Father of Teeth, has five peaks, separated like an uneven row of molars by steep ravines. We had reached the lowest projection and were gazing at the green ridge close ahead, when something quite unexpected happened. A dark mass, not a hundred yards away, suddenly began to move. I recognised them in the same moment as I heard Reuben's warning hiss. 'Gorillas', he whispered, apparently as surprised as I was.

We stood quite still, staring at them. It was their size that struck me—their immensely powerful bodies and their blackness. I longed to get nearer, but there was a steep little hollow between us, and the gorillas had already taken alarm.

Silently, almost crab-like, they dropped on their hands and with many backward scowls went slowly up the ridge and out of sight; last of all a big female with a young one riding like a jockey on her back.

We found the tracks they had been using strewn with black droppings. Their nests, built low like cradles among the tree heathers, were deserted.

'Gone back to Rwanda,' grumbled Reuben, pointing south into a gully. But he was delighted to have come across gorillas again. Perhaps the guide business would revive.

The slopes now steepened, and dark heathers gave way to a dense, bright green thatch of giant lobelias and tree groundsels which ran riot over the remaining knolls like some crazy and long neglected vegetable garden. We had to do a little crawling here, for Sabinio's last tooth is patched with steep little ledges of loose and greasy soil. I was glad to rest when at length we came to the top.

From a height of 11,900 feet we looked down into the Congo. As soon as I saw it, I had a strong desire to go there. The fragment that lay below was, it is true, only another piece of Africa—shaggy, tufted and brown, steaming a little, stained and ragged like an old door mat. But it had disturbing and dramatic associations. There were those scraps of old writings about it, embedded in the memory. The shadow of Conrad's Kurtz: Roger Casement's report on how Belgian government tax collectors used to lop off a man's right hand; that frightful moment when Grogan came across abandoned cooking pots with half-roasted human limbs in them.[1] And there were the present gross disorders.

I looked at my map, and on it drew a circle round Karisimbi.

As we sat there I saw that gorillas are not the only creatures that feed on the cool juicy plants through which we had threaded our way. The tall lobelias (whose stems, if you slash them, exude clear water and a creamy latex) were spangled with tiny malachite sunbirds which prey on the insects that breed and live within the protective flowers.[2] Like jewelled ribbons, the birds were flitting with streaming tail-feathers from one powder-blue spike to another.

Going down required a little more care than coming up. Night fell before we were off the mountain, and we had just

[1] Colonel Ewart Scott Grogan was the legendary, long-lived Irishman who, in 1898, as a Cambridge undergraduate, walked through Africa from north to south 'to prove himself worthy of his New Zealand sweetheart'. He settled in Kenya in 1904 and lived there for over sixty years. 'Let each man with means and muscle for the fray go forth at least to see what empire is,' he wrote in the preface to his book *From the Cape to Cairo*, London 1900. He concluded, 'A good sound system of compulsory labour would do more to raise the native in five years than all the missionary efforts for the last fifty.'

[2] The sunbird is said also to strip insulating hairs from the leaves of the high altitude 'cabbage' groundsels and to line its nest with them. See Dr Malcolm Coe's article 'Above the Forest on Mount Kenya' in *Africana*, Vol. 3, No. 5, Nairobi, March 1968.

91

re-entered the bamboo forest when we were startled by alarming noises of destruction.

'Elephants,' said my two companions.

Nothing would induce them to go on—elephants were *mbaya*, bad. So we went back a little, lit a bright fire, and settled down to doze. I slept badly with the fire roasting my feet and my back chilled. We were still nodding over the embers when, long after the elephants had gone crashing up the valley, the first birds began to twitter.

Muhavura

Our next objective was Muhavura (The Beacon), highest of the three volcanoes. To get there we had to traverse the intervening Mgahinga saddle. Here at dusk we had another encounter with smugglers.

I was leading, and the smugglers must have been very craven indeed, for as soon as they saw me come—alone—round a bend in the track they bolted into the bush, throwing down their head loads, which we retrieved after a search and carried into our shelter for the night.

We found that the six heavy bags were stuffed with tin grains. This disappointed me, for had it been coffee I would have kept some for myself. Reuben, though, became uneasy. The smugglers, he feared, might try to seize their property in the night. He went off to get a policeman.

He came in the morning with an escort, drank up our tea, and with much mock straining under its weight valued the loot at over £150.

'Who buys the stuff?' I asked Reuben.

'*Wahindi na Waharabi*,' he replied, 'Indian and Arab traders— and all the other contraband too: gold, ivory, coffee, Belgian cigarettes and beer. The Greeks have also got their fingers in the pie.'

We had to labour uphill next day through a dense forest overgrown with brambles, creepers, and lianas that festooned the trees like ships' ropes. No one for a long time had passed this way. We sent back for an extra porter, and both of them had constantly to slash a path. Their strength astonished me. Balancing our gear on their heads, and carrying a pole and a spear in one hand, with the other they hacked tirelessly with their curved pangas. The smell of crushed and severed plants was as sharp as ether.

My role was a despicable one. I waited till a tunnel had been slashed, and ducked through it.

We camped for the night by a thicket of beautiful hypericum trees whose foliage, in the day, had glowed with golden blossom. A tree hyrax croaked and screamed. I awoke soaked with dew to find my companions scraping out the *posho* pot.

Above the forest we came to another weird barricade of groundsels and lobelias. Reuben and the porters hacked cruelly at the frail, juicy plants. Their severed stems exposed rings of bleeding creamy pith with a tangy smell. The groundsels were of many shapes, some like sturdy tobacco plants, others with woody trunks that forked into lyre-like growths bolstered with great cushions of dead leaves.

By noon we were at the top of Muhavura (13,540 feet). Its gentle platform encircled a crater pool of blackish water, and gave a splendid view that was sharpened in the rain-washed air.

Along the arm of the western Rift the heads of other volcanoes were lined up far into the Congo's purple mist. Karisimbi, the highest of them, seemed to steeple into a cauldron of golden fire and smoke; Kigezi, on the Uganda side, revealed blue lakes coiled among the striped tumuli of Bakiga farmers. Immediately below us the tracks of smugglers were clearly visible on the saddle.

I told Reuben that I was going to climb Karisimbi one day. Would he come with me?

'No,' he replied, 'the people over there are *gasia*, thieves and trash, *kondos*. They would murder us, or put us in gaol.'

Reuben

On the way back, before we went on to the Travellers' Rest, Reuben took us into his hut to drink Primus beer. He had turned his parlour into a small private museum. All his souvenirs were there: the framed certificate of honour he was awarded in 1962, his badge, and a photograph of himself standing on a lawn in Entebbe in a double-breasted suit to receive them from the Governor. There were newspaper pictures of a young gorilla—another 'Reuben'—which he had found orphaned in the forest; it died soon after it was sent to Regent's Park zoo.

By the time we started for the Travellers' Rest the beer had taken effect. Reuben grabbed a bicycle and pounded my empty water can as though it were a drum. Mr Baumgaertel was not amused to see him come singing into his garden.

'Go home, Reuben,' he said.

'Reuben', he remarked to me, 'is getting old and foolish. As for chasing smugglers, he ought to mind his own business. One day someone will put a spear into his back.'

To me at any rate Reuben had been a delightful companion. Unruffled, tireless, and shrewd.

The grass fires were out when I drove back along the Masaka road. The charred landscape lay burnt and torn as though by gun fire. But life was creeping back. Purple starlings lined the verges. The setting sun shone on the dark markings of a topi antelope standing behind a blackened mound. When it moved it dragged, painfully, one of its legs.

Near a village I passed a drunk—or a madman—declaiming in the road. He had taken off all his clothes, and people were laughing at him. A little later I was facing the hazards of a night drive in Africa: big lorries loaded with charcoal and plantains belting along the crown of the road, and almost invisible files of villagers meandering through the shadows at the edge of the tarmac, to unlit huts among leafy trees.

CHAPTER 10

Nyiragongo

Mr Baumgaertel

When, some months later, I returned to Kisoro, Uganda's frontier with Rwanda and the Congo had just been reopened and business seemed back to normal.

At the barrier three big German lorries, returning to Kampala, were being searched by the Uganda customs while their Sikh drivers looked on gravely. When the contraband Belgian cigarettes, the Primus beer, and the dismantled Land Rover engine had been discovered, and they were fined £200, the Sikhs paid up with good grace.

The atmosphere was amiable. In the evening the Uganda customs officials, their Irish colleague, and the Sikhs all drank beer together in the bar of the Travellers' Rest. They were oddly assorted. Paddy, a big russet-haired man with a paunch, wore a hairy pullover and shorts that appeared not to be his own. The pullover was too small and exposed a drum of flesh round his navel. His white calves bulged like turnips above his socks.

The Sikhs wore jeans that clashed with their turbans and serious, bearded faces. Their hip pockets were lumpy with bank notes. The African officials had taken off their jackets. They all had one thing in common. They were thirsty.

Mr Baumgaertel had recovered his humour. Now that the frontier restrictions had been removed, his rantings were a thing of the past. He fetched his gorilla books and discussed some of the visitors he had known. He liked the modest ones— such as Alan Moorehead and Miss Donisthorpe; and the real experts like Schaller, the American. It was the mean and the conceited he couldn't stand: the ones who expected Reuben to tramp all day for five shillings and no food; the Dane who had boasted of his gorilla pictures (they turned out to be monkeys); people who were rude to the hotel's tame 'pygmy'—an old, ugly man who begged for cents.

Mr Baumgaertel's huge watchdog prowled happily among the gorilla books and bottles. In the town, beyond the barrier, everything would now be shuttered. The Indian storekeepers would be drinking sweet tea with milk in their back parlours, their wives, crosslegged on the floor, chattering shrilly, the children asleep on made-up beds among the packing cases. In the hotel garden, the damp night air brought out the sweet smell of moonflower blossom.

The frontier

The object of my journey was to climb Nyiragongo. It stands inside the Congo border, and on Mr Baumgaertel's advice I was going to take the longer Goma route through Rwanda. The lonely road running direct from the Congolese frontier post at Bunagana to Rumangabo was, he thought, still too risky for Europeans.

The only evidence, next day, that I had left Uganda and entered Rwanda was that Africans spoke French, one drove on the right, and the road was spattered with loose volcanic stones. The same pipe-smoking Bahutu people were trudging past in old felt hats and coats. The same untidy plots were shaggy with banana groves, maize and vegetables. The same white-collared crows were honking over rows of eucalyptus trees, and crested cranes flourished their yellow crowns among elephant grass sprouting from muddy black earth.

One by one I began to round and then pass the great volcanic cones capped with cloud that stretch in a crooked file—there are eight in all, comprising the Virunga range—from Muhavura in Uganda to Nyamuragira in the Congo.

Then at the bottom of a hill marked by a Catholic shrine I came to the lakeside at Kisenyi. This small town—the lake is said to be free of bilharzia—used to be a popular holiday resort. But it had been dying for some time. There was no one about except a soldier who shouted at me. The lake with its fringe of gaudy shrubs, bungalows and a few hotels, was grey and silent.

I bought some Congo francs from a tubby Belgian hotelier with a massive African wife. Her complexion, after many years of bleaching it, had turned yellow. He, in spite of his thirty years on the equator, looked as pink and well preserved as a prosperous grocer at home. The meal he gave me was entirely unsuited to a tropical climate: very fat pork chops, boiled red cabbage soaked in oil, and cream tart.

Now for the test. Waiting for me in a shed at the Congo frontier, I found half-a-dozen young men wearing smoked glasses and fancy shirts. They were sitting round a transistor set that was in full blast, evidently enjoying their authority and determined to make a profit out of it.

Their technique was the cat-and-mouse game—humiliating, time-wasting, and expensive if one weakened. I could not enter the Congo, they said flatly after some discussion. I was told to get back into my car and drive several times round a tree.

One of them then took me to be questioned by a more senior official. I leant against the chair by his desk; it disintegrated noisily into three pieces. No, he said, I could not travel farther. Indeed, as I was already on Congolese territory without documents, I was in trouble. He told me to circle another tree and practise parking. I was then left to brood, with a soldier to watch me.

When they thought I had been sufficiently softened up the youths called me back into their hut. They stared at me like stage inquisitors. I noticed that the wall calendar was a year out of date. They wore expensive wrist-watches. They were calculating how much they could squeeze me for.

'You can have your visa,' one of them suddenly announced. 'It will cost you a hundred and fifty shillings.'

I couldn't help laughing. 'Don't be so bloody silly,' I said in English, and then, '*Messieurs, je vous payerai vingt shillings, pas de plus.*'

My twenty-shilling note was accepted, everyone relaxed, and I was about to go when another fellow came out of a roofless shed. 'Currency control,' he said. What he really wanted was another pound for himself. He got nothing.

It was now the soldier's turn. He had been peering at my baggage and I felt more sympathetic to him than to the others —he was the sort of man whom in other circumstances I might have recruited as a porter and shared a camp fire with. I put a tin of sardines into his hand, and without looking back drove swiftly into Goma.

Goma

Goma—a collection of banks and poorly stocked shops—was modern, unfinished, and already decomposing. The arcaded pavements were still littered with steel reinforcing rods left uncovered by the builders. Rubbish was heaped behind the *boutiques*. The new bank façades were chipped. In the suburbs rows of cheap cuboid houses stood among grease, weeds and wrecks of cars.

There were touts everywhere, and young men in fancy shirts, among them a few Europeans—I took them to be Greeks and Belgians—carrying briefcases with the seedy, defeated air of small-time salesmen who would go on putting up with humiliations in the hope of a little profit and of better times to come.

Their women, in these tough, chaotic conditions, looked I thought unwisely conspicuous. The dyed blonde hair trailed behind their ears like plastic straw, and they wore tights in cream and sky-blue that showed the outlines of underwear and trembling flesh. In Brussels one would have taken them for tarts doing their shopping. Here in Goma they seemed to be asking for trouble.

I went into a bar and looked out at the half-dozen battered cars parked in the town centre, at the cigarette touts and the chocolate-skinned women. The smartest of the women had brightly patterned lengths of cloth twisted round their hips. They had wrapped their spiky coiffures in bulky turbans. They had high-heeled shoes and large, soft, beautiful eyes above wide lips on which the red make-up looked mauve. I suspected their cobra-like embraces would leave a wound. They would make off with your clothes as well as your money: and if there was any argument, bash you with a shoe.

The Tourist Information Office was a sham. An immense

barefoot Watutsi in an old army greatcoat guarded the door. It was run by a solitary girl who sat in a chair in the centre of a large, bare room. The literature she had was several years old. She giggled when I asked her about Nyiragongo, and let me admire the mosaic of reticulated partings that patterned her scalp.

The Rwanda roads had been bad, and I had passed the wreckage of a fresh accident—a Swedish lorry upside-down in a pool of crushed vegetables—without which no day would be complete. But the cindery road I now took north of Goma had entirely lost its surface. It was like bumping over a lava flow.

It was dusk when I reached Rumangabo, headquarters of the Albert National Park administration. There was no one about so I stopped outside a fine stone building and sat on my old Turkish stool to boil coffee. I was being watched, of course; and soon six handsome women with babies on their backs came up softly to share my sugar. They were the wives of park officials all of whom, they said, were away. But the Director himself was expected from Goma.

Rumangabo stands on a pleasant hill splashed with coral trees, and with a dramatic view of Mount Mikeno ducking and reappearing through wraiths of restless cloud. Here the Belgians put up luxurious stone buildings for the Park officials. But the gardens had run wild, chickens hopped through doorways, and there were goats in kitchens that used to hum with a refrigerator. There was no electric current, and no piped water. The whole complex of expensive European architecture was being turned into a happy African village.

The Director, when at length he came chugging up the hill in a battered Volkswagen, was enthusiastic and helpful. Visitors, he explained, were so rare that he had no organisation to deal with them. He found me a bed near the guard room and promised me his best guide.

Gitebe hut

Jean called early next morning. He carried a panga, a thin blanket, and a haversack stuffed with green beans. From the beer shop at Kakomero we picked up three thick-set Bahutu porters and set off for Nyiragongo's truncated cone. I could see

99

it ten miles away smoking in thunder-cloud: a big black lump rising from a blue-green sea of scrub and climbing forest.

Not far from our start point we crossed a section of the 1954 lava flow. It had left a grey scar that was furry now with lichen and sprouting fresh ferns and shrubs. I soon found that my companions were extremely nervous.

'The elephants here,' said Jean, whose forage cap, short khaki coat, and boots distinguished him from the others with their ragged thin shirts and bare feet, 'are *méchant*—they will attack.'

There were clearly many of them about, and buffalo too; from now, until our return four days later, we trudged along narrow game tracks churned, pot-holed and fouled by their passage. We made constant detours. I was discouraged from talking, idling, or stopping to rest.

Five hours' march, through thickening undergrowth and hypericum-spotted woodland that rustled with small invisible birds, brought us to Gitebe hut: a semi-dismantled shed with a stove and four rough beds spread with dry grass.

The porters lit a fire under the base of a fallen tree and while the beans were cooking they sang—for my especial benefit—a doleful church chant in French. Above the fretwork of forest leaves, stars came out in a clear patch of sky.

'What are stars?' one of the porters asked me. When I declared that every star is a sun, and that our own sun is but an insignificant member of this incalculable host, they grunted with astonishment. They questioned me about Uganda? Was it really a paradise of food, peace, and work?

'The Congo', one of them said, 'is a bad, hungry place.'

'*C'est à cause de la République*,' added Jean. 'And yet,' he went on, 'a Congolese minister earns 100,000 francs a month.' The sum seemed so immense that he found difficulty in expressing the figures in French.

I asked him what the ministers spent their money on. 'Whisky,' he said malevolently, 'which they mix, not with water *comme les blancs*, but with *pombe*.'

I would have liked to sleep outside but, said Jean, it was strictly forbidden. So the porters barricaded the empty window spaces and in smoky darkness we went to bed.

Baruta hut

The trail next day took us up a steep ridge congested with magnificent trees—tall podocarpus and hagenias with russet panicles hanging like grapes from upcurved branches: trees of large stature, yet funereal and discoloured in their ugly pelts of streaming lichen, swollen by creepers, and hung with lianas that stretched like trip wires through vast beds of stinging nettles. When it began to rain the elephants' footmarks filled with water, and plodding up the track was like stepping in an endless row of foot baths.

The Baruta hut stands near a small crater pool on a hump immediately below the 11,450-foot cone. Jean apologised when he saw the broken windows and the beds covered, not with mattresses (as the faded old guide notes promised), but dusty lichen beards. 'Pygmies must have broken in,' he said. '*C'est à cause de la République.*'

It was a cold wet spot. The undergrowth glistened and dripped and the porters shivered miserably as they tried to start a fire in the broken stove. But rain had cleaned the air. Far below, near the lava flow that had cut the porters' feet and now gleamed like a reef exposed at low tide, we observed small dots of tents. 'Game rangers,' said Jean, 'chasing poachers.' It was, he explained, partly the poachers' fault that the elephants were so bad tempered.

Immediately to the east, Karisimbi and Mikeno peaks stood up very clearly, and, at their foot, a grassy plain spotted like some crazy golf course with craters, domes and pyramids marking minor eruptions.

The gorillas on Karisimbi and Mikeno, said my companions, were very dangerous. They would grip a man by the wrist, whirl him round their heads, and batter him to death.

I told them that gorillas are said by Europeans who have studied them to be quiet, shy creatures.

'They may be afraid of white skins,' remarked Jean, 'but not of black!'

We spent a bad night in the hut. It was cold, and filled with sour smoke from the useless stove. In the morning only Jean and one of the porters were willing to go farther. The mist had blown away, and the top of Nyiragongo was revealed as a blunt and sturdy cone, covered almost to the rim with diminishing vegetation that showed very green against the black and cindery rock.

The crater

We tramped at first through dripping hypericum forest where the elephant spoor ceased at last. Then came a mass of twisted heather trees, many of them felled by violent winds, woolly everlastings, and senecios which finally shrank in size and petered out in bare lava rock. A short scramble up this ugly black slope, and we were at the crater rim.

The next moment I was confronted by a sight that was beautiful and terrifying. Looking over the edge, I found myself poised above a huge and steep abyss—obscured, alas, about midway down by a mattress of cloud.

Outside it had been quiet. Here, within the cindery lips, a thunderous sea-roar rose and fell from the invisible bottom.

It was some time before the sun burnt up the sleeping fragment of cloud. It was worth waiting for. The whole of the crater was now exposed, dropping very steeply for 1,300 feet or more, via a projecting gallery, to a lava bed with a great boil on it. The hot entrails of the earth were violently erupting. Steam belched constantly from the fumaroles. I could see now where the explosions came from. One of the fumaroles was tossing out gobbets of fiery matter with a thud and protracted echo which pulsated round the crater as though it were an immense inverted bell being struck by a sledge-hammer.

I could spot nothing growing inside this suppurating fistula except a single kniphofia near the ledge where we were standing out of the wind. I stayed a long time, fascinated by the belching demon, its fiery throat, its calcined vents and mighty voice.

In the morning my companions hurried me relentlessly—'Il faut souffrir,' said Jean—back to Kakomero, pointing silently with their pangas at fresh elephant tracks, beckoning me to hurry, to halt, or to steal softly away from the big heads that lifted their umbrella ears towards us through tangled foliage and stems.

I had fallen behind with Jean when we came to the last lava flow. There was no sign of the porters except for their loads, scattered among ferns, and the footmarks of the elephant that had scared them. It was some time before they returned. One of them had badly gashed his foot.

They sat down and refused to go on. Their haggard, friendly faces had turned grim. They wanted an extra 300 francs each—and judged this to be the best moment to press for it.

But Jean had already worked out the next move. 'They're trying it on,' he whispered. 'Offer them an extra 100 francs each, they deserve it—and give me 200, but say nothing.'

Soon everyone was smiling. The man with the gashed foot forgot his wound, one of them lifted my own rucksack on to his shoulders, and we raced downhill to the park boundary.

My car was safe. Many grubby little fingers had smeared it, but nothing was missing. Only my plimsolls, slashed by lava rock, had disintegrated for ever.

At Kakomero I stopped with Jean at the beer shop. The *Conservateur* and his game guards, whose tents we had spotted from Baruta hut, had already arrived and were drinking in a back room among a stack of beer bottles. Their transistor set was hammering away, and they had two pretty girls to amuse them.

'Say goodbye quickly to the *Conservateur*,' said Jean, 'then come away—otherwise you'll be stuck with them till next week. The party's just starting.'

At Rumangabo I put up my camp bed under a tree and was woken by a bugler sounding reveille. A guard was watching me. He had been washing his feet in a small tin of water, he looked hungry, and he wanted tobacco.

Return

Now I was driving back to Goma, past the 1914–18 Belgian military cemeteries at Kibati (inscribed gravestones for officers and NCOs, black wooden crosses for the rest), past the sweet-potato fields, the coral and pawpaw trees, the wide-mouthed women with soft eyes and big baskets of green maize cobs on their heads.

As I passed through Rwanda, the late afternoon sun was casting rays of dazzling light that seemed to go right through the skin of people walking towards it and bring out copper tints as though the pigment beneath were pink- and ochre-streaked. I had the illusion that these were no longer black men, but Caribbean Indians. I passed Belgian-built fountains and Catholic shrines, huge cabbages, dracaena trees and empty petrol pumps. When I stopped to change a wheel a man with a yaw-hole in his knee insisted on helping. He left little smears of pus here and there which, when he had gone, I carefully wiped away.

I took a last look at the Virunga volcanoes from the Kanaba gap, fifteen miles inside Uganda: a row of cloudy shapes that marched off among countless terraced hillocks into a watery haze. Now that I had been to the top of one of them, they no longer seemed operatic, inaccessible, and protected by chaos. Farther down the valley, towards Kabale, long-horned cattle were clustered like bugs on little patches of grass. In the shade of hedges schoolboys were waiting warily with packets of smuggled Belgian cigarettes for sale.

Not far from Mbarara I gave an old man a lift. The road was sometimes blocked by fine Ankole cattle, accompanied by tall men whose stature and thin Hamitic noses and lips reminded me of the Watutsi in Rwanda and the Congo. '*Iko maziwa mingi*,' said the old man; 'No shortage of milk here.'

The chocolate and piebald cattle, bunched closely together as though yoked by invisible harness, jostled along through a cloud of flies. In the long grass where they were grazing off the road, their huge curved horns stood up against the sky like antlers.

CHAPTER 11

Karisimbi

Rumangabo

My trip to Nyiragongo had given me a taste for more of this strange frontier landscape. From Baruta hut I had had a close view of Karisimbi steepling above a plain pockmarked with craters. It was the highest of the Virunga mountains and I had wanted to climb it ever since, from the top of Muhavura, I had seen its purple crown.

By the time I was free to go again to the Congo, the March rains had set in over Kampala. Drumming rain was stirring night swarms of winged termites to leave their red pyramids and perish in a brief, suicidal migration. The heavy showers drenched early morning workers as they trotted along muddy lanes holding banana leaves and newspapers to protect their heads. Books on shelves collected a little more mildew.

For a hundred miles I drove through downpours that splashed the road with foam. It blew off in vapour almost as soon as it hit the hot tarmac. When the sun came out, the chocolate earth smelt like burnt toast.

In Ankole the new cattle ranching area, recently (with the aid of American machinery) stripped of trees to eliminate tsetse fly, had turned from a dry ochreous waste into green prairie. Lightning was illuminating the tops of volcanoes as I drove over the Kanaba gap. A petrol tanker that had skidded into a bamboo thicket was still burning.

At Kisoro next morning a Uganda customs official tried to dissuade me from going farther. 'The Congolese frontier police are'—he searched for a word—'fickle. They will take away your passport and you will never see it again. But if you must go,' he added, 'then travel via Goma where there are Europeans who can help if you are in trouble.'

I chose, nevertheless, the direct route into the Congo, and drove up to the customs shed at Bunagana hoping for the best. In an effort to make it look like a real *maridadi* office, its shelves had been stacked with old and useless receipts. The typewriter was broken, but not the transistor set, which was thumping out guitar music.

I had little trouble in passing through; for the two senior officials were preoccupied with counting a vast pile of old bank notes, and the youth who asked for money did not press me when I declined. The soldier who searched my baggage for '*cartouches*' found nothing incriminating. I was given a receipt for my passport. An official carefully sealed my camera with wire, which he trimmed with a pair of garden shears.

Fifty miles farther on I found Rumangabo apparently unchanged since I had last been there. There was still no electric light or piped water. Everyone was amiable. The *Chef de Poste*, who commands the numerous park guards, welcomed me with a bottle of beer and some jazz tunes on his transistor, then put me up for the night in the house of the former Belgian Director: a large, once splendid, but now uninhabited mansion with a fence of coral trees and a cemented tennis court that had long split into rubble. Like a butler alone in a haunted house I roamed its corridors with my lantern trying to prepare a meal.

When I told the *Conservateur* that I wished to climb Karisimbi he replied that no one had been to the top since independence. Karisimbi was strictly *interdit*. Provided, however, that I undertook to go straight up and down, he would in my case waive the rules. He agreed to let Jean accompany me as guide.

The start point next morning was Kibumba village. While Jean looked for porters—they were not enthusiastic for Karisimbi, they said, was too high and cold—I sat outside the village school to watch the children arrive.

It was raining. The children had brought a single roasted maize cob each for breakfast. They had running noses and their navels protruded like stick-ends from the narrow swollen bellies. They pressed round my car, fascinated by the wealth inside it: the tins of food, the boots and books. It was a travelling shop.

I did not envy the six African teachers as one by one they ducked out of their huts into the mud and rain. Glumly they made their classes fall in and sing in French an Uhuru anthem while the Congolese flag was hoisted on a pole. Their thin shirts were wet when they went into the class rooms and began to write on the blackboards. I could see the children watching the words and figures with the rapt stare of television viewers.

The three pipe-smoking Bahunde porters, when at length they arrived, disdained my maize meal and filled instead a sack with beans and small sweet potatoes. A park guard with a spear joined us as escort. Two crested cranes watched us vanish slowly, unwillingly and already wet, into the wall of bamboo scrub that seals the foot of the mountain.

The reek of beer that clung to the porters would not wear off till the following day. We followed a path so boggy, so churned by elephant and buffalo, that I gave up trying to skip the black mud holes and was soon coated to the knees with slime.

Beyond the bamboo undergrowth reared a magnificent rain forest of broad-leaved neoboutonia trees, which looked from above like a vast orchard of green umbrellas. Then tier upon tier of hagenias with tusty pendent blossoms, the great flaring branches swollen and bolstered, as though bandaged, with lumps of moss on which rows of red-hot pokers stood like exclamation marks.

We slept in the rain by a gorge roaring with water, but the porters could make a fire out of anything. They had soon stacked lichen and kindling at the tip of a fallen tree stem, and once started the fire fed steadily along it through the night. Overhead sounded the doleful thrashing of wet leaves.

Kabara

At 10,200 feet we came through hypericum woodland to Kabara meadow. It was a grassy clearing with the sun on it, a wooden cabin and a pool trampled by buffalo. Forty years ago, on this sheltered saddle between Karisimbi and Mikeno peaks, Carl Akeley the American naturalist had been taken ill and died.

I walked over to his grave. It bears a cemented slab. The forest had lent it the shade of a hypericum shrub that was dressed in golden flowers.[1]

Here too, among the lichen-draped trees, George Schaller, another American naturalist, camped in 1959–60 while making his remarkable observations of gorillas, many of whom he got to know so well that he identifies them by nick-name.[2]

But the cabin is now partly wrecked. 'Watutsi!' exclaimed my companions as soon as they saw its charred roof.

They told me how the tall, pastoral Watutsi had taken advantage of Uhuru to intrude from Rwanda with their cattle, destroying vegetation, scaring the gorillas and disturbing game. *'Ce sont des ennemis,'* said Jean, not surprisingly for he is a Bahutu as well as a park guard.

After the squelching game trail, it was delightful to tread the firm grass of the meadow. It stands within a horseshoe of hagenias. Sunbirds were flitting among the gold-spotted hypericum. I brewed tea and watched Michel, our escort, take off one of his boots.

'Regardez,' he said, pointing to where the sole hung loose in front, 'a fish head with its mouth open.'

The repair was simple. He prised a long nail from the cabin door and drove it clean through instep and sole.

Rukumi hut

A thousand feet above the saddle, at the foot of Karisimbi's perfect arched cone, with Mikeno towering opposite like a rusty *Pickelhaube*, we came to a mat of alchemilla surrounded by tree heather and giant groundsels in flower. Here, draughty and forlorn, stood Rukumi hut. Its furnishings had gone. All that remained were scraps of cotton mattress stuffing that blew about the floor. 'Watutsi!' repeated my companions.

[1] Mrs Akeley was with her husband when he died (1926). She has described in *Congo Eden*, London 1951, how in 1947 she returned to Kabara to tend her husband's grave. He had called Kabara 'the most beautiful spot on earth.' Albert, King of the Belgians, camped there during his attempt (which narrowly failed) to climb Mikeno, in 1932.

[2] *The Mountain Gorilla: Ecology and Behaviour*, University of Chicago Press, 1963, and *The Year of the Gorilla*, London 1965.

Here, though, after hours of claustrophobic green twilight, we had at last a view. The sky had cleared, showing the tops of the two still-active volcanoes Nyiragongo and Nyamuragira, floating above a white cloud quilt like black hummocks in a snow field. To the south-west Lake Kivu lay in a grey bowl of hills. With nightfall the Plough appeared, dragging its tail like a weary kite. A faint fist of lights indicated Goma town. The rest of the enormous landscape was in darkness.

It was bitterly cold in the hut, I was dirty, and I did not enjoy my tinned herrings. I lay awake wondering why I chose to suffer in this manner. How pleasant it would be to turn back and go home.

To that, of course, the immediate objection was that as soon as I had descended I should despise myself for having given up, and I should be nagged by an urge to return. I deduced, then —what I already knew before—that it was a sort of vanity which drove me on.

Perhaps all this nose-poking into strange places was merely fulfilment of the child's craving to climb the apple tree next door, to explore that forbidden wood with the warning notices 'Trespassers Keep out ... *Zabroniony* ... *Eintritt Verboten*'—to escape from nanny.

And the reward? To see the massed green umbrellas of a rain forest, or black fissured hills standing like upturned islands between the tribes, or a tree heather rooted like an Irish harp in a ravine?

But writing about it adds a burden to travel—may even spoil it. To have to identify, when tired or in a hurry, D'Arnaud's barbet bird or a ground orchid, to have to memorise shape and colour of a landscape, or the feather in a mud-helmet—like the constant urge some people have to photograph, the habit can become obsessive.

It would be simpler just to walk—but for me, at any rate, duller; the clues would stay hidden. For a tree is not merely a tree. It is a eucalyptus planted by some forestry official to drain a swamp, or a fire-charred whistling thorn hung with punctured galls and a parabola of weavers' nests. A bird is a stork with a woolly neck, or a fiscal shrike. That black-skinned farmer in his cotton field is not simply swinging a tool. He is using a curious Nilotic hoe, bent in the middle and with a heart-shaped blade.

Pedantic, restless and inquisitive, the traveller with a book in mind is not only a sort of spy; he may become a bore.

I set out early for the top with Jean, who was wearing my spare socks as gloves. In cloud, rain and mud we plodded up crumbling terraces of well-grown tree groundsels waving bright yellow flowers among the strange spears and spikes of lobelia. Mikeno dropped slowly behind us. From below it had seemed enormous; seen from above it was clearly Karisimbi's smaller brother.

Then the mist thickened, turning the lobelia stems into ghosts of tall pikemen, blotting out the game trails and Jean. Stumbling and wet, with the blue dye from my old sweater soaking into my shirt, I was no longer enjoying myself. A bush buck startled me, bursting suddenly out of the gloom and running off like a demented spirit.

Towards the top we came to banks of steep orange moss that collapsed underfoot like rotten sponge. Then unexpectedly, at the end of a lava pitch, we were treading the black dome itself. At 14,782 ft. we were at the highest point of the Virunga mountains.

Alas, the Rwanda valleys were hidden in cloud and there was no protection from the wind. Someone had blown up the summit shelter and its débris was strewn among buffalo bones. We had plodded up; and now we must plod down.

Before us, next day, lay the long descent down a soggy trail. There was not much to break the monotony of the green glades—the wan butterfly petals of balsam and a few tiny flashes of sunbirds, nothing more. A slip landed one in a bed of stinging nettles. We looked like muddy animals. But to my companions' relief we saw no fresh traces of gorilla: their droppings were already old. At the end of the day I was glad to hear voices of children at play in the bean fields.

Looking forward to comfort, I drove in the morning through sparkling coffee plots to Rutshuru township. All I found were some huts selling bolts of cloth, and a Luxemburger sitting alone in his scarred hotel.

Rutshuru

He was a thick, grey-faced man with a mat of hair on his hands, which were trembling with the morning hangover. He readily gave me beer and a plate of *Speck* carved into little white cubes. Our conversation went like this:

'How's business?'

'Bad. No tourists. People are afraid to come to the Congo.'

'There seems to be plenty of beer about.'

'Yes, but not everyone pays for what he drinks.'

'Have you a car?'

He pointed to a Volkswagen van standing in the yard. It had two flat tyres and looked sick. 'No engine,' he said.

'When it rains,' I said, 'you can paddle it.'

Two young Belgians came in, a man and a girl, both very pale and slim, and both wearing almost identical shirts and jeans.

'*Décolonisés*,' sneered the proprietor, 'poor types, probably school teachers.'

'*Hör' mal*,' he went on. 'I've known some of these new fellows take an African woman in there'—he nodded towards the outside latrine.

'Where's your wife?' I asked.

'Gone to Goma to have her hair done.' He turned towards a plump young African woman who at that moment was bending down, deliberately revealing the backs of her brown, polished thighs. 'For the time being I'm using that one.' He grinned. 'Screwing her is like grabbing a tiger by its tail.'

We were joined by a lugubrious Spanish doctor employed by the United Nations at a local hospital. He was anti-British.

'England,' he pronounced, 'is responsible for most of the world's troubles.' He began to list them: Cyprus, Aden, Israel, Vietnam, Rhodesia . . . 'You sell arms to both sides and then exploit the mess.'

'The Portuguese', he continued, 'are the only people who know how to run Africa. Smith is right.'

'The Africans', he said finally, 'are monkeys.'

'*Richtig*,' said the Luxemburger, '*laute Affen*. Beer and women is all they care about.'

III

'And motor cars,' added the Spaniard. 'If they see a car or a woman, they must climb up.'

I could get no sense out of the doctor. He considered me an intruder and—if it was true that I had climbed Karisimbi—a lunatic. But he did come out with one scrap of professional information. 'A protruding navel', he said, 'is regarded here as an adornment—mothers pull their children's navels to make them longer.'

The Travellers' Rest

Back across the border in Uganda I felt an immediate sense of relief. No one shouted aggressively at me for a lift. Gangs of men filling in pot-holes stood readily aside to let me pass. At any of the little *dukas* I could buy something useful with my money. Mr Baumgaertel, his face pink with lunch, was playing draughts with an Australian while a Swiss visitor read his gorilla book.

'Africans', I heard Mr Baumgaertel say, 'have beautiful skins—much nicer than ours.'

'I'd rather be in London,' said the Australian.

'Well,' said the Swiss, 'it's for you to choose: Z-cars and cocoa—or cockroaches.'

The Spanish doctor, I recalled, had repeated that old stuff about monkeys. What is a generalisation worth? When a man tells you he 'likes Africans', it may simply mean he's fond of his servant—who is clean, loyal, apparently honest, and willing to wash his underwear, at 120 shillings a month with some paraffin and sugar thrown in.

Porters, Kachagalau

Reuben (guide), below Sabinio

c. Dracaena trees, Sabinio

10a. Gorilla nests, Sabinio

b. Giant Lobelia, Muhavura summit   c. Vegetation just below Muhavura summit

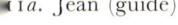

a. Jean (guide)

b. Tree heather on Nyiragongo

c. Guides at crater wall, Nyiragongo

d. Lichen-covered trees, Nyiragongo

12*a.* Descending through forest, Nyiragongo

b. Mufumbiro volcanoes seen from Kanaba Gap

CHAPTER 12

Morungole

Kaabong

The Buganda landscape is a still-life of banana trees painted in emerald squares and oblongs on undulating chocolate soil. Its glaring evergreen colour is chequered by scarlet flowers, the white blossom of coffee shrubs, purple dresses of women. The owners' huts are rooted firmly within their plots. There may be a church anchored to a nearby hill. It is a solid, static landscape, with an atmosphere of permanence, of regular food and domestication; and there is money, invested in schooling and old cars, in a tiled roof and good Sunday clothes.

In Kigezi and the Congo border country, rain and mist enfold forested tumuli in black shadow and a blue-grey wash. The innumerable hills, piled one upon the other, enclose you like tumbling waves. No sooner have you breasted the top of one than you must descend into the trough of another. The elusive view which you hoped to see from the next knoll is likely to be blurred or lost in aqueous haze. Away from the contour strips and the roughly cleared scrub where mosquitoes buzz, forests of bamboo and trees swollen by creepers shut you in.

Karamoja is different. In its clear light and dry air you can see for miles across immense tracts of grass and scrub. It is a restless landscape, alive with the small moving figures of cattle and herdsmen, of game and flitting birds. Even the cattle kraals are transient. Here and there among the stones are the ashes of a wanderer's fire; or a water hole trampled with spoor and splayed footmarks, on which green scum is floating. It is a country to set one's feet in motion. A twenty-mile trek through the grass is nothing. The morning's landmarks, slightly altered in angle and aspect, will still be there at night.

113

Of all the regions I had seen, Karamoja was the one that most attracted me. Now I had come back, driving along the dirt road that runs from Moroto towards the Sudan border. It was a lonely road, vaporous in patches with drying mud. For over a hundred miles the only other vehicle I met was a van driven by an Italian priest—he waved his cigar butt at me—from one of the Verona Fathers' mission stations that are scattered about Karamoja. But the thorn bush, though cruelly scorched by long drought, was not at all deserted.

When I stopped to look at a gang of marabou storks grotesquely brooding like hunchbacks on stilts round a heap of freshly picked bones, I saw that I, in turn, was being studied from behind a stone by two striped hyenas. The white rumps of scores of Grant's gazelle were twinkling in the bleached grass along the roadside, and bushes trembled with dikdik in scuttling flight.

It was already dark when I reached Kaabong, in the Dodoth tribal area (the Dodoth are one of several interrelated Nilo-Hamitic pastoral tribes that make up the 'Karamojong cluster').

I called immediately on the young African ADC. He was wearing an embroidered *kanzu*. His room was furnished with some government chairs, a shelf of law books, and several tiny ornamental neck-stools. He showed me himself to the small corrugated-iron rest house. While he was demonstrating how to unscrew the lock, a hyena went past with a blood-curdling cry. 'You are not', he remarked, 'in Kampala now. Keep the windows closed.'

I sat outside to cook my meal. In front of me the Plough, its stars enormously magnified, seemed to stretch across almost the whole of the northern sky. From time to time I heard the laughter of the hyena as it capered through the scrub.

I learned next morning that drought and the resultant failure of food crops had forced the ADC to provide an emergency distribution of maize meal. Families were being made to earn their portion by doing a little work—which seemed to have devolved upon the women, for over a hundred men had collected in the grassless square to watch wives and daughters tramp to and fro with poles for a building site.

Even in the Verona Fathers' patiently tended fields the crops had died. But a Scottish veterinary officer who lived alone on a hill showed me a flourishing acacia which shielded his aluminium rondavel from the sun. 'The only decent tree for miles,' he said. 'I throw my bathwater on it.'

From his hut I could see the strangely eroded rock prongs and turrets that are scattered round Kaabong, and over thirty miles away the top of Morungole which was my objective. Below us women were drawing water from a bore hole. As they worked the pump handle, sweat would be dripping down their faces and breasts into the cans.

The gombolola chief smelt of beer and he was fat—evidence that he was a stranger, for the only fat men one sees among the Dodoth are policemen, priests and shopkeepers from other parts. When I told the chief that I wanted someone to accompany me to Morungole, he immediately fetched three men who ran out of a hut ready to start that very moment, though they carried nothing but their snuff horns, a panga, and a tiny stool belonging to Lokutai, the leader.

The herdsmen of Karamoja are used to journeying light. They are tireless walkers but poor porters. Men consider it undignified to hump a load, and their decorative coiffures prevent then in any case from carrying on the head. My companions looked unhappy shouldering my small bundles of food and gear.

The sun was blasting out of a clear sky when we set out from Kalapata on our twenty-mile tramp to the foot of Morungole. Weeks of heat and drought had blistered the land. All that survived of the grazing was a threadbare mat, chewed and pounded by cattle. I soon noticed that my Dodoth escort was nervous when sighting strangers, wondering whether they might be Turkana, who not long before had been savagely raiding the neighbourhood. I did not enjoy myself at first. There were many small irritating flies, my knees seemed arthritic, I annoyed my companions by sometimes sitting down to rest under a bush.

None of the stream beds we crossed held water. But at a small spring containing a black and gritty dribble we were joined by a party of Dodoth from a neighbouring ring of huts. The girls were wearing chain belts, brightly burnished, which jingled musically like harness. As they insisted on walking behind me, almost treading on my heels, I felt obliged to hurry. It was dusk when we halted at the thorn fence of their encampment. Scrawny white cattle were being driven inside bringing a cloud of flies which settled in a black film on our belongings.

The headman came out to greet us. He was very black, affable, and muscular. His hair was teased into an immense orange-coloured bun with a feather in it. His cloth cape flapped uselessly over his shoulders, shreds of dried grass adhered to his penis. With the westering sun afire behind him he looked like a Caliban from the flaming underworld.

He brought me a wooden bowl of milk and invited us to sleep inside the kraal. I declined. The dung, the flies and the children discouraged me, and though Lokutai grumbled I chose a spot upwind.

A little later over a fire I was enjoying that sweetest hour of the day when one's companions cut sticks to stir their maize meal into a thick, bubbling porridge, the ground heat radiates swiftly starward, and flies have ceased to torment. After they had eaten, I watched Lokutai pick up a smooth round stone and grind the tobacco I had given him into snuff.

I lay awake listening to the restless sounds, amplified by the still air, that came from the fenced huts: the groan of goats and cows, shrill, impudent laughter of women, and the grunting voices of men.

We left early, before the cows filed out through a hole in the *boma* and the flies came back.

Morungole

Mount Morungole, a bushy 9,020-foot lump with several knolls, was now above us. On its lower slopes we passed a group of herdsmen lying in the brown grass with spears and the polished mashie-shaped sticks with which they whack their gentle cattle.

The men had freshly washed and greased themselves. Gloriously naked, sleek and graceful as leopards, they would have made a fine team to head a protest march against the processes that are giving modern man his soft, deodorised and chemically preserved body—and against all those modern economists who prefer cash crops and decry the 'backwardness' of pastoral life. (The British, some say, deliberately conserved Karamoja as a sort of 'human zoo', and are to blame for its primitive state.)

Like the Kurds, among whom I had formerly travelled, these people were their own masters, free to follow the grass and water and to roam at will a tribal territory. Only the Dodoth were handsomer than Kurds. A Kurd has to cover himself in thick clothes which wear out into unsightly rags and patches. His women put on long drawers and frowsy skirts. The smell of a company of Turkish infantry on the march is a smell of feet spoilt by bad boots. The Dodoth did not want our insanitary clothes.

Their women had small round heads which protruded from immense ruffs of metal and beaded rings. Their hair was matted in a crest. Their teeth, scrubbed with fibrous sticks, were white as milk. Their breasts had the perfect shape of small gourds. They spat adroitly, with a flicker of crimson tongue between dark lips. The married ones, in place of the young girls' dangling chain apron, wore in front a leather flap embroidered with beads.

We gave them a few pinches of our snuff, gripped thumbs, and went our way.

On the higher slopes acacias grew green and unravaged, and proteas were in flower. Baboons barked gruffly at us; buffalo had churned the barely trickling stream beds into slime.

A small dark bird suddenly flew into a bush and set up an agitated chatter. As it flitted noisily from tree to tree, we followed it, for it was a honey guide; and, when it stopped a hundred yards on, the Dodoth looked for the cache of honey. There it was, embedded in the black earth, waiting to be dug out with the panga. My companions looted a dozen wafer-shaped combs and had devoured them, with grubs and soil, within a minute or two.

The sound of cowbells had long dwindled, and near a clump of cedar trees we lit a bright fire to see us through a cold night. I was getting to know my companions a little. Both Lokutai and Luara were dejected. They had no cattle, for the government, said Luara, had seized them when they did not pay their taxes. The youngest porter had spent a year at the Verona Fathers' mission school in Kaabong. He spelled out his name—Marco—by scratching it on his arm with a twig then rubbing off the grey marks as though from a slate. They all chewed sticks, and picked things up with their toes.

I envied Lokutai his minute stool, which in a country where the ground is hard and thorny, and trousers are not worn, was invaluable to comfort. He now propped his head sideways on it, pulled his only piece of clothing—a length of brown *shuka* cloth—round his hips, and fell instantly asleep. The others, having loudly cleared their throats, lay without snoring. A buffalo snorted once in the night.

An overgrown gully led to the summit. It had three precipitous sides and an open crown mottled with rusty-flowered aloes. A single giant heather was glued to it like the *Gemsbart* stuck in a Bavarian farmer's hat.

Lying there in the sun, the Dodoth pointed out the landmarks spread across rolling ochre valleys: the eroded black hills of the Sudan, the smoke of grass fires towards Kidepo Game Park, the country to the north-east of those formidable Turkana raiders ('They use firearms', said Lokutai, 'brought from Ethiopia'); immediately below, small circles of cattle camps, and that growing feature of East African landscape—the sparkle of sun on corrugated iron roofs. Somewhere down there, at Pirre, I had heard that Colin Turnbull, the anthropologist, had set up camp among the Teuso.[1]

Dr Turnbull was not the first anthropologist to reside in this neighbourhood. Five years before, an American woman had spent several months among the Dodoth, recording their habits, from bleeding cattle through a neck vein pierced by a

[1] Dr Turnbull is probably best known to the layman through his book on the Ituri pygmies (*The Forest People*, 1961).

blocked arrow to their reactions to western religion.[1] The herdsmen of northern Uganda, with their proliferating live-stock and love of raiding, are an embarrassment to government but they are one of God's special gifts to the anthropologist.

Descending, we were again invited inside a *manyatta*. It had a strong fence of cut thorn and pieces of *euphorbia candelabrum*. Cattle pens lined one side of the enclosure, on the other were the roofless partitions for families, down the middle a row of cooking fires crowded with children. When I noticed that our porridge pot had turned black with flies I made an excuse to leave.

We walked slowly homeward. The go-away bird was calling, and I saw for the first time a ground hornbill, ponderous, turkey-like, with scarlet splashes on its neck.

Kidepo

Back at Kalapata I removed, apprehensively, the galvanised roof strips which some boys ('to prevent evil men from breaking in') had draped over my car, and a few hours later I was sitting by my camp bed in a corner of Kidepo Game Park.

The staff was not yet ready to deal with visitors in a sophisti-cated way; the lodges were unfinished and there was no catering. But they welcomed me, and gave me a drum of water.

An Acholi ranger accompanied me on my drive round the park. We saw plenty of game: elephants darkly plastered with mud, lumbering towards a water hole; ponderous buffalo; giraffe, hartebeest eland and fleet little oribi. The borassus palms, the tall grass untrodden by cattle and the furrowed bulwarks of the Sudan were beautiful. And yet, imprisoned within my car, I did not feel properly of it. The animals seemed to have distanced themselves, like fish seen through the panels of a tank. The ranger with his service rifle, who detested the local tribes ('rowdy savages') and the poachers from across the border, was an intruder too.

I spent the whole of the next day watching the sun wheel up and down the sky. Four hundred yards away a group of

[1] Elizabeth Marshall Thomas, *Warrior Herdsmen*, New York, 1965.

hartebeest stood motionless for hours in the slowly lengthening shade of thorn trees. Behind them elephants dotted the brown grass like humps of rock.

I was happy. As happy as a sun-starved Swede who wakes in the Northern night to find himself on a Greek island.

I had climbed a hill, and I was idling while other people worked, trotted along subways, banged typewriters, telephoned, operated machinery, counted money, and went to the dentist. And the chain of events that had brought me from Europe to this piece of grass on a large map had been simple: two or three typed letters, a half-hour interview, a small car with a sound engine, a few pounds' worth of camping gear, and average health.

A little before dusk Mr Pegg, the Warden, came over to see who I was. He looked a little doubtfully at my little bed and box of food. 'No tent?' he remarked. But he did not tell me to go away. When night fell Orion was dazzlingly bright, and towards Morungole grass fires were writhing like red serpents along the contours of the hills. 'Be careful,' the warden had told me. 'There are lion about.' But my only visitor was quite harmless. At dawn, as I was preparing breakfast, I heard a scuffle and looked round to see a striped grey squirrel making off with my biscuits. I let it keep them.

CHAPTER 13

Adilang

Jinja–Soroti

The 180 miles of tarmac running north of Jinja to Soroti cut through familiar types of landscape. At first hedgeless rectangles of the tedious sugar cane throw back dazzling shafts of sunlight. The cane cutters trudging home with their heavy pangas, their old felt hats and tired, sweaty bodies look like miners coming off a shift. Madhvani's big sugar lorries are constantly breaking up the hot, thin road surface, and there are sometimes fearful collisions.

Then come maize and cassava, cotton and coffee plots: among them, like smooth ornamented pillars, borassus palms with fan-shaped leaves and big orange fruit. Along the roadside *mvule* trees, tall and solitary, suspend dark bundles of foliage over chocolate earth that is spotted with the pale, trailing mouths of ipomoea. The thatched mud huts of *shamba* owners are screened by pawpaws whose fruit, if not picked in time, will be mauled by bats and mouse-birds.

Uncomfortably hot, dazzled by glare, irritable yet alert for cattle and wobbling cyclists, the motorist notices little of it. Its myriad small sounds—except for the sudden piercing trill of a cricket, or at night the tinkling bell-music of the frogs— are lost in a rush of wind. On the long journeys across East Africa's growing network of fast roads, one is always in a hurry. Night falls quickly, throwing verges and leafy bends into blackest shadow. It is the destination that obsesses: the bath and sundowner.

Like other small towns Soroti has a few parallel streets lined with Indian-owned stores, some beer bars where the juke box is turned up loud, and an outlying residential area with government bungalows, a rest house and golf links.

It is, almost, an imported fragment of India: an Oriental trading centre where goods are unloaded and sewing machines are pedalled by African labour—at once a tribute to Indian enterprise and a warning of readjustments to come.

As the road, now gravel strewn, sweeps north through Lango and Acholi the country grows drier and emptier, villagers— they are Nilotics—dark-skinned and powerfully built. It was already night when I came to Adilang and began to look for Kalisto.

An Acholi homestead

Kalisto was one of my students: an enthusiast who ran the college debating society, read widely, and was going through a stage of dislike for women, politics, and the Roman Church. I was to stay with him for a fortnight.

It was not easy on a black night to ferret out, among miles of moonless scrub, the exact, tiny glow of firelight that indicated his father's compound. When I found it, at last, Kalisto was waiting for me, bare-chested, with a lantern. He had cut forty yards of bush to clear a way for my car. His hut was clean and dry.

Kalisto's father, Mr Okwonga, was a lanky ex-soldier. He came over in the morning, wearing shorts and a very faded jacket, and welcomed me in formal phrases. Like a good many of his neighbours in this south-eastern part of Acholi running along the Labwor hill border with Karamoja, he had served with the King's African Rifles in Abyssinia and Burma.

The dour, dark-skinned Acholi men have a tradition of military and police service. Their strong Nilotic physique, uncomplicated outlook and mutual loyalty, coupled with lack of economic opportunities in a long-neglected district of earth roads, bush and primitive millet and cotton plots, have predisposed them to a soldier's or policeman's life.

This has not, of course, endeared them to the Baganda— Uganda's most numerous and sophisticated tribal group— who call the Acholi and other northern peoples *banaggwanga*, foreigners, and resent both their connection with recent government centralisation policy and their prominent role in the security forces which were used to overthrow the Kabaka.

Two of Kalisto's four sisters were at home—a married woman with a cheerful homely face and the prominent splayed front teeth that are often seen in the north, and a girl of fourteen who limped ('She went to the Verona Fathers' hospital for an injection', said Kalisto, 'and someone stuck the needle in the wrong place.') Kalisto's mother was a smiling, work-worn woman, thin and erect. She had a chronically swollen leg which gave her pain. ('Mother', Kalisto told me, 'says she stepped on poison.')

Kalisto had done much better than most local youths. He won a place in the well known Roman Catholic boarding school at Kisubi (after which he wore shoes and gave up farm work) and would soon qualify in Kampala as a secondary school teacher.

His bachelor hut was cool and comfortable. His father, following Acholi custom, had built it for him when he was eighteen: a round mud and wattle building with a roof of thatch and bamboo poles resting on a ring of forked stems. No nails were used. The rest of the household were living 150 yards away in a dusty compound spotted with cow droppings and with hive-like granaries on stilts.

I settled down to a routine of being spoilt. Every morning I sat on my old Turkish stool outside Kalisto's hut, shifting it from time to time away from the sun. The bush was trembling with heat, puffs of hot, dry air burnt the sweat off one's body. The bare rock faces that closed the skyline shone in the sun as though sprayed with dew. Not far away there was an outcrop of stone slabs where the family drew its water in pots and washed clothes. Among its stones, rock hyraxes with blunt hairy faces sunned themselves, hid, screamed and whistled.

Twice a day, Kalisto's sisters brought us food. They knelt to proffer the tray of boiled chicken, gritty millet dumplings and maize porridge flavoured with groundnut or simsim sauce.

A calabash of *pombe* was always to hand no thin industrial fluid, but a thick yellow-brown millet brew, sour, strong, satisfying as soup, the delight of thirsty men. We had many visitors: neighbouring plot owners with a present of eggs or a chicken, youths on bicycles who wanted to practise their

English, passing strangers who like sparrows would drop in for a smoke and a pull at the calabash.

I looked forward to the evenings. The gusty, hot wind that blew up in the afternoon would drop to a cool breeze, and when the moon rose bright there was improvised music and dancing in Mr Okwonga's compound. Brothers, sisters and neighbours assembled softly out of the shadows, the young men in white shirts and shorts, girls in simple frocks or a skirt and brassière. They would face each other. Then the *okemi* players would start to strum, and the dancers advance.

For an hour or more they would shuffle and gyrate round the fire, rarely touching each other, preoccupied with the intricacies of their own separate convolutions. The big splayed feet with cracked and horny heel-pads moved softly in a scuffle of dust. Thin dogs came up, seeking chicken bones. Over the dark fields fireflies drifted like sparks. The pulse of crickets seemed to echo the clicking of the *okemi*.

The *okemi* is a flat wooden box on which metal keys—they may be made of bicycle spokes—are fixed in varying lengths. The young men twanged them in such marvellous harmony that the quick, rhythmic notes sounded like tinkling drops of water.

But older men prefer the *nanga*, which is a harp strung with fibres from the flesh of a monkey's tail. In the intervals between the dancing they strummed it gently and the words they sang, in soft hoarse voices, were often lugubrious—of youths who could not afford the bride price, of the girl married off to an ugly husband.

When the moon sank we went home. The young men with their long, scarred legs vanished back into the shadows, blowing cow horns, the dogs licked up the *pombe* dregs, and I slept under the butter-nut tree outside Kalisto's hut. Sometimes a sudden gust of wind would spatter dust into my face. But it was generally so quiet that I could hear the tiny thud of a leaf falling.

Kano

Kalisto had never climbed the hills that lay along the skyline, and Mr Okwonga strongly advised us not to try; 'There might', he said, 'be enemies up there.'

Nevertheless we set off one day for Kano, a high peak of the Labwor range, which gives some protection to this part of Acholi from Karamojong raiders.

At its foot we asked two villagers to accompany us. Kano we found to be covered with coarse shoulder-high grass, thorn scrub and proteas charred by old grass fires, and the trailing solid-stemmed lowland bamboo that is prized for building. It was rough going, and there was no trail. But our Labwor guides, who were carrying spears, enjoyed themselves.

In the forest zone they cut fresh spear shafts; then with a flaming grass torch robbed bees of the honey they had stored in a dead tree. The golden combs running with sweet honey they gave to me. The combs that were dark, rubbery and grub-infested were the ones they preferred. 'The grubs', they explained, 'make a man potent.'

From the top of Kano, Kalisto's homeland was revealed as a rough green mat scarred by small patches of cultivation. There is no land shortage here. When they feel like it farmers simply move to fresh tracts of adjacent bush which they clear by burning and slashing. Cattle were not grazed on the range. 'Too risky,' said our companions, pointing towards the Karamoja plain running east to the misty hump of Mount Moroto.

Napono

A little to the north run the Napono hills, overlooking a few lonely dwellings among borassus palms (the leaf fibres are stripped for basket making) and cotton fields whose crop helps to pay for school fees, clothes, sugar used in beer brewing, and the charge for medical treatment made by the Verona Fathers at Kalongo.

One day we climbed Napono peak too, and from it saw the roofs of Kalongo mission glittering under the Arabic-named 'Rock of Winds'. Ninety miles to the north, the Agoro mountains of the Sudan border, where wild date trees spring from eroded gullies, were standing black above the smoke of bush fires.

It was long after dark when we stumbled back to a hut at the foot of Napono. The owner, though we were strangers to him, stirred the fire and made us sit down. His wife put a calabash of warm beer and a drinking ladle before us, and skins were laid out to sleep on.

'Travel', said our host when I tried to apologise for his trouble, 'is a serious and dangerous thing.'

The beer was thick and sour, and so welcome that I closed my eyes, as one does in prayer, to concentrate on those first greedy gulps. The firelight was shining on the woman's swollen breasts. Two mangy dogs came out of a hut and sniffed at me. I fell heavily asleep, and woke at dawn to find the calabash had been refilled.

In the morning we covered the last twelve miles at leisure. Schoolboys, as they do all over Uganda, were trotting tirelessly through dewy grass to school—a five-mile run is nothing to them. We passed a dispensary with its cluster of sulky patients suffering from the minor ailments—diarrhoea, festering sores, heads cut in a beer fight—which they are willing to entrust to the care of an African dispenser.

A small British-built reservoir, that had once contained clear water, was now spangled blue with water lilies. It had attracted familiar birds: scuffling lily-trotters; herons and buff-backed egrets sharing a stump; the pied kingfisher with his aggressive beak stuck like a dagger on the spotted body.

Then, near Kalisto's home, we startled half-a-dozen rock hyraxes that were lying among the stones like big hairy slugs. 'People believe', said Kalisto, 'they carry leprosy.'

Verona Fathers

A young Italian priest showed us round the Verona Fathers' Mission at Kalongo. It is a large, self-contained station which includes a school, a very busy hospital with a crowded maternity clinic, an Italian surgeon, and a training centre for nurses; and a church with an organ and a waxed cement floor.

When I was left alone I went into the church. It was cool and smelled of disinfectant. Its size alone must have impressed villagers who spend their lives in poky huts.

I sat in a pew idly wondering what Graham Greene might have noted in his diary.[1] The calculated piety of the swarthy

[1] See Annotated Book List.

cherubims and the plaster Madonnas as pretty and graceful as film stars? The microphone that would make the priest sound like Moses thundering from his hill? The broken bell tower which the lay brother in charge of building maintenance had not mended? The priest grumbling to me about stolen hospital blankets and a colleague's new tape recorder that had been traced to a patient's hut forty miles away?

The incongruity—or cruelty—of making black women with large breasts and shaking buttocks into nuns?

I personally like the Catholic priests and missionaries I have met in East Africa. As I do not call on them in order to pray, I associate them less with religion than with hospitality, medicine, and expert local knowledge. They are—like small military detachments—practical people obliged to look after themselves in lonely places. They are originals. Their gossip is different, for they are free from private money and domestic entanglements.

Their enemies, on the other hand, may accuse them of opting out of the rat race so that they can concentrate on saving their own souls; of exploiting, among Africans, refined forms of Western superstition; of behaving like wrong-headed school-masters who have denounced local customs that they cannot on principle accept, thereby, in a great many instances, doing grave harm to African society.[1]

Acholi is largely within the Verona Fathers' Mission field, and religion as well as politics have brought dissension; for political feelings are roughly divided along religious lines, with the Verona Fathers strongly supporting the Catholic-orientated Democratic Party, Protestants the government party of the Uganda People's Congress. In several villages rival party flags were flying from the tallest trees. A large DP banner was hung just outside Kalongo Mission station.

The Verona Fathers' close connection with the Democratic Party has not endeared them to the government. Of late the authorities (in line, it is true, with official inter-denominational policies in schools) have drastically curtailed direct Italian participation in education. Not long ago they deported several Verona Fathers on charges of meddling in Sudanese politics.

[1] See J. Kieran's recent article in *Race*, January 1969 (London).

Acholi life

In the cool evenings, with the lightning flashing on the horizon, I often sat talking with Kalisto and his father.

'We in Acholi', said one of our neighbours, 'don't like the Baganda. They are rich and conceited. They have for years looked down on us as savages, instead of being grateful to Acholi soldiers for the blood we shed for Uganda in the last war. Our province has been neglected.'

'People say', he went on, 'that Buganda is like its women— beautiful but corrupt. And why should there be a Kabaka? The common man doesn't want kings any more.'

There in a nutshell was another small proof of the tribal ill-feeling—in this case one that may be said to involve the wider issues of Nilotic and Bantu rivalry—which is the bugbear of any African government centralising policy.

I asked Kalisto what souvenirs Acholi soldiers had brought back from the Abyssinian campaign. 'Italian jaw-bones', he answered, 'with the beard attached, to bury in their shrines.'

Acholi may have been neglected in the past. But there are strong signs of change even in this remote Agago area where, almost by accident, Kalisto's father had come after his war service to farm unclaimed land.

Young men ride English bicycles along the rutted dirt roads. Fields are now being scratched with iron ploughs pulled by a pair of oxen (millet, though, is still weeded with snail shells). Women use tin pots and pans as well as the less durable gourds and earthern jars (if you see a woman with a big orange calabash strapped to her back, you may be sure there's a baby sheltering underneath it). Lengths of cotton tied at the waist to leave the breasts bare, and for men a cheap white shirt and khaki shorts, have replaced the skins worn not long ago.

Soap smeared on the body to make it shine (it may be brilliantine for town girls) is preferred to the old simsim or shea butter-nut oils (but twigs are used for toothbrushes). It is less common now to scarify the chest and abdomen of young girls, or to extract incisor teeth from the lower jaw. Kalisto refused to have this done when his primary school teacher warned him that he would speak English with a lisp.

But it is a rude life. People still sleep rough and almost naked on skins spread on a hard mud floor. No one cares much for ornament. The women—big, sleek, clean and bare-breasted —shave their heads close and are content with a cheap bead necklace. They are very dark, and have large feet. When they smile they show strong, white teeth with gaps.

Iron-legged men walk through the bush carrying spears, bows, or sticks, and perhaps a drinking tube inside a cane. They smell of beer. They have the self-assurance of men who—as soldiers, policemen, messengers and night-watchmen—have seen something of the world. They do not fuss or fawn over foreigners.

There is, too, a surprisingly large number of small primary schools in the district—some of them, though, no longer in use (in the earlier days of Protestant-Catholic rivalry, schools were often duplicated), others with neat lawns and football pitches which boys have to shave with pangas.

Here young African teachers live and prepare their evening work in thatched huts by the light of an oil lamp, with a transistor set switched on to Kampala. It is a lonely life. Gulu, the capital, is over one hundred miles from Kalisto's village, along bumpy roads.

Kalisto seemed to be living his double life with balance and good sense. In Kampala he was a relatively important person. As president of his college debating society he met VIPs and wore a smart suit. He read *The Times* and Professor Ali Mazrui's books on political science. Here at home he was a village youth. Every other day he walked through a mile of scrub to wash his shirt, shorts and underwear at a spring. He put them on again as soon as they were dry. He sat on the ground under a tree with the old men. He slept in a thatched hut whose only furniture was a bed, a small table, a clay water pot and enamel mug, and a tin box with his books in it.

Kalisto, on the other hand, was privileged to the point of being spoilt. He did no farm work, he had sisters to wait on him, and he had privacy. No one, not even his parents, would enter his hut without permission.

All day Mrs Okwonga sat in her husband's compound grinding and pounding the gritty meals which she cooked in a big black pot while Mr Okwonga, in his ragged old jacket, ambled about looking for beer and gossip.

He owned three cows, some goats, chickens, a dog, and he had a plough. His cotton and millet fields were nearby. Two miles away was an African *duka* which sold paraffin, carbolic soap, matches and cloth.

A poor, rough—yet in many ways almost idyllic—life: so long as crops yielded their harvest, and one did not fall seriously ill. A life based on a disciplined social and family relationship, and with—for men—plenty of leisure. It was a sad thing, though, said Kalisto, that his father had no other sons. Daughters inevitably left home to marry. Without sons to look after them in their old age, parents would end their lives wretchedly.

On the last night a dozen young men came with their *okemi* and a *nanga*. It had been raining. The earth smelt musty, and was strewn with the papery wings shed by flying ants. The night before, Kalisto had caught them in scores. We had fried and eaten them for breakfast.

I sat on my Turkish stool, surrounded by a small tinkling cascade of music. My lantern flickered on the everted lips and shiny black faces of the young men, on their dusty cracked feet and threadbare shorts on the long, unevenly pigmented fingers scurrying faultlessly over the keys. The singer was an older man with yellowing eyes. In his soft, cracked voice he sang songs like this:

> We like the young girls,
> Not those women over twenty
> Who are already fat
> And smell badly.

And this:

> Spears once shone like stars,
> On the plain thy foes fled.
> Bent spears we brought home,
> Spears red with blood.

The tunes they twanged on their rough wooden boxes over-whelmed the persistent screaming of night insects. They would have strummed all night. But a cold wind blew up, shaking leaves off the wild fig tree and spurting up patches of black dust. So the young men took their nailed boxes and went back into the scrub, blowing a cow horn to frighten the dark. The three cows had broken out of their kraal and we had to chase them back before we went to bed.

Juke-box

When I left with Kalisto in the morning the last people I saw were some haggard Karamojong resting under a tree. They had gone hungry for a long time. Their rib cages showed like wire, and they had walked for two days over the Labwor hills to find temporary work for a few bags of grain. Three men from the leper centre near Patongo waved fingerless hands at me. As I turned on to the gravelly main road to Lira, a notice 'Be aware of flying stones' reminded me of hazards to the windscreen.

A hundred miles farther on we came to Soroti and went into an Ismaili bar. It was Saturday. Thirsty African clerks were lining the bar. I had been living among thin men, and noticed they were fat. The juke-box was turned up loud, and two light-skinned women in *busuti* gowns were wriggling themselves in front of it.

'Prostitutes!' hissed Kalisto. 'You don't find their sort in Acholi.'

Kalisto has some intolerant ideas about women. ('I hate prostitutes!' he once cried, startling everyone during a class reading of Isherwood's description of Fräulein Kost eating chocolates with her Japanese lover).

I enjoyed watching the women gyrate in front of the juke-box. They were pretty, and slightly drunk. It was the bottled beer I found disappointing. After those calabashes of warm *pombe* gruel it tasted like a thin cold medicine.

Jie raiders

Kalisto's home was no longer a peaceful, bumbling place when I revisited him some months later. The news was

131

alarming. Jie raiders, for the first time in several years, had appeared. They had been stealing over the low saddle near Kano to attack homesteads after dark. They had killed old people and children who could not run away, and made off with cattle.

The very first morning, I was roused by the ululations of an alarm call sounding from homestead to homestead, and by men hurrying past with bows and spears. They were back in the evening to report that bands of Jie were lying up in the hills.

The raiders came again during the next two nights. A detachment of Special Police moved up to Patongo, thirteen miles away. But they were too few and too late. Within twenty-four hours everyone—except for a few obstinate old men—had fled from our neighbourhood, taking their cattle, bicycles, clothes, and bundles of food.

Kalisto's father was one of those who stayed. 'I was the first to settle here,' he said, 'and I'll be the last to go.' His cattle had gone off with a hired boy, and his wife and daughters had walked twenty miles to friends.

Kalisto and I went to the raiding area. Acholi families scatter their homes. Each homestead consists of a large hut, which the parents occupy, and of smaller huts for their grown-up children. The compound has food bins and a small cattle kraal. Sandy foot tracks strewn with fallen butter-nuts lead through the scrub from one family compound to another (they may be separated by half a mile) and to the small cotton and millet plots.

Every homestead we came to was deserted. Hoe handles, bundles of cord and thatching grass, lay about. Some of the granary bins were half-full of sorghum. Inside the huts the clay pots stood empty on their moulded earth stands. The doors, panelled with flattened petrol tins, had been left open. The staked cattle kraals were empty enclosures of churned mud and dung. Chickens and guinea fowl were feeding on scattered grain, the old cotton plots were flowering, the millet fields unweeded.

Kalisto was very upset. 'The crops', he said, 'will be lost this year. People will be too scared to come back. The Jie have rifles—if only the government would give us firearms!'

The Jie came again—much nearer: and it was likely to be our turn next. That night, the half-dozen men who had stayed behind crowded into Kalisto's hut with their spears and bows. Mr Okwonga brought a calabash of beer.

But it was soon clear that my companions had gathered for mutual comfort rather than action. 'If the Jie come,' Mr Okwonga said to me, 'don't on any account go out unless you want a spear in your back.'

As the beer began to take effect, tension relaxed. By midnight everyone was asleep. In the early hours I heard a commotion not far away; and when something very quietly pushed the door, I put my hand round a spear handle, wondering what to expect. It was only a dog.

Kalisto, when I drove him back to Kampala, was ashamed and downcast. 'The government', he said, 'doesn't care about us. We are too small and too far away.'

Longorok

A week later Kalisto wrote an account of the situation for a Kampala weekly, *The People*. This is the gist of what he wrote:

'For weeks Longorok has been pillaging isolated Adilang villages. He strikes between dusk and midnight. This enables him to retire into Karamoja before sunrise. Nobody cares to chase Karamojong at night.

At night the Jie surround the huts in a homestead. Each spearman guards a doorway. One man opens the cattle kraal noisily to provoke the owner. Some foolish farmers have run out of their huts to attack the raiders but they were immediately speared to death.

Lamwon is a village in Adilang. A week ago Longorok fell on the village at sunset. The men were away at a *pombe* party, and finding only women and children at home he slaughtered three women, three children, and drove off the cattle. A primary schoolboy aged six was speared three times.

Those who have fled from Longorok described his gunmen as stark naked, the spearmen as Jie. Adilang elders believe that only Turkana have the habit of being naked. Again, only Turkana are likely to have rifles, which they have acquired from Abyssinia. But the gunmen could be Jie who have got rifles from Turkana, and go stark naked in order to be taken for Turkana.

What is left of Adilang at this moment? Property worth a great deal of money has been abandoned. Families are trekking to Pader Palwo sub-county. The result may be famine next year. Crops and cattle will be lost.

The police alone are not an effective deterrent. When I left for Kampala on May 17th some herds of cattle were again stolen in the night.

Even if the police were effective, as soon as they go Longorok will again be on the war-path. It is well known that the Karamojong must raid and kill a person to be initiated into manhood. The government cannot eradicate this custom overnight. Education will one day accomplish this, but it will take years.

Adilang elders want to help the police control the situation. Let the government encourage Adilang farmers to protect themselves! Adilang is the home of ex-servicemen who were discharged after World War II. Many Adilang men fought in Abyssinia, some reached the jungles of Burma.

Can't we defend ourselves, if we are encouraged to and are given guns?'

Postscript (*May 1969*)

Kalisto is now teaching at a secondary school in Kitgum. His headmaster is an Irish Verona Father, his neighbour (also a teacher) a former R.A.F. Bomber pilot who was shot down over Ploesti and rounded up by Romanian peasants carrying scythes. Kalisto tells me that the area raided by the Jie two years ago has not been resettled.

CHAPTER 14

Lomwaka

Soldiers

There was a sound of firing from the Kabaka's walled palace on Mengo hill when I drove out of Kampala towards Jinja. The Kingdom of Buganda was falling, its leaders and armed bands being rounded up. I had been warned not to travel, as crowds of 'hooligans', it was said, were making the roads unsafe.

'Two of your people', a police officer told me, 'have just been lynched. If you see a mob, stop, look, and be ready to turn back.'

But the road was deserted, village stores shuttered, the banana *shambas* framed only a few timid faces. The one embarrassment I had was from three armed soldiers manning a road block at Mukono.

A crowd of dejected people was sitting under guard by the wayside, and the soldiers were in a state of nervous excitement and anger which made it highly dangerous to cross their path. It meant nothing to them that I was white. It seemed to make them angrier. One of them tried to grab me by the nose. I was relieved to get away and once over the Nile at Jinja to leave Buganda and its troubles behind.

When I got to Mbale, I asked an Indian bar-owner what news there was from Kampala. 'People say', he told me, 'that the Kabaka is dead—and good riddance too.'

'The Baganda', he added, raising his voice to impress the customers, 'are a bad people. The Kabaka is especially bad. He gave firearms to hooligans. A ruler who provokes unrest in the country is no good.'

Another Indian spoke softly in my ear. 'The whole business of attacking the Kabaka's palace', he said, 'is deplorable. The Baganda, for all their faults, are a civilised people. They have treated us well.'

I slept under a spreading tree at the side of the golf links. When I awoke some labourers were going by. They laughed and waved to see me entangled in my pyjamas and mosquito net. Buganda's nightmare was not theirs.

Kitgum–Lomwaka

At Kitgum, 150 miles north of Soroti, I camped in a field next to an outfit of the Tanzanian Diamond Corporation. A bare-chested Englishman was in charge. He gave me fried sausages for supper, and told me that Moroto had just installed its first juke-box in Patel's bar. 'I went to the opening night,' he said, 'and some bugger stole 600 shillings out of my bum pocket.'

Indian traders as well as missionaries have followed the northern highway with its broken old milestones ticking off the distance to Juba. Up-country, where they feel less protected than in towns, the Indians close early, and in Kitgum they spend the hour of dusk sitting over cards on reed mats outside their stores. They are a small, mainly Ismaili community owning between them a lorry or two and a white mosque.

They also run two bars one of which, 'The Acholi Pride', was crowded with lorry drivers and soldiers in floppy hats. The Kabaka's picture had already been taken down. The barmaids had been brought from Mbale. Their thick bodies were bursting from very tight, short dresses. They were the only African women in Kitgum who dared to wear them.

The Agoro hills, where I wanted to walk, stood another fifty miles to the north. From Padibe I could see them sealing off Uganda's border with the Sudan. I drove towards them, along a greasy cotton-soil track, until I was stopped by a bog. There was a store and some huts nearby. The storekeeper very soon found four men to go with me, and we set off on a ten-mile walk to the rest house at the foot of Lomwaka peak.

The way led across a flat plain clustered with fine shea butter-nut trees. They have dense crowns and fruit like green plums from which the precious oil is extracted. Blue bee-eaters flashed over the path. Men in torn singlets and tough women with heavy bare breasts came out of their huts to see who I was.

136

A sharp climb above the plain brought us to Lotuturu rest house.

It was a cold, broken building whose doors and shutters had been burnt as fuel. But it gave a splendid view. To the south a plain lapping against ridges and inselbergs; above us a row of hill tops dominated by Lomwaka.

At the forestry camp, labourers were using heavy old Nilotic hoes with the shaft bent at right angles in the middle and a heart-shaped blade. We crossed a stream, and started to climb.

The grass was thick and high, the ground strewn with hidden stones and thorns; and by midday my companions said they had had enough. I had already suspected they were duds. The oldest of them had a terrible swelling round his throat and ears. He had come to enjoy a short walk and food. We left him sitting on a stone in the sun.

The youngest porter had already gone back to the plain for eggs. Of the two who were still with me, one had gashed his foot, the other grumbled that my Crown Bird cigarettes were not good enough for him.

We were sitting under a wild date palm enclosed by a sea of wild grass which gleamed here and there with the red flowers of *gloriosa simplex*.

'We're tired,' said the two Acholi. 'We're hungry and thirsty. It's dangerous to go farther.' They had already, I noticed, finished off their bottle of water. I had not touched mine.

I suggested camping for the night. 'Impossible,' they said. 'The Didinga might kill us.' (But Madi Opei, where Didinga had in truth been raiding and murdering, was over thirty miles away.)

So I gave them some of my water, and left. The sky was clear, the mountain green, and protea flowers had opened like white pincushions. After a time a few tall groundsels and lobelia spikes showed I was getting high. Then towards the top the grass thinned, and I scrambled quickly over the last ridge. A pair of mountain reed buck ran off. I was looking down at the Sudan.

Valleys, ravines and hills—green and blue shading to black—were tumbling at my feet. I would have liked to go on. There was miles of walking country in front of me. But having hurried to the top, I had to hurry back again.

5*

It was already dark when I joined my companions and we crossed the little black stream by the forestry camp. We heard shouts, the shrill laughter of women, and drumming. Lomwaka had been utterly still. This was an ugly, drunken noise, and we circled round it.

Back in Kitgum, the diamond searchers were still camped in the field. I sat under a tree listening to a woodpecker's laughter and partridges calling. Some women had been brought in to wash clothes. Their attitudes, as they stooped with their buttocks pointed sharply upward, were unconsciously erotic. They had scarified faces and wore waist beads under their skirts.

Before I drove off, I called at the Verona Fathers' mission, which had been settled in Kitgum for over fifty years. I was surprised to see a large portrait of the Queen hanging over the coffee room. The Father Superior pointed out that he was an Italian-born, naturalised British subject. He spoke Cockney, and encouraged at lunch the relaxed male atmosphere of an officers' mess. Everyone smiled proudly at his story of the Irish priest who, only a day or two earlier, was said to have knocked down an armed rebel on the Masindi road. A policeman had come up and shot the man dead.

Kidepo

From Kitgum a bad and lonely dirt road meanders north-east towards Kidepo, through a waste land stripped brutally of trees to check the tsetse fly. This was no place to get stuck in with engine trouble. At the end of it, I was immediately aware of having crossed into Karamoja. The grass had been trampled by vast droves of cattle, and no one wore European dress.

Among the Karamojong one never knows what stage of the human body one will see next: a hag with stringy hair and breasts, shrivelled like a smoked fish; a lovely young woman with a Mongolian slant to her eyes and a small face split in a dazzling smile, legs slender as young banana stems, breasts small and round, wearing a trailing cow hide cut away in front

and at the back fitted smooth and dark as the flesh itself round
the top of the buttocks; an old man, hollow-cheeked, dirty and
stark naked; or a young man sleek and proud, his hair done in a
huge orange bun stuck with feathers, his long coal-black limbs
shiny with grease.

Here were all sorts, trekking along the wayside or squatting
with cattle. I stopped at a village to watch some men dancing
in a cloud of dust. They were jumping high into the air, and
like stiff-legged marionettes hitting the ground with a shout
and a rhythmic thud that made it tremble.

I found the new Warden of Kidepo game park arguing in his
office with an Esso agent—a Luo from Kenya—who wanted to
erect a big pole with a sign on it outside the petrol pump by
the park entrance.

'I won't have it,' the warden was saying. 'My visitors come to
see animals not advertisements.'

When I asked him if I could travel through the back of his
reserve to climb Zulia, he was not enthusiastic. 'The area is
flooded,' he said. 'You wouldn't get through.'

At the petrol pump I found the Esso man already surveying
a site for his pole. I asked him for news of Kampala. 'There has
been a great explosion in the Kabaka's palace,' he said cheerfully. 'It killed the Kabaka. He had been shooting soldiers with
a machine-gun given him by the British.'

The handful of bungalows for the park visitors had at last
been finished. But there was still no catering, and owing to the
rains, no visitors. I learned that the clerk, who on my earlier
visit had asked me to take his photograph, had been gaoled for
pocketing entrance money. I went back to Kaabong.

CHAPTER 15

Zulia (1)

Kaabong

About once a week the police at Kaabong send supplies to their detachment at Pirre. For this purpose a track has been cut from Kalapata over a spur of Mount Morungole. The track has been roughly hacked out of rock and sand. It needs a tough Land Rover to make the jolting trip. When stream beds are full it is impossible.

The police agreed to give me a lift to Pirre; and, while I was waiting at the tin rest hut for their truck to leave, I was joined by an Australian professional hunter from Kenya and his clients—an American married couple of Greek origin. They were not interested in shooting game but in photographing it, and in doing at the same time some profitable business in native carvings, spears and other bric-à-brac.

The Australian was in his late sixties. He wore a clean bush hat and he was gentle and patient. He set up the camp beds, cleaned the lantern, cooked the beans, washed up and boiled coffee; and his fists, though huge and covered in red hairs like a Hemingway character's, did not tremble with whisky.

'You young fellows', he said to me after supper, 'don't know what you've missed. East Africa used to be a glorious country—game galore. Nowadays poachers use trucks. Great mobs of game have been slaughtered just to make fly-whisks from the tails. And the country's full of jumped-up chaps in *maridadi* suits—and Socialists. 'I daresay you're one yourself,' he added with a grin.

He gave me a packet of Crown Bird cigarettes and a piece of advice. 'Don't trust the hyena,' he said. 'When you sleep out put your head against a tree, and have the lantern burning at your feet.'

140

Pirre

We had been bumping and grinding along the flank of Morungole for a couple of hours when the police driver stopped. 'Over there', he said pointing into the bush, 'a British police officer was shot dead by Turkana.'

The spot he was pointing to looked like any other: a slope spattered with scrub, stones and tough grass. 'The Turkana,' added the driver, 'still make trouble. That's why we're here.'

I had been told that Dr Colin Turnbull was still at Pirre. Englishmen who have travelled thousands of miles at great expense to find privacy can be very snooty with intruders. What, I was wondering, would Dr Turnbull think of me? Would he be rude, coldly polite? Would he resent a stranger walking clumsily about *his* territory?

I decided that if he looked put out, or scowled, I would give him my bag of limes and depart immediately over the hills.

From above, the Teuso village of Pirre looked like a bunch of haycocks. The adjacent tree cover had been felled or mutilated. Dr Turnbull was living in a thatched hut surrounded by a double stockade. His red truck, which one might have mistaken for a fire engine, was parked under a tree hung with weavers' nests.

I needn't have worried about my welcome. 'Come in,' he said. 'I'll make tea. You're my first visitor.'

The hut had a sloping earth floor so that empty tins, candle stumps and other objects rolled down against the wall. The furnishings were home-made, the bed was broken.

'Don't look so horrified,' said Dr Turnbull. 'I sleep and work in my truck.' He was wearing rather elegant white shorts and needed a hair cut. He had a pale sun tan and numerous small sores on his legs. His delightful charm and friendliness put me straightaway at ease.

He introduced me to Joe, the young coloured American student who was helping Dr Turnbull in his research and gathering material for his own thesis. Joe was wearing an old hat and raincoat. He was, he told me, fascinated by his work. But it was a hard and uncomfortable life, and he was homesick for the tender, fleshy women of Buganda.

According to Dr Turnbull, the Teuso (they call themselves Ik) number about 1,500 of whom 500 live in Pirre, the remainder around Kamion on the Turkana escarpment. They are hunters and gatherers by tradition: slightly built, unaggressive, and—because they have no cattle wealth—poor; a tribal remnant, not yet identified, distinct from the Nilo-Hamitic pastoralists of the 'Karamojong cluster' who surround them, and possibly, it was thought, related to an early Bushman people. One of Dr Turnbull's jobs was to try and identify them.[1]

Dr Turnbull's account of their present situation was a gloomy one. The Teuso, he said, were going through a difficult time. Stricter surveillance of the Sudan border and encroachment of the Kidepo game park boundaries had drastically curtailed the area which they were free to roam. They were compelled to rely increasingly on food crops. But these, grown on poor patches of mountain side that lacked water and were roasted by strong sunlight, were not enough.

The strain of constant hunger which had recently reached starvation point following two years of drought had so demoralised the Teuso that families were no longer sharing food or providing for elderly parents.

'It's most depressing,' said Dr Turnbull. 'They snatch and steal food from each other. They go off into private places to eat by themselves. "Goodness" means having a full stomach. You'll notice they're so distrustful of each other that within their village each family hut has its own stockade. The children and old people naturally suffer most. At three, children are expected to find their own food. The old people are simply ignored—they accept it as their lot.'

Our hut stood against the fenced village. After dark I could hear a murmur of voices. 'The catechist', remarked Dr Turnbull, ironically, 'is taking prayers. No doubt they're all thanking

---

[1] Professor Tucker, of the School of Oriental and African Studies, is reported to have found links between the language spoken by the Teuso and Ancient Egyptian. Dr Turnbull has written, 'The Ik speak a language that is quite definitely not Sudanic, as previously tentatively classified. Professor Tucker believes it to be closer to Cushitic, though some may see similarities with Khoisan languages' ('The Ik: Alias the Teuso', *The Uganda Journal*, Vol. 31, Part I, Kampala 1967). Dr Turnbull's article summarises some of the facts he ascertained about the Teuso during his stay with them.

God that a white man has arrived, and praying you've brought them some food!'

The Teuso coughed often in the night. When they crept in the morning from the little huts where they had slept naked among strewn ashes of fires, their thin, prematurely wrinkled bodies had a grey, spidery look.

Soon a straggle of hungry children, and emaciated old men and women unable to plod uphill to work a plot or drag themselves to the government maize meal distribution centre a day's walk away, were haunting Dr Turnbull's hut for scraps.

Like the neighbouring Karamojong the men wear nothing but a length of cloth tied at the shoulder, the women a creaking cow-hide that trails at the back, with a flap in front (unmarried girls hang a chain apron round their waists). They use beads and lip plugs, and pattern their bodies with keloids. Women mat their hair; their small heads, shaved at the sides, protrude from an extravagant collar of hoops. They strike one at first as a cheerful community; their outwardly happy-go-lucky demeanour conceals their wretchedness.

Zulia stands on the Uganda-Sudan border like a big boundary-stone. Dr Turnbull had no trouble in finding four volunteers to accompany me there.

The leader, Atun, was a small neat man with a wrinkled face. He, alone in all the village, wore shorts and a shirt. His daughter was the prettiest of the girls. Her beads were brightly polished and she had a taut little stomach bulging over a clean leather flap. Joe told me she was doing well out of an affair with one of the policeman, who gave her food. Atun was also profiting from the connection.

'You can trust Atun,' Dr Turnbull said as we left, 'but make him carry his fair share of the loads.'

Kidepo boundary

The track led at first along the edge of Kidepo game park, past a cleft in the hills used by Turkana raiders from across the Kenya frontier. The grass was high, the sharp seed pods pricked like small thorns. Rain had brought colour to the scrub. White and yellow blossom obscured the needles and hooks of many acacia trees. Their stems glistened red or pale green under black, scaling bark.

I soon found that the Teuso were enterprising but erratic guides. They stopped frequently to gorge berries; stalked, with spears and a bow, a hartebeest (it bolted at forty yards); poked tirelessly at the termite mounds, and wandered off to examine dozens of half-dead thorn trees for honey.

We rested at midday at a tiny water-hole in a sandy stream bed; the spot had been trampled by game and the water smelt and tasted like urine.

When we stopped for the night Zulia was still far away. My companions made camp expertly. They tore up sheaves of soft grass to lie on behind an improvised thorn fence, and lit a hot, smokeless fire on which they stirred and cooked the cow peas and maize flour till it turned into hot bubbling porridge. Then, when the stars brightened, and they had scraped out the blackened pot, each man made his own little fire and they stretched out in a row, quite naked, to sleep.

As usual I had placed my camp bed some yards from the fire, for I did not need its warmth. I had boiled and eaten a thick oatmeal porridge soaked with milk and sugar. My gear was arranged around me and the night breeze was rustling my hair. All the familiar bright stars were looking through the tough, small leaves of trees.

For a few minutes I watched the firelight flicker on the scabby bark of a thorn tree and on the four spears and quiver of arrows propped against it. As soon as I put out my lantern I was asleep.

By next day I had quite recaptured the rhythm of walking hour after hour in tall grass and elephant spoor, and over ruts and stones. Only a small fraction of my mind was involved in placing one foot before the other. The rest of it was free to dream, to fidget with a hundred thoughts, to observe the colour and shape of objects.

Atun went first, carrying his bow and quiver of arrows. We were distracted by honey guides. The Teuso encouraged them with a clucking noise and from time to time Locham, the youngest, chased after them and brought back a few poor combs of honey. The bush was noisy with hornbills and black and white crested shrikes. Purple solanum flowers with a big

a. and *b.* Mt Mikeno from Rukumi hut

c. Lichen and moss-draped forest on Karisimbi

14a–c. Vegetation on Karisimbi peak

. View of Mt Mikeno

. Nyiragongo from the plain

16a. Mikeno from Rumangabo

5. Congo volcanoes

yellow berry climbed among the grass. When a small breeze blew, the thirsty-looking dracaena trees that stood in groves along the dry gullies seemed too tired to shake their crowns of leaves.

Zulia stood now right ahead: a solid mass of overgrown rock with a few wooded bumps on it. A ridge congested with a forest of flower-tipped *euphorbia candelabrum* took us to its base.

Camp

We camped on a ledge a few hundred feet above a spring. My companions had found a tortoise which they baked, then hacked off the carapace and ate. Not a leaf stirred in our high, sheltered dell; but far away, on the exposed ridges above, wind was soughing.

We had seen neither hut, field, nor any person since coming down the little spur on which Pirre stands. I liked this deserted grassland and the changing shapes of the hills that partitioned it. I was getting to know my escort and the parts they played.

Atun, the *mzee* (elder), was guide; he took the largest *posho* helpings and smoked most of my cigarettes. Locham looked for food. Lolim, who was the strongest, carried the heaviest load. Lochere was the handyman who levelled off the camp site and chopped fuel. They carried dagger-shaped knives. Lolim and Lochere had huge gaps where the lower incisor teeth had been rooted out. Their ears were full of perforations; and all of them were heavily marked with keloids.

They were—like other northern tribes of Uganda—uncircumcised; and it occurred to me that without the protection of a foreskin, they might have thought twice before plunging naked among the needle-like thorns of the bush.

On the march and in the rosy firelight their bodies, that their sweat constantly washed, glistened with thin muscle: only the buttocks, on which they sat cushion-like, were grey with dust. When they spat they ejected suddenly and without clearing the throat a thin pencil of frothy spittle.

The crest

In brilliant weather we climbed next morning through protea scrub and scattered stands of wild date palm, cedars, and giant tree heather. The proteas were coming into blossom, their

145

white flower-heads peeping timidly out of a green cup. Towards the top, the aloes had shrunk to a rosette of dwarfed red leaves on a stump.

The top of Zulia (7,048 feet) is a series of grassy bumps and depressions. Like a trespasser on a rooftop I felt exhilarated to be gazing down on all this mass of lonely border country whose lawless cattle-raiding tribes encircle the Teuso: to the northeast, the Turkana plain running through a shimmer of swamp; north, a stout barrier of heights securing the Didinga lands of Sudan; beyond Pirre, Morungole's tilted summit ridge with its sentinels of giant heather overlooking Dodoth cattle camps.

In this wild enclave neither Pirre police post nor the new Kenya frontier guard (whose white building I could see gleaming many miles away) can give complete protection. I sat on a stone with Atun and asked him about the Turkana.

'The Turkana', he said briefly, 'are *adui* (enemies). The Dodoth are friends.'

In recent months, he went on, the Turkana—some of whom carried rifles—had twice overrun Pirre. The first time they came in peace; they took over the area for a few days to water and graze their herds. On their second visit they stole Dodoth cattle, and there had been fighting in which Pirre police post was involved.

The Teuso survived, he explained, because, owning few livestock, they were not worth plundering. He did not add, though, that by making themselves useful as 'spies' to Turkana and Dodoth alike, the Teuso cunningly exploit their situation on the raiding gateways of three countries.

Kidepo game park rangers, Atun said, were another nuisance. They kept a sharp watch on poachers and put them in gaol. The Teuso, he grinned, knew how to outwit them; but Didinga were often caught, their cattle and spears confiscated.

For supper Locham brought back two young hornbills tied wretchedly round the neck. A night wind blew up, drowning the tick of night insects, and the stars showed patchily through hurrying clouds.

Rain

Returning the way we had come, we were chased all next day by thunder showers. When the first storm clouds appeared, bouncing from hill to hill, Atun took out a plug of wood given to him by the witch doctor, scraped it on a finger nail, and blew the dust towards them. But we were soon drenched. So he stuck his *dawa* on the tip of his spear and propped it against a tree with the blade pointing at the streaming rain curtain—which hovered, then to his delight swerved by.

'The rain', he giggled, 'will now be striking the Bwana from America.'

At dusk it again rained heavily, and while we were making a night shelter of hacked-off thorn branches I found it warmer to strip than to shiver in sodden clothes. I tried to pretend I was a bather briefly caught out on the English coast on a wet day. The Teuso felt the cold too; but it was their heads they were careful to protect, wrapping them whenever it rained in their small brown cloths.

The rain had brought colour into the pale yellow thorn blossom; even the grey dessicated arms of the *euphorbia candelabrum* looked greener. The sodden droppings of leopard and hartebeest were enthroned with gaudy butterflies. We had startled a great many sand grouse, quail, and flocks of helmeted shrikes.

But it had not been a very good day. My companions had mutilated dozens of trees in their search for honey; the caches were all dried up—*mafuta hapana*, said Atun, no fat in them. And his *dawa* had not made all the rain clouds sail away.

A downpour soon fills the dry stream beds of Karamoja with thunderous, short-lived torrents. When we climbed the last ridge to Pirre, its ford was already blocked with débris. The bed, when we had crossed it earlier, had been dry and spattered with Teuso excrement that contained semi-digested corn. In the pools of water left behind by the rain, my companions now bathed and rolled happily like dogs in sand.

Baboons were raiding the small terraced plots which from below had looked like untidy scars of a landslide strewn with broken tree stems. Under a tree we passed some wasted old men and women sitting motionless as lizards over tiny red embers on which nothing was cooking. Atun, Locham, Lolim and Lochere had, at any rate, come home with full stomachs.

Pirre again

I found Dr Turnbull and Joe packing for a trip to Kampala. The hut looked as odd as ever with its broken chairs, the two rolled black umbrellas (one of them rather expensive) hanging on a nail, the empty medicine bottles, and the sloping mud floor where cockroaches scurried at night.

The radio had announced from Kampala that the Kabaka was still missing. 'The Baganda', remarked Dr Turnbull, 'are now paying the price for having accepted the white man in a big way and for trying to go it alone.'

I asked him, after supper, how he had managed during the raids on Pirre. He had stayed, he said, in his hut while there was shooting and spears were flying about. One young Teuso had been shot in the stomach. 'The others, of course, left him to die. I made him some tea.'

Dr Turnbull knew about Atun's magic plug of wood for exorcising rain. The old witch doctor, he remarked, was dying. But he had not yet decided whether to impart the secrets of his trade to his son, with whom he was on bad terms.

In the morning the stockade had to be taken apart to let out the red Land Rover. A crowd came to see Dr Turnbull and Joe off. Not underestimating Teuso cupidity, the last thing they did before locking up was to place some deterrent magic of their own in the centre of the hut floor.

We jolted past the metal huts of the police post where stout, well-nourished men in shining black boots were lounging with their wives. I took a last look at the village. Some small black figures in scraps of cloth were crouched over wisps of smoke, and the sun was catching the tiny steep plots strewn with rubbish and old tree stems.

CHAPTER 16

Zulia (2)

Famine

Moroto is over 300 miles from Kampala. I got there, intending to revisit the Teuso, long after dark and looking forward to a quiet sleep in the rest house garden. But High Life jazz, enormously amplified, was blaring from an adjacent barracks, and though I walked half a mile to put up my camp bed on a grassy space, the hammering of electric guitars followed me. I grumbled about the noise to a night watchman, who laughed. 'It's the same every night,' he said. 'What else is there to do?'

Forty miles from Moroto I stopped to look at three pairs of ostriches which ran off with a high stepping action, waving their tails. With their long bare necks they looked like teapots. Farther on I scared a cheetah off the road. Three months had passed since my first visit to the Teuso. In the meantime the thorn bush had turned greener, the grass in the ungrazed no-man's land separating the Jie from the Dodoth was high, the ground sprayed with purple, white and cream coloured ipomoea; and red aloe flowers waved at bush height like pennants.

The ADC at Kaabong was in a state of nervous excitement. The Teuso, he told me, had been dying of starvation at the rate of five a day. It had just been decided to set up an emergency food distribution centre in Pirre itself, since the present one at Kaseli was too far and people were collapsing on the way. A minister was due to land at Kidepo air strip and to visit the area that very day. The ADC was off to meet him and I had just time to climb into his truck. It was loaded with 500 lb. of maize meal.

149

In Pirre a crowd of hungry people was waiting to grab the food sacks and within an hour cooking fires were mantling the hillside in smoke. An emaciated old man who had fallen down was carried back to Dr Turnbull's hut by his son ('I had to cuff the son,' said Dr Turnbull, 'to make him help.') The old man's bones showed like sharp rods through the wrinkled flesh; his eyes were gummy. Dr Turnbull propped him up and fed him with a sweet banana and tea.

The crops, I learned, were not ready; and much had been spoilt by pests. A number of villagers had died since my visit—the 'non-productive' ones, children, old people, and the witch doctor, who had not passed on his secrets to his son.

The survivors looked wretched: dirty, emaciated, hollow-faced. The women's breasts had shrunk to flaps, their bellies were a mass of wrinkles and folds. The children were skinny and pot-bellied. They coughed badly.

'The government food ration', said Dr Turnbull, 'will be mostly eaten by the stronger ones. The Ik cannot survive long at this rate. Yet they refuse to be resettled in a more fertile place.'

In the evening we sat over a fire in Dr Turnbull's compound. 'I was of course happier', he said, 'with the Ituri pygmies. They were gay, relaxed, and had plenty of food. These people are always tense and busy.'

I asked him about their sex life. 'Sex to an Ik', he said, 'is simply an occasion for getting rid of semen.'

Joe advised me against sleeping out in the compound, as there were leopards about—a child had been snatched from a hut—and the police had recently shot two. In the night I heard a snort followed by a twitter of startled voices. There were other noises—the rustle of the big brown cockroaches and the hum of a mosquito looking for tiny rents in the old army mosquito net I have carried about with me for twenty-eight years. I repaired it a long time ago with safety pins. Its yellowing envelope of Indian mesh does not keep out all the mosquitoes but it gives me a feeling of privacy.

Kamion

In the morning I said goodbye to Dr Turnbull and Joe and set off for Kamion where I was told Teuso are scattered on bumps and ledges along the Turkana escarpment. My old companions were much thinner and less energetic than before, declining to chase the honey-guide birds through thorn scrub. We camped for the night in a glen, near a green puddle edged with clear water that had to be dug for in black sand. Around us stood tier on tier of *euphorbia candelabrum* with cream coloured rings on their stumpy fingers. The trees, said, Atun, were useless: the white juice was *kali*—bitter and poisonous. Yellow-flowering cassias were in blossom, and ipomoea was threading its twine in and out of bushes and dotting the ground with shallow, mauve trumpets.

The porters were ravenous. As they boiled a mass of *posho* and beans, they watched it and each other as closely as dogs round a bone. Atun took the largest portion, piled it on a leaf, and walked off a few yards to eat alone. He was, I noticed, better equipped than on our first journey. He had brought a government maize meal sack to sleep on, and a spoon which I assumed had once belonged to Dr Turnbull.

We had a six-hour gentle walk next day up and down bushy ridges. We were travelling along the edge of rain clouds that blew in constantly from Turkanaland and moved towards the Sudan. My companions did their best to keep me dry. They cracked fingers, clashed their spear heads, puffed *dawa* and brandished thorn branches at the misty curtains of rain, and knew exactly where to find a rock to shelter under. When the rain sometimes wetted us in spite of their magic, I grinned at them and they grinned back. Yet they were very serious about the puffing, the finger cracking, and the King Canute gestures with which they stroked and wheedled the air.

At our second camp we stayed near a village and were pestered by scroungers. Atun wisely deferred the meal till they had gone.

We were walking now past scattered fields. My companions were unscrupulous foragers, taking uninvited a few tobacco leaves or red peppers from one plot, some maize cobs and heads of sorghum from another, which they put instantly into the embers of a fire—Lochere carried a piece of slowly burning wood with him—and ate.

At midday we rested outside a Teuso village. A baboon was

raiding one of the plots and Lolim went after it with a spear. The baboon—in grotesque parody of greed, guilt and furtiveness—ran off with a cob in its mouth.

The ravine below was steep, slippery and eroded. Huts and skilfully terraced crops were pitched on its walls, which echoed with the cries of children scaring off crows and baboons. Here were witch-like women with babies clinging like the young of animals to their teats. A boy with a battered medallion round his neck was strumming an *okemi*. Some of the women were cooking millet. From every pot my companions took a helping.

Then suddenly, at the top of the next high ridge, we were standing in a strong, cool breeze on the edge of the Turkana escarpment itself, Here, gloriously and precariously perched, was a small village. But it was not easy to find a place to rest in; there was excrement under every wind-bent tree and shrub.

An old man, a dusty black gnome quite naked and wrinkled, came from nowhere to sit with us. His eyes were running slightly with pus. His white hair was reddish-brown at the sides, as though nicotine-stained.

We looked down into the plain hundreds of feet below and he showed me landmarks: far away, a Kenya police post; tracks winding up the cliff face used by Turkana raiders, whose favourite gateway this is into Dodoth cattle country; the steep split rocks where baboons raise their families and hide. The bushy plain was a scalp bristling with tufts of peppercorn hair. Over it moved the slow shadows of clouds, some in human shape like giant figures of ploughmen. Sogwass, to the east, stuck its hump across the sky. 'Come again,' said Atun when he noticed me looking at it.

The old man's village was stockaded; and within, each hut had its separate fence, turning the settlement into a small labyrinth of thorn protected hives and holes. The breeze that swept up the escarpment was swaying the lengths of rope which, to exorcise rain, the Teuso suspend like clothes lines round their dwelling clusters.

This was another of East Africa's beautiful places. Here the Teuso, scruffy, shrewd and cheerful, have perched themselves bird-like above the world of government and strangers. A high cliff is their watch tower. Beyond the ravine beds, where water is crannied in cracks and sockets, lies a grazing chessboard. An unmanned frontier runs past. A stage has been set for those gangs of obsolete raiding men who come and go at night with files of sweating cattle.

We walked along the escarpment edge, then went steeply down a gash where the sun struck blindingly against hot rock, and at the bottom water was trickling over smooth stones. Children were at play here: boys like shiny spiders, and little girls in tinkling chain aprons and with their heads shaved except for a narrow comb on top.

A youth in shorts spoke to me in English. He had been to school in Kaabong. 'When are the Europeans coming back', he asked, 'to stop our people dying and being killed by Turkana?' He believed, apparently, that the 'great revolution' taking place in Kampala was a prelude to the return of British administration.

We had to climb again, one laborious step upward after another, to get out of this shaft and its fierce trapped heat. Women were now descending to fetch water in pots and cans balanced on the head. The trudge back would be a cruel, exhausting task that lined and aged their faces and drove sweat into their sunken eyes. We halted for the night on the lip of the escarpment.

Lightning was glowing over Turkanaland when I went to sleep. At 1 a.m. I was roused by rain—pitiless rain that was cold, dense and steady. The thin trees were useless for shelter. There was nothing to do but keep the fire going and stay near it. Atun put the calabash over his head, the *posho* sack round his shoulders, and with his feet almost in the fire sat bowed and silent. The others had fled. I smoked one damp cigarette after another and watched the blue dye soak out of my old Turkish sweater into my shirt. It was a long night, a night that took away one's zest. We moved at dawn into a tiny hut at the edge of a field.

The hut was meant for crop watchers. But there was no one there, and my companions, after shouting a little at the big black crows that skulked among the millet stalks, went into the field to do some cadging of their own.

Then a young wife came, her skin and beads shining with rain, and she sat with me on a log. I was a tramp, with stubble and broken buttons and sodden black pumps. She had a leathery smell. But her bare thigh was smooth and warm against mine, her smile was brilliant, and as we crouched under the thatch we were suitably matched. Atun caught my eye and giggled.

Kalapata

When the sun came out I stripped and was soon dry. I had lost weight and felt well. A long walk through tall grass took us away from the escarpment into Dodoth country two miles from Kalapata.

I chose a camp site on a knoll overlooking big, flat-topped acacias and flowering scrub that was full of birds. Their noise woke me early and I looked over the edge of the knoll.

Just below me a pair of plantain eaters were chasing each other from tree to tree, landing clumsily with their tails up and a loud cackle. Golden weaver birds were fussing about nests that swayed like round fruits at the tip of the slenderest branches. There were shrikes and drongos, and a speckled woodpecker with its protracted, agitated cry that tailed off in metallic laughter. Those black dots on the ground were guinea fowl; and that ridiculous curved beak in low, laboured trajectory was a hornbill.

I could hear D'Arnaud's barbets calling, and put my field glasses on them: two small yellow birds with heavily spotted heads facing each other on a branch. They were doing their pantomime. While one almost jerked its head off with the effort of song, the other lifted and waggled its tail, showing the red patch underneath. Their chorus—an unmistakable series of brisk, penetrating notes repeated up and down a scale over and over again—is a sound that goes on echoing in my head long after I have finished a walk.

In this lonely place the din of the birds seemed overwhelming. How often have I listened to that shrill, grating discord of squeaks, twitterings and whistles!—confused, unmelodious, scarcely recognisable as song: a hubbub of small piercing sounds set off by an occasional deeper and more powerful trombone note—the bray of the go-away bird or the loud squawk of a casqued hornbill.

It is a virile noise, of rivalry and self-assertion; and I admire birds because, unlike us who are earth-bound and have to creep about the ground, they have freed themselves from its tyranny. They can fly and soar above dirt, war, smallpox and congestion. And they are rightly suspicious of man, keeping well out of reach when he approaches with his wheedling smile, his small boy's cruelty and his incalculability.

When the final phase of the Cassino battle opened one night in Italy with a mighty concentration of gun fire, I was lying on the ground among Polish infantry forward positions; and I fancied I heard a nightingale singing. I wished that I was so small a target; that I could soar at will above the steel splinters that would soon come raining back. Birds, during their short, nervous lives, have the advantage over us. Now, however, I was above the birds, prying down at them and their nests.

We were cooking breakfast when two tall men with spears came softly across the knoll. They were Dodoth, looking for tobacco and empty tins. I could see their cattle grazing below; and they had brought flies with them.

Kaabong

In the absence of cattle we had been walking through tall, untrampled grass. Now, when we turned towards Kaabong, we were back in pastoral country. Small, irritating flies attacked our faces, droves of voracious livestock were mauling the ground. Their Dodoth herdsmen, dandified and gleaming with grease, seemed huge compared with my escort. These swaggering athletes have learned, though, to scrounge unashamedly from travellers—a result in part of contact with tourists who drive along the highway to Kidepo game park and will bribe them to push their car out of a bog or to pose with bared genitals for a photograph.

A storm drove us to shelter in a ruined Catholic chapel that was crowded with goats; and then in a field hut, together with cows, where Atun made a fire by tearing thatch off the roof.

155

The cows had had their ears carved into the shape of cock's-combs and they wore bells whose cup was a small tortoise shell.

Near Kaabong my companions discreetly removed the blades from their spears. They were tired when, late at night, we trudged past the lights of the Italian mission, climbed down a broken span of the bridge which the flooded river had washed away, and lay down in the rest hut.

I said goodbye to them in the morning, at the Somali store. I was sorry to see them go: four small, worn men carrying a panga, a patched calabash, a bundle of food for the trek back to Pirre, and, in the folds of their skimpy brown cloths, some empty, invaluable tins.

CHAPTER 17

Villa Maria

Banana shamba

Kalisto had brought himself to my notice by his enthusiasm. He read almost anything he could get hold of: Thesiger's travel books, the Communist Manifesto, Camus, Hemingway, long-winded treatises on *négritude*, the hysterical stuff of Frantz Fanon. As secretary of the college debating society he persuaded diplomatists stationed in Kampala to address students on Rhodesia, the Berlin Wall, Israel (a Soviet Embassy official concluded some references to colonialism with the usual film of Georgia—all grapes, sun-baked churches, the sword dance, and handsome women with Indian profiles. 'Surely', I heard one student whisper, 'these Georgians aren't Russians!' 'No,' said another, loudly, 'they too were colonised.') Kalisto also ran the college magazine until he offended Northern students by printing an attack on their bride price customs.[1]

Hesbon Lubega, another of my students, was an unobtrusive Muganda. He wore glasses, spoke English with a slight stammer, and had been educated at a junior seminary. One day he brought me the manuscript of his 'novel'. In the style of many African novels it was full of beer, whores and night clubs ('the fat girl brought the beer. Stephen squeezed her hard . . .'). A London publisher's representative told me I should encourage Hesbon. So now I was driving along the Masaka road to visit him.

I found Hesbon in a banana grove where he lived with his parents and three younger sisters and brothers, in a neat house with a tame vervet monkey on the roof. His father wore a *kanzu*, his mother was cooking in a smoky shed. The house was pitched on the slope of a valley enclosed by green hills that

[1] See End Note (1).

bristled with banana plantations. A mile away I could see the buildings of Villa Maria mission station through thick clumps of trees.

I spent a week walking about the banana groves, listening to Kiganda songs on the gramophone in the evening, and drinking banana beer out of a jug.

In this neighbourhood, as they do elsewhere in country districts, the Muganda villager lives in a mud and wattle hut inside a small compound surrounded by his banana trees, with a copper leaf bush or some scarlet canna flowers to decorate the space in front. Today the grass thatched roof has more often than not been replaced by corrugated-iron sheets, which are a status symbol as well as being less hospitable to vermin. The unglazed windows are sealed against thieves, mosquitoes and prying eyes by wooden shutters.

It was quiet, cool and shady in the banana plantations. The green fronds wave and tremble incessantly like restless arms of many windmills. It is oppressive too, if you are not used to it, to stay for long within these damp, slightly rank smelling groves where the ground is strewn (for humus) with rotting leaves and stems, and serried plants—twenty-foot banana trees, coffee shrubs and cassava, wild date palms, pawpaws and bark-cloth trees—intercept the sun and a view of open country.

At night the groves were a black and rustling labyrinth laced with little paths that led to the glimmer of an oil lamp in a doorway—a nightmare to little children who fear snakes and spirits, and to stumbling drunkards.

The green banana or *matoke* plantain is the Muganda's staple food. He never tires of it. The hard, peeled plantains, tightly wrapped in their leaves, are steamed into mounds of hot yellow mash whose sour-potato flavour is set off by a groundnut or other sauce. Mrs Lubega spent much of her time preparing this and the side dishes in her draughty cooking shed. Before the family knelt or squatted to eat they covered the hard mud floor of the parlour with clean fibre mats. Wrapped in its huge leaf the *matoke* was then opened and spread before them, and eaten—dipped in sauce—with the fingers. Meals were a serious and important occasion. Mr Lubega liked his family to eat slowly, deliberately, and in silence.

The immediate consequences of such a meal, and of the banana or pineapple beer that precedes it, are a distended stomach and an overpowering desire to sleep. The children slumbered where they sat. Alas, the effects quickly wear off. Too soon one is hungry again.

Diet, of course, as well as climate and occupation, influence physique. Unlike the tall, lean and mobile pastoral tribes of northern Uganda, the Baganda, rooted within the few humid acres of their plots and tied to the settled neighbourhood of their clan, are often round-faced and fleshy, with stout handsome women whose rolling hips, in middle age, are accentuated by the loose, vividly coloured *busuti* gown that is their national dress.

Among them it was easy to spot Wahima, and the Watutsi refugees from Rwanda who have been settling in the area. They were taller, they had the thin noses and lips that sometimes give them a cruel and predatory look, and their women— oddly fattened about the hips—had faces that reminded one of black Madonnas.

The church

Hesbon's district has been strongly influenced by the big Roman Catholic mission at Villa Maria. Like his neighbours, several of whom were catechists who wore their heavy crucifixes like regalia over the breast, Mr Lubega had turned his parlour into a small private shrine. The walls were pasted with prints of Pope, bishops and Madonna, and he had a crib made of painted banana leaves. He was strict about saying Grace before the two daily meals. On Sunday everyone walked in family groups to church.

The chime of the bells filtering through a screen of tall *musizi* trees startled me. The bells seemed out of place in this sensual landscape which would have been more suited to the pounding of a drum struck near a wisp of smoke. But there was nothing dull about the cheerful faces of the congregation, the brilliant gowns and rolling bodies of the women, or the big home-made church.

When I went one quiet morning into the church, I immediately felt the force of its homely yet powerful personality. The roof alone is remarkable. It is supported by huge, crooked tree stems that were cut and dragged by volunteers from a forest several miles away. Mr Lubega told me that the White Fathers had rewarded these toilers with medallions. 'Cash or cloth', he remarked, 'would have been more appreciated.' The steep valley climbing up to the church is still called, ironically, 'Not Worth A Medallion.'

Gaps have been cut in the thatched roof, under its layer of gleaming corrugated iron sheets, to discourage cockroaches. Though it was long past Christmas, the crib—like a prize exhibit—had not yet been taken away. Its Mother and Christ-Child, shepherds and wise men had ivory-white skins. There were four confessional boxes, an organ with a dust-cloth on it, and a sensational painting of the holocaust of Ugandan martyrs in which youths were soaring heavenward above crackling flames.

Anchored to its hill, a leviathan among the small native huts, the church is a monument to those bearded white foreigners who came with their printing presses, their sun helmets and spine pads, and for better as well as for worse have changed the lives of Africans for ever.

Villa Maria mission has a secondary school, a convent and a hospital. They are enclosed by ornamental trees and shrubs planted with affection. The frangipani embalms its skeletal grey ribs in fragrant stars of tinted blossom. Thevetia lifts soundless yellow trumpets. Red spirals hang from an Australian bottlebrush. There are tulip trees, cassias, and mounds of prickly Spanish bayonet.

Nowadays, though, when the *musizi* and *mvule* trees decay, they are no longer replaced. The avenues show gaps.

Many local youths are attracted, at least initially, to the junior seminary at nearby Bukalasa where they get a good secondary school education. The discipline is a hard test of character. 'No running up steps,' said Hesbon, who had attended it, 'no mango picking, second thoughts about celibacy.' Those who stay the course go on to study for the priesthood at the adjacent major seminary.

Customs

The Baganda do not disfigure their bodies, a fact which surprised early white visitors who had passed through neighbouring districts of naked, scarified people. They regard torn ear lobes, lip plugs and tooth extraction as barbarous. It is said that their dislike of mutilation was one reason why the Baganda resisted early pressure to accept Islam, with its insistence on circumcision.

For the same reason the atrocious mutilations—cutting out of eyes, lips, and the like—which the old Kabakas and their chiefs used to inflict on their subjects for the most trivial offences, were all the more feared and loathed.

The older generation are still careful to cover their bodies. Exposure is immodest—a tradition that dates back to the edict of an early Kabaka who ordered that each peasant should plant bark-cloth trees, and that everyone should be clothed. In rural Buganda men wear the *kanzu*, a white Arab-type gown with square neck-line; women put on the majestic and gaily coloured ankle-length *busuti* with its loose sash and butterfly sleeves.[1] In Hesbon's neighbourhood, only schoolboys and imported Rwanda labourers put on shorts. Mr Lubega told me of one old chief who used to thrash any man he saw improperly dressed. 'Why do you show me your legs?' he would shout at the fellow. 'Have I not legs too?'

Wild fig trees with smooth grey boles—Mr Lubega had several on his land—are still stripped for rust-coloured bark cloth. The cloth used to be universally worn, and was a traditional marriage gift. Today, I was told, it is used mainly as bed covering or for shrouds. If a man dies in hospital, his body wrapped in bark cloth, is brought home in a taxi or strapped to the back of a bicycle, to be buried in his plot.

The Baganda tend to be soft spoken, proud, and reticent; and one cannot stay long among them without noticing their courtesy—which their friends admire, their enemies distrust.

It is courtesy of the old-fashioned, time consuming kind that delays people who are in a hurry and is unsuited to the *tempo* of town and office life. On my walks with Hesbon the greetings were protracted: a phrase of welcome followed by a series of soft grunts in different keys.

Beer drinking is a social duty: sharing it a neighbourly ritual based on rules and reciprocal hospitality. I was asked into

---

[1] See End Note (2).

several huts to drink. If the men were away, their women saw to our needs and watched silently while we drained their sour, yellow brew.

Everyone in turn must stamp and ferment his best *mabidde* plantains—which is done in a boat-shaped bath of hollowed wood—till the juice has changed to alcohol. There is no need for a man to advertise his brewing. The neighbours know, and have their beer tubes ready. In the cool of the evening they assemble softly out of the banana groves to drink it.

At one hut, towards dusk, the owner was not yet back from work. But a small crowd of thirsty men in *kanzus* was already sitting on the grass to await his return.

'Perhaps', said Hesbon to me, 'the owner has seen the crowd and is hiding till some of them go away!'

As we were favoured guests the man's wife immediately asked us in. Other followed. The beer was served in an enamelled jug and kettle. Two old men had brought their drinking tubes tucked inside their jackets. We all sat on the floor.

'An aeroplane flew over today,' said one of the old men. 'There must be something in the wind.'

'I have heard', added another, 'that the Kabaka and his friends will come back this month.'

'Who are these friends?' I asked.

No one seemed to know. 'They may be Americans,' someone said. They were all, I realised, living in a dream world of fantastic gossip.

When we left a woman gave me a basket of eggs. It was a black night, and I feared I might stumble and break them.

'Is it true', I asked Hesbon, 'that Baganda women won't eat chicken or eggs for fear of becoming barren?'

He laughed. 'That's what the old people say, but the truth of the matter is that men are greedy. They want the best food to themselves.'

With Kalisto and his family, in Acholi, I had spent the evenings outside the huts, sitting near a fire. The night air had been cool; we were a dot among vast scrub, a tiny unit of a scattered society that had no substantial possessions and had made its homesteads out of the trees, the grass, and the baked mud. It seemed right to sit on a log out of doors, to make use of space—of the enormous starlit space.

Here among the banana trees, the coffee shrubs and cassava, people went indoors after dark, windows were shuttered, the door bolted against those crowding shapes and shadows of the night. It seemed natural to lock them out, to insulate oneself from that oppressive vegetable world within a private place lit by a cosy lamp.

Mr Lubega never tired of the gramophone. He would bring it out after supper and play, one after another, its repertoire of a dozen Kiganda songs. They had a catchy rhythm, the words were often witty and mocking. When two elder daughters and friends called in, there was improvised solo dancing.

The mode of dancing was to waggle the buttocks. To heighten the effect (which, in the old days, would have been more transparent in a grass skirt), Mr Lubega made us tie his jacket round our hips.

'The bigger the buttocks,' he explained, 'the better the waggle. Now see how useless my son is—his buttocks are too small!'

I was using Hesbon's room: a cubby-hole with a homemade string bed and a suitcase for his shirts and books. During the night I would feel the banana beer fermenting inside my stomach, and go to the latrine. It was a clean, thatched pit forty yards away. The crops always smelt rank after dark, and were full of scuffling sounds.

Bride price

Inevitably we talked one day of bride price, which—when it is still exacted—the Baganda pay mainly in cash. Partly because of Church pressure, and, of course, of changing attitudes brought about by their relatively widespread level of education, it is generally a much lower sum in Buganda than elsewhere. The local bishop, said Mr Lubega, had in fact told people to limit bride money to 120 shillings.

However, 'If the girl's father', he explained with a smile,

163

'demands 500 shillings of a young man, and the young man says "no" and quotes the bishop's price, he will simply be told "Go, then, and marry the bishop's daughters".'

One of his sons, he added, had been asked to pay 900 shillings for his bride—which he had beaten down to 600. 'You have to be a fool or a fanatic', he said, 'to be satisfied with a paltry sum.'

Among young Africans, bride price is a much argued subject —a favourite of debating societies and newspaper letter writers; and opinions on it closely reflect a person's educational experience and tribal connection.

Some complain that it is a burden the young man cannot afford; and that it is debasing for a woman to be 'bought like something in a shop'.

Others argue that the bride's parents deserve compensation for having reared the girl, only to lose her services; that she herself is proud of fetching a good price; and that the bride money puts her under an added obligation to work hard for her husband and to be faithful to him.

Yet among the Baganda, marriages often fail. Mr Lubega's experience—two out of three married children have been deserted—is not uncommon. The Christian marriage rite, he said, without the backing of the law, was less effective in enforcing a permanent bond between couples than were the old tribal sanctions when a man's wives were bound as food producers to a plot and adultery was fiercely punished.

Though church marriages were the rule in his district, customary 'divorce', he said, was in fact an easy matter. If an ill-treated wife went back to her parents the husband would have to buy her back with cash and a present of beer. If he did not fetch her within six months she was considered free to take another man. It was a situation that quite often occurred when a man went off for a few months to work in Kampala, and his wife felt she had been abandoned.

Change

The influence of Uganda's capital, Kampala, which is in Buganda territory, is naturally eroding much tradition. 'It turns all girls into harlots,' said Hesbon, whose 'novel' had dealt excessively with this theme.

City influence has, for one thing, revolutionised women's fashion and habits. It has popularised long, straightened hair looking, say those who don't like it, like wet rats' tails (the true peasant woman has her hair neatly cropped), wigs like a fireman's helmet or a bushy kite's nest, short, sheath-like dresses, slimming, independent wage-earning, prostitution—and now, among wives of the new élite, prams and car-driving.

The city attracts men seeking money, excitement, or a hiding place. Not all of them find jobs. Some swell the host of thieves —a parked car, the cash box at a ginnery, are never safe. (It does not do, though, for a man to be caught stealing from other Africans. In the countryside he may be beaten to death. In town he flees for his life to the nearest police station.)

Kampala, goal of the educated African, is often the poor man's doom. If he gets drunk and falls down, it is much safer for him to do so under a village tree than in a back street of Mengo.

Like any other people, imperfectly, and in their own way, the Baganda have come to terms with their surroundings. The owners of these chocolate coloured acres have leisure, plenty to eat, cheap home-brewed beer. They have got rid of most of the vervet monkeys that used to plague their crops. Small African-owned stores have sprung up along the lanes. The *shamba* owner has a Japanese transistor set, his wife a smart *busuti* robe. A primary school, a dispensary, and a bus are never very far away.

The European would no doubt fault him, in spite of all this, on the score of comfort: the guttering oil lamp too dim to read by; the earth roads that are churned into mud during the rains, dusty when dry; the monotony of the dict; the women's interminable chores of tending the food crops, and peeling, pounding and preparing meals over an open fire.

Mr Lubega, on the other hand, must think the European excessively burdened by gadgets. He was astonished that I could produce from my luggage such things as penicillin powder, binoculars, a corkscrew, even a pillow.

Politically the Baganda have been passing through a difficult time. They are the most numerous and most progressive of Uganda's tribal groups, their territory the most prosperous. Nineteenth-century explorers and missionaries already commented on the relatively high standard of their civilisation. The Christian Church, British administration, and education quickly took root among them and thrived. The holocaust of early Ugandan martyrs—thirteen Catholics, it has been calculated, and thirteen Protestants—who were burnt on Namugongo hill, is an honoured memory.[1]

Aware of their advantages and favoured by the British, the Baganda for too long made the mistake of underestimating other tribes—especially the tough northern peoples who preponderate in the country's armed forces and whose talents are at last being widely developed through education. Political leadership has of late passed largely into northern hands. The Baganda have lost their Kabaka, their kingdom, and their assembly.

Nevertheless the Muganda peasant farmer still keeps a picture of the ousted Kabaka on his wall, among the family photographs that show his children stacked about him like a school football team. It is only natural that men of Mr Lubega's generation should be the last to remove it.

I had my last view of Villa Maria from one of its gentle hill tops. The banana gardens were a green bay through which the red paths were cut like tunnels. Dark tresses of *mvule* foliage, the scarlet petals of coral and tulip trees, made splashes of strongly contrasting colour.

Ibises were wailing over the papyrus beds where the Lubegas drew their water in pots and cans. I could see, in a patch of elephant grass, a crested crane dancing before its mate. When I approached, the pair flew off with a sad, mewing cry.

[1] See Faupel in Annotated Book List.

A few white-clad figures of men were walking very slowly through the green waves that filled the valley below.

I had the conviction, at that moment, that this must be one of the world's pleasantest corners: a warm climate and regular rainfall; fertile soil for both food and cash crops; submissive women to work the *shamba* and bear children; all the basic comforts in reward for a little work; opportunities of schooling and of paid jobs for children; the knowledge that one's relations would help in time of trouble; the honour—somewhat tarnished—of being a Muganda.

All this has helped to make the Muganda peasant farmer's life a relatively easy one, and by some Central and East European standards almost idyllic.[1] It has helped also to mould a people: easy-going, somewhat sybaritic, cultured and intelligent.

The immediate future, though, now lies very largely with the men from the north: from Lango and Acholi, from Teso and the West Nile. They are rightly anxious to centralise, to reduce provincial separatism in favour of the one-nation concept. Long denied the opportunities of the Baganda, and brought up in hard surroundings, they are determined to prove themselves, to show what they can do.

Epilogue

Some time after my visit, Hesbon wrote a piece of verse in which an old Muganda farmer laments his change of fortunes now that the Kingdom of Buganda has been abolished and its laws and administration brought into line with the rest of the country's. Here it is:

THE POOR OLD FARMER

The poor old farmer
More desperate than a widow,
Gums toothless with age,
To his poor son he spoke:

[1] Some of the most primitive dwellings I have ever stayed in were in Montenegro: piles of stones, unhewn, unplastered, with a mud floor and lumps of wood for furniture. Many of the Kurds of eastern Turkey spend the winter in underground burrows foul with smoke and cattle dung.

'Son, unlucky you are.
The soil that our ancestors fattened,
Their bodies shining with good food,
With tomatoes, *matoke* and milk,
My son, all has gone with the time:
For money we knew not of old
And now, money is life for all.

Didn't I, my son,
When the Kabakas were still kings,
Follow them to battle,
Naked to hips,
With shield, spear and spike
To their victories over the Banyoro?
In return for bravery and courage,
To this land with red bent spear I returned
With a herd of cattle,
Miles of land
And a troop of women,
One of whom, my son, bore you.

But all that is gone,
Gone like the old skin of a snake,
And your turn has come;
But the fruits of your time, the modern time,
Are too high for you to reach.
Spear, shield and hoe were my tools—
Wit and school should be yours.
Alas! the school is a rich man's place
And for me, poor farmer, with coffee
Cheap as stones,
There's neither money nor bursary.
O fat bellies are favoured most!

No, my son, heir you cannot be,
And when the soil my blanket has become,
My land you cannot have.
Heirs of the Bazungu
To our thrones have come.
O woe is this modern time!'

NOTES

(1) Are the Baganda immoral?

The article ('Are the Baganda Immoral?') which got Kalisto into trouble with the northern students was written by a Muganda. It was polemical, and deliberately overstated its case. The same words, spoken in public debate, would have raised a laugh. In cold print they were taken as abusive. Here is an extract:

'Baganda marriages, it is said, break up very easily. Many girls get pregnant before marriage. Swarms of young men and girls are to be found prowling everywhere.

True. Yet not very long ago the situation was not so different from the north. Divorce was a dream, sexual intercourse outside marriage rare. But modern ways have ousted the old. Formerly by the custom of Buganda a divorced woman had nowhere to go. Nowadays she is welcomed back by her parents. Even if they refuse to take her in, she can bury herself comfortably in the city. And searching for her there will be like looking for a needle in a haystack.

As for the husband, it is easy for him to get another wife. It costs him hardly anything.

In the north, on the other hand, husband and wife are glued together by custom. The wife is nailed to her husband by that enormous bride price. Naturally such couples are inseparable. The girl's parents cannot afford to refund the bride price, nor does the man have enough cattle left to buy another girl. What has morality to do with it?

No wonder girls are cherished in the north. They are the family investment, as coffee shrubs are to a Muganda. Think how many head of cattle a girl is worth! So if young men are not allowed to mess about with a girl, it's not because they are highly moral, but to avoid compromising the bride money. Yet a rich Muganda will give away his daughter without asking for a cent.

In the north, parents still arrange their children's marriages, and antiquated custom demands that brides be virgins. Should the Baganda, for the sake of 'morality', go back to antiquated customs too? Must some Baganda copy the old ways of kidnapping women so that husbands may once again become dutiful watchdogs over their daughters and wives?

To say that the Baganda are immoral is failure to recognise what modernisation has involved. If a community dare not give up its old custom of living in family clumps for fear that boy will meet

6*   169

girl; if it refuses to give up bride price business because heads of cattle are the guarantee of a stable human relationship; if it prefers the rural life to any other—regarding the latter as profligate—then that is its own affair.

But where material civilisation grows, so does immorality. Many women in Buganda are financially independent. What do you expect of such a woman?

And it seems to me that others are following in the wake of Buganda, ascending the same ladder at an even quicker pace. The odds are against them conserving their old ways. The Baganda as such are not immoral. Environment makes us what we are: for better or for worse—immoral?'

(2) The Busuti

The *busuti* was developed in Buganda from the earlier bark-cloth *shuka* (which was a length of material tucked round the armpit, leaving the shoulders bare) by adding to it a square neck and short sleeves (the yoke).

It is said that a Goan tailor in Kampala named Gomes made the first *busuti* at the turn of the present century and that it became a national dress after the wife of Daudi Chwa II wore it at her coronation in 1908.

CHAPTER 18

A Night Out

On a journey I have always liked sleeping out on the ground. It saves money, and there is the excitement of waking up in a strange landscape with the early morning sun on it.

In Norway and Finland, on the old Arctic highway to Petsamo or Hammerfest, I have often rolled up in a blanket among the dwarf birches, and under stars like ice crystals watched the Northern Lights flicker across the sky. In Persia, while sleeping at the end of a Caspian rice field, I had my trousers and bicycle pump stolen. Once, in a wood near Marlow, I was woken by a man poking me. He stepped back in alarm when I opened my eyes. 'I beg your pardon, sir,' he said, 'I thought you was dead.'

The war—in which I saw service in warm countries—only encouraged me in the habit of dossing down anywhere. My memories of countries tend to be associated with waking up in strange places. In Serbia and Macedonia I can expect children and old men to discover me in a corner of their stubble field. They will give me scraps of sheep's cheese (the Greek farmer offers grapes). In Lower Austria, when the Red Army were still there, I once, through miscalculation not bravado, spent an uneasy night among some frogs at the edge of a Soviet military airfield whose searchlights constantly fingered the ground around me.

The Turkish peasant, finding me asleep near a graveyard, used to be concerned and yet suspicious. Was I a spy? Belgium I associate with a vegetable inhospitality. The country is so covered with cabbages that it is difficult to find a corner in which to lie down.

Lying out in East Africa has an atmosphere of its own. The birds and the stars are delightful companions. One is, nevertheless, an intruder in a teeming animal and insect world full of invisible eyes which do not approve of one's presence.

Until a few years ago I had the habit of travelling slowly. I walked, pedalled a bicycle, or took country buses. But ever since I bought a car I have been under the same temptation as anyone else to rush through landscape like a madman.

This, I know, is an insult to beautiful country and to the village people, the children and the animals who have to jump out of one's way. So I rarely drive far without stopping under a tree.

Now, after motoring for some hours through scrub country in north-eastern Uganda, I felt I had had enough. So I turned into the bush and got out in the shade of an acacia. Up to now, with my eyes glued to the winding red-earth road for ruts and pot-holes, I had scarcely noticed the landscape. It had unrolled itself vaguely in a film of drab thorny plants and mud-coloured gravel, apparently deserted except for an occasional guinea fowl.

But as soon as I stepped out of my car, the bush showed itself to be startlingly alive. It hummed with insects and was full of the flash and chatter of multi-coloured starlings and of weaver birds that were darting in and out of coconut-like nests.

It was mid-afternoon. A loud and repeated bleat I recognised as the cry of the go-away bird, occupying its favourite position on the flat crown of a thorn tree. I watched the high, stiff crest nodding and twisting like a cockade on its grey head. The pale belly feathers were a tight white apron. Not liking my presence as I sat on a stool and prepared to brew tea, it flew to another look-out post a little farther away.

Then, in a thicket of creepers, a glimpse of orange caught my eye. It might have been a discoloured leaf. But no, it was the tip of a big, grotesquely curved beak, slightly opened: the hornbill's. When I stared at him he took off with a clumsy, dipping flight, and I was left alone with the dangling weavers' nests.

Meanwhile ants were tickling me. In or out of doors one is scarcely ever free of ants (I find them in my refrigerator and in the bath). Here the galls which hung like black plums on the whistling thorns were infested with them. I looked at the galls. Two long white spikes stuck horn-like from every ugly swelling. From the punctures in them, minute ants were scurrying in hundreds.

Most of the scrub was thorny acacia and *euphorbia candelabrum* that grew among sharp-pointed aloes and coarse grass. The acacias were of all sizes, some with golden flowers, others half-strangled by creepers or the parasitic loranthus which grafts itself on the branches of the host and then adorns them with its own bright tubular blossom. The acacia has much to put up with: drought, grass fires, goats and browsing game, parasitic plants. It is chopped for firewood and fences. Bees store honey in its dying parts, and it is mutilated by honey gatherers.

The cactus-like *euphorbia candelabrum*, on the other hand, with its bare upstretched arms, is generally left alone unless it is felled in a massacre of trees to clear bush of tsetse fly. Its branches are sometimes stuck in the thorn fences round cattle kraals. Africans say that the copious white latex is an irritant to the eyes; over a large part of Africa it is used as an ingredient of arrow poison.

Loranthus is a favourite of sunbirds; and soon, with a red and emerald flash, a sunbird alighted on a tree to probe the yellow tubes with its tiny, down-curved beak. At dusk other birds showed up: red-billed wood-hoopoes, drongos, troops of noisy francolins. A woodpecker with a scarlet splash like a caste mark on its nape, hammered on a tree. The small dikdik antelopes, when they saw me, bolted for cover.

I had noticed that the sandy ground was marked with game spoor and the pale droppings of a leopard. After dark there would be hyenas about.

Some people say that hyenas keep away from man; others relate how the hyena, with a single bite, has robbed many a sleeping person of a piece of face, or foot. So, alone in the bush, you lie down for the night with mixed feelings, wondering what the animal world has in store for you; the ear at first sorting one sound from another till all the trilling, the creaking, the scraping and the rustling is confused at last into a single sleepy cradle song, and you have dozed off.

Now, as night fell, I was glad of my blanket. Moths and flying ants, beetles and stick insects battered and burnt themselves against my lantern glass. I stared back at the stars which, like inquisitive eyes, were watching me through the acacia branches. The Plough was standing on its head. Opposite, down the line of the Milky Way, like a reeling diamond, glittered the Southern Cross.

When, later, I was roused by the crackling of twigs and leaves, it was the green eyes of a dikdik that my torch beam reflected. Perhaps the hyena with its weird, chilling cry had come and gone. Only night-jars flew bat-like among the trees. Some of the stars had disappeared behind cloud. If it rained I feared my car wheels would spin in the morning in red mud and the ford at Amudat might be too high for me to cross.

But the rain held off, and I found next day the single rutted lane of Amudat full as usual of lounging Suk. Here, under the eyes of the police, the men have to carry sticks instead of spears. In their loose cloth capes, their beads, and their painted mud caps surmounted by a feather, they stalk and idle about like warriors out of a job.

Their women, with the immense collars of metal and beaded hoops piled round their necks, look at a distance as though they are wearing brightly coloured shawls, or breastplates. The head is a black urn on a garish saucer. The hair style—shaved at the sides, matted in a crest of strings on top—accentuates the strong cheekbones.

The pleated hides (much more durable than cloth) that trail behind from the hips are generally greasy and tattered, and creak unpleasantly when they walk. Their ornaments, scari-fication, and torn ear lobes may be considered barbaric by out-siders. Yet the effect is very striking. Suk women with their finery on and their skin burnished with fat are as gaudy as turaco birds.

A visit, though, to the small BCMS hospital (twenty beds), just beyond the police barrier, reveals a story of ailments. Trachoma is widespread. Brucellosis (or undulant fever) enlarges the spleen. There are many neglected cases of malaria, amoebic dysentery and jaundice. People get festering sores and injuries. A doctor sees the darker side of the cheerful African: the wounds and the polio, the diseases that spoil the muscular body, his neglect and ignorance of them.

I found Dr Cox the English missionary doctor and his assistants working in a small compound where relatives of the patients cook food over tiny wood fires. The blankets were threadbare, and the operating table an interesting relic. A plaque shows that it was originally presented to the people of Britain, in 1941, by the town of Juneau in Alaska.

But the missionaries (they are Bible Churchmen) are grateful for the money and the modern drugs which the government gives to their hospital. They do not grumble except (a little) about the neighbouring Verona Fathers' practice of recruiting children who, as Dr Cox puts it, 'are still too young to know what religion is all about'—so many souls lost to his own unadorned type of Protestantism (which, however, the Verona Fathers say is no religion at all!)

Dr Cox is a cheerful, athletic man who lives with his family in a tin-roofed bungalow surrounded by thorn bushes and noisy barbets.[1] The Verona Fathers run a small school on a dirty hill ravaged by goats. I found the two priests snoring over empty coffee cups.

Not far from Amudat the skyline is blocked by the wooded Kadam massif. In its neighbourhood, tall grass and broad-leaved trees replace dessicated scrub. Beyond the Didinga settlement I watched some turaco birds scrambling in a copse. Their chorus of penetrating brays is a sound one never forgets. Then at the foot of Namalu saddle I saw a lion by the roadside. I went past it, and turned back. Now there were three. On my third run I stopped and counted a pride of nine. The big-maned male gave me a bored look and they all retired a few yards into the grass.

Namalu marks the end of Karamoja. Young people here are already discarding skins and skimpy lengths of cloth for western clothes. Even Moroto, eighty miles farther north, is changing. A drove of women in tight town dresses has already arrived there, the juke boxes are blaring, and at night the new, yellow street lamps blaze over the plain like the lights of a liner at sea.

---

[1] Dr Cox has since left the district.

175

Another two hours' drive and I was approaching Mbale. Crowds of excited Bagisu youths were trotting along in file in the shade of the big wayside *mvule* trees, drumming and chanting, their bodies hung with grass and leaves and smeared white with clay. They were screwing up their courage for the mass circumcision rites that in a month's time would initiate them to manhood.

I reached Kampala after dark to find the streets lined with excited Africans. A week of rain and raw, misty nights had brought the grasshoppers out. Stripped of their wings and legs, and fried with pepper and salt, they are eaten as a delicacy. Great crowds of men, women and children with sheets, cellophane bags, and newspapers were trapping them as they whirled, spiralled and spun like snowflakes round the street lamps.

In their joy and excitement, people were darting across the road after the insects. One little group, however, was sitting sad and silent near the body of a dead boy laid out on the pavement.

The motorist who had knocked him down would, of course, be cleared in a court of law. People have no right to crowd the carriage way like lunatics, not even if the grasshoppers have come to town. The rights of the motorist must be respected. Still, from the boy's point of view it was murder.

7a. Carl Akeley's grave, Kabara

b. Porter on Morungole summit c. Weavers' nests on palm

18a. Lichen-draped Hagenia tree, Karisimbi

b. Summit of Napono

9a. Kalisto in front of bachelor hut

b. Kalisto and family

c. Kalisto's relatives

20a. Teuso escort collecting berries near Zulia   b. Climbing for honey, Zulia

c. My Teuso escort   d. Teuso children on Turkana escarpment (with *okemi* musical box)

PART II

PEOPLE

CHAPTER 19

Three Peoples (1):
Africans

We were sitting in a burnt-up meadow among the dark Acholi. The Sudan border was an hour's drive away.

'Africans become whiter', said my companion, an unmarried English geologist, 'the longer you stay in Africa,' adding, 'You know, I find African girls rather attractive.'

Later, I wondered which girls he had in mind. The doe-eyed ones with Moorish features and fattened hips? The smart Kampala girls with make-up and stretched raven hair and brassière-supported breasts? The black and robust northern women with their jolly smile and big white teeth?

There was at any rate some truth in my companion's well-worn adage, with its implications of *rapprochement* at many levels.

When I first came to Uganda I was, as I realise now, strongly, even absurdly, conscious of the African's colour—and in a lesser degree of his other distinctive physical features. I suspected that physically, and perhaps mentally too, I was a person apart. I was not adopting a superior attitude. I simply felt we were different sorts of animal (his sweat had a musky smell, mine sour; he was glistening and hairless, I was a pale ponderous cow).

The Indian, by comparison, with his regular profile, straight hair, and tanned to pale complexion, seemed one of us.

I felt conspicuous and sometimes embarrassed among a crowd of Africans. Being preconditioned—by years of exposure to myth, gossip and prejudice—to find the African inefficient, slow or uncomprehending, I was ready to fault him and easily irritated.[1]

---

[1] Burton's tirades, and Grogan's ('if a native is told to do anything, and it is within the bounds of diabolical ingenuity to do it wrong, he will do it wrong') are typical contributions to this myth. See Annotated Book List.

With familiarity these feelings began to go. I got used to taking my place in a slow-moving queue of messengers and nondescript Africans at a post-office counter. I began to move about more slowly. I accepted—though at first unwillingly—the rebukes of African traffic policemen (the few who wore Middle East campaign ribbons I considered to be old friends). The dark fingers of my Luo servant gripping a dish by its rim ceased to disturb me. As I got to know my students better, I began to identify myself with their thoughts and hopes, their complaints, their sense of humour.

Very soon I felt at home in the city, for which credit must go to the African. I found him sociable, good humoured; he loves talking, and he has time for you. It was easy—at certain levels—to communicate with him. And since in Uganda almost every African who has been to school knows some English, the language problem was generally far less than it would have been to a Scotsman in the south of Italy.

But there are, of course, limits to total communication. The African has not watched television in a Birmingham home. Even if he is well educated he cannot be expected to discuss cricket, the Berlin Wall, stamp collecting or space rockets with the facility of a European whose mind since childhood has been cluttered with an encyclopaedic store of facts and mechanical skills. Not many Africans read *The Sunday Times*. How, then, can they keep up with the ephemeral minutiae of our small talk?

I found basic differences of attitude, too. African politics, quite naturally in this early stage, do not revolve smoothly round concepts of democracy and social welfare. They have to do with rivalries, both personal and regional, with love of power and its material rewards. The private crudities of our own European politicians are more skilfully hidden. And the government of Uganda has more exciting aims than we have: national unity, popular education, survival. Politics are an adventure which requires men of daring.

Nor are there any illusions, among Africans, about the basic meaning of the white man's role in Africa. It is considered to have been synonymous with colonialist exploitation. White interest used to be the slave and ivory trade, land grabbing, low wages and profits from monopolistic coffee.

Today people assume that the old interest is still essentially unchanged, though it may be disguised in part as aid (with strings) or hidden behind a façade of insincere protest against Rhodesia and South Africa.

As for national prosperity based on proper planning and development, the Uganda African wants it very much—but primarily for his own tribe and district; and he grumbled when the government introduced a Development Tax to help pay for it.

Christianity? A great many would prefer it without monogamy. East Africa's 'unique heritage' of wild life? The African is not interested in giraffes, and certainly not sentimental about the hippopotamus. He has probably never seen a lion, and doesn't want to. If a rabbit scurries on to the road, he is likely to run over it.

'Picturesque tribes'? He sees nothing noble or anthropologically fascinating about the naked herdsmen of Karamojong. He is inclined to wince at the thought of them. Not only are they 'savages', of whom he is ashamed; they are a great nuisance —cattle raiders and possibly murderers, too.

So one's early dialogue with an African—until one knows how to tread—may well be at cross purposes. The brakes are on. I found it better, at first, and politer, to avoid painful issues, easier to share a joke, to criticise something disliked in common (taxation, astute Indian traders, car thieves).

Even now, over five years later, I believe that to probe into an African's mind and personality—and this must in some degree apply to any people whose background has been radically different—one would have to swop bodies, women, ancestors, diet, and tribulations. As it is, we can only see each other first sifted through ourselves.

To complicate matters, one's African friend may have a double personality: one for you, for the lecture room, the sundowner; another for his home in a forest clearing where, perhaps, his polygamous father consults the witch-doctor and his brothers in ragged singlets hoe a plot.

It was getting away into the countryside—discovering it for myself on foot, getting the hard, salty feeling of it into my skin— that finally made me feel at home.

Glimpsed briefly through a car window, the green or ochre East African bush tangled with tall grass, with spikes and shaggy ant-hills, strikes you as impenetrable and hostile.

You gaze in trepidation at the miles of awful scrub, a non-swimmer deterred by a huge and lonely ocean.

You get out of your car to change a wheel, and you are immediately lacerated by a thorn. A snake (though more probably it's only a lizard) whips through the grass; or you stumble awkwardly in the red mud. A man with a panga emerges from behind an ant-hill and watches you silently. You feel at a loss in this apparent wilderness of ticks and thorns. It may be all right to drive through it in a reliable car. Unthinkable to walk in!

Once I had made a few up-country journeys on foot, I was cured for ever of my apprehensions.

There came a point when I was no longer looking at my travelling companions as different anthropological types but as ordinary people with whom I was sharing an experience. Mine, in any case, was the subordinate role. True, I supplied the cash, the *posho*, and the incentive. But being dependent on their astonishing knowledge of bush, forest, and direction, I felt among them—and I still feel—less master than pupil.

Such episodes, however, were fragmentary. It was the Africans I saw every day, my students especially, from whom I learned most; and though I had overcome my own early inhibitions about colour, some of my students, I found, had not got over theirs.

A chapter they read of the geographer Lebon and a look at Coon helped to put this right.[1] There they had it in print, what to a layman at any rate seems an obvious truth, that a man's physical characteristics are nature's way of adapting him to his surroundings.

So it is right and proper for the African to be darkly pigmented, to have everted lips, a large mouth and wide nostrils (and to move slowly, and sweat and drink freely). Wrong and inefficient, in equatorial Africa, to be white or pink (and in a hurry); it is the European who is the albino, the misfit here.

And what is colour?

[1] See Annotated Book List.

The variety of shades to the African's skin—from copper to chocolate, from ochre, sepia and brown to deepest jet—make nonsense of the single word 'black' to describe it.[1] I have seen how strong and penetrating sunlight brings out the reddish undertones in an African's skin. There are lighter and darker areas on the same body, for the pigment may not be evenly spread.

As to its aesthetics, how well matched is a dark skin to brilliant colours of dress and adornment! The body's dark sheath obscures the freckles, the blue veins and small blotches of discolouration that show up on a pale surface. It gives a rounded and statuesque effect to muscle. The untanned white man has, by comparison, a naked, bloodless look.

Women

Uganda is said to have some of the most beautiful women in East Africa. A few Europeans marry them. A good many have been to bed with them. Some white people are put off, others attracted—to the point of erotomania—by the physical difference.

The Uganda woman, as far as I can judge, has no false modesty—or at any rate her reserve and her coquetry are prescribed by code. She well understands the secret of her power over men and wields it frankly. The soft, glossy skin, large eyes and powerful sexual organs are part of an armoury not to be ashamed of. She has the arms, shoulders and breasts of sculpture. She is both sensuous and tender. She has not been brought up to bustle and run about. She takes things with her hands gently. If there is a virago behind the soft voice it is not for everyone to see.

To a Western eye she has defects too: a tendency to bulge, a bridgeless nose.[2] She can be obdurately sullen, cook and live untidily. She may not put very much emotional or moral value on fidelity. Her prime job is to bear children. Our Western

[1] Africans themselves are very sensitive to their own different shades of colour, which may denote tribal origins. 'He's very black,' the Baganda may say of a man from the north. A light complexion is the fashion among many Uganda women. If nature has been unhelpful, and they can afford it, they use bleaching cream.

[2] This would apply in particular to the 'Bantu' type.

183

brand of romantic love is alien and unsuited to her; it idealises emotion, inflates a woman's status, and so cannot at present be a working formula for survival in most of African society.

As objects of desire, of envy, of strife, or of property, African women—as anywhere else—are naturally associated with violence and crime. The Karamojong murder and steal cattle to get honour and bride price. Men brawl over the rootless women who flit about African towns.

Four or five years ago, street girls were plentiful in Kampala. Then the police stepped in and took them off in van-loads to be locked up for a month. Today they are more discreet. They attach themselves to a bar.

The tarts come from many parts of Uganda (though not often from the north) and from outside: from Kenya, Rwanda and the Congo. They are not, generally, the haggard shrews of the old Edgware Road, of Colonel Beck's Warsaw or of seedy post-war Düsseldorf. They are mostly young. They have vitality. And they will drink with you glass for glass. They are, of course, avaricious; and they may have a man waiting round the corner to empty your pockets.

They live—unless they have been unusually successful—in rented shanties and cubby holes on the outskirts of the town with a heap of old *matoke* peel near the door. The main piece of furniture is likely to be a strong bed, screened by a curtain hanging from a rope which is loaded with cheap dresses and underwear. The girl has a transistor set and oil lamp, a few cooking pots. She puts her hair in curlers, scratches her ear with a match-stick, and slips her earnings inside her brassière.

It may be risky to visit her, for there will be thieves, pimps, and drunks about. When she has a customer she turns up the transistor and barricades the door with *debes*. She generally has children, who have to sleep on the floor among the scurrying cockroaches. They are the bonus of her trade. But if pregnancy is unwanted, she gets aborted. She probably eats twice a day— tea with milk and sliced white bread at breakfast, steamed *matoke* and scraps of cheap meat before she anoints herself and goes out at dusk.

The green lanes and untidy side streets where the girls live, with their scattered, stained houses and ragged banana groves, look cheerful and harmless enough by day. The few quiet Indian families who may share the neighbourhood will give it, almost, an air of respectability.

At night it turns sinister. The greasy earth, the broken tarmac and old sheds give out a smell of rubbish and urine. People come and go softly in the dark. There are sounds of quarrelling and of high, jeering laughter. A door opens, and the yellow light of a lantern shows a woman standing near an old car tyre. She is wearing a single piece of bright cloth round her body. It won't be long before she finds a customer.

Her customers are mostly Africans or Indians—the latter understandably, for their own women are jealously guarded. Respectable Europeans try to avoid these districts. Insulated on a residential hill they do not need to know about the existence of an African town. The untidy plots where old car wrecks are slowly overgrown by grass, the smelly little streets where dogs ferret among decaying rubbish, are not their territory.

Violence

Violence is, of course, not unique to Uganda—or to the shanty towns of Nairobi and Johannesburg. But its quality is not everywhere the same.

In Poland there was, I remember, the sad, quarrelsome violence of men living in a poor, cold and muddy country surrounded by formidable enemies. In Italy there are knifings; in Turkey, rape, earthquakes and floodings.

A special quality of violence in Uganda is that it lies so close to the surface of everyday life; and that it is no one else's business. It is bound up with vitality, zest and physical robustness; with the growth of municipal slums and of a cash economy that is widening the gap between rich and poor; with cars, and with the fact that a man here will drink till he falls down.

Violence is inherent, too, in the petty thefts and burglaries which are endemic to the neighbourhood of towns; and which like plague destroy one's confidence in other people—for among the ordinary passers-by there must be potential thieves.

Sooner or later one has to recognise its presence and come to terms with it: develop the safety-first instinct; be callous. A mob chasing a suspected pickpocket in the market, a crushed body in the road, are none of your business.

From time to time, soon after I arrived in Kampala, I used to hear one of my neighbours (a civil servant) beating a woman in the night. He would beat her off and on for an hour or so. I thought at first I ought to intervene—perhaps murder was being done: until I discovered that next day everything would be back to normal, *maneno kwisha*, the row over.

One is warned, as a householder, not to grapple with a burglar—he may 'slice your ear off with a panga'; as a motorist, not to stop if you knock someone over—whether you are to blame or not, you may be set on by a mob.

I have seen men chased and badly beaten in the street, a target for anyone's foot, fist or stick. A country dispenser may not know very much about medicine, but he will be expert in treating heads cut open in a beer fight.

At all hours, but especially after midnight, men with torn bloody shirts, women with bruises, limp past the guards at Mulago casualty reception station. These people are not the gangster type, but ordinary poor citizens.

A woman screaming in the night? No one interferes. She may be a bride, or only in labour. It is her husband's or her lover's affair. A drunk lying in a muddy white shirt across the gutter? It is nothing to do with you. A crushed dog, mongoose, or cat on the road? A man doesn't identify himself with an animal. It should have kept out of the way of the new post-Uhuru tyrant—the man behind the steering-wheel.

In the back streets of Mengo, when a Congolese whore in a ragged turban gets beaten up, people stand aside and jeer. Away to the north, Jie cattle thieves may be spearing a child.

The Indian, if I mention these things to him, grins. 'Africans', he says simply, 'are cruel.'

A European is more likely to ascribe it all to bad living conditions, or to lack of education. Africans can be reformed. It is, after all, the 'transition period' in which a man must either earn his five shillings a day or sleep on the ground like a dog, and starve.

To this I would add an impression of my own. Where Europeans have at length, and very gradually, developed a wide-ranging social conscience that stretches human pity right down to the street dog, an African reserves his true conscience for a friend, a member of his family or clan. For the root of his survival, where all else fails, is the blood relationship.

As for environment, badly paid men who live within sight of wealth are almost bound to rob. The loot is there for the taking, in those vulnerable suburban bungalows, in the flimsy *dukas* and the lonely up-country ginneries; and the chances of being caught are small. It is there, too, in villages after the cotton and coffee crops have been sold, pathetically insecure, in small wads of notes stuffed into a mattress or buried in a tin.

Woman beating? A man may claim that an idle, unfaithful or disobedient woman for whom he has paid money deserves, like Okonkwo's wife, to get a drubbing.

Rowdy, gin-sodden London with its typhoid and cess pits was accepted at a time of England's wealth and greatness. Violence seems to be connected with vitality and the male prerogative as well as with poverty.

Problems of education

I have said that it was from my students especially that I learned most. Through them I could identify myself with exciting hopes and ambitions.

In the meantime, eighteen months after it had been begun, our training course for non-graduate secondary school teachers had been transferred (in March 1965) from its temporary refuge in Makerere College to the old Primary School Teacher Training Centre at Kyambogo, a few miles east of Kampala. When Kyambogo was upgraded and renamed the National Teachers' College, our original handful of students was increased to 100 and then to 400.

It is said that we don't, at Kyambogo, attract Uganda's brightest school-leavers; that the best of them go on to Makerere College, or reject teaching as a dull and unambitious career.

This may or may not be true. My own belief is that a body of two or three hundred literate young Uganda Africans is a fascinating deposit. Prospect in it, and you will find startling riches: athletic and dramatic talent, painters and musicians,

187

eloquence, a natural gift for writing free verse.[1] They will be immature by Western academic standards, but mature and experienced in other ways—in, for instance, the basic struggle for survival which from childhood up will have included much private knowledge of birth and death, illness, sex, and violence.

It is because one half of his life is closed to the outsider that our knowledge of the African student remains limited. We know that a young man's (still more, a girl's) path to higher education is generally strewn with immense difficulties: family poverty and perhaps hostility, factors of illness, of geography and communications. But what can we know of the details of such private struggles?

I have stayed in the country homes of several of my students. Yet I cannot properly visualise the difficulties they have had in educating themselves. It struck me as heroic, and almost unreal, to find a young man trying to read about the Greek City State in the corner of a dark and crowded hut surrounded by miles of bush, on a diet of a single daily meal of *posho* and sweet potatoes, while his brother shivered with malaria.

I have also seen many hundreds of little boys, and girls, all over Uganda, *running* the five miles to their primary school in rain and drought. They may have had no breakfast. With their bright eyes, an exercise book and a pencil, they trot tirelessly on bare feet through the tall grass, over stones and mud, to a crowded old building with earthen floor and broken windows. At home they have no proper bed to sleep on, no light, and they are kept awake by noise.

On the other hand, for the lucky ones who live in or near a town, there will be a bus service, even a bookshop (if they can afford to use them) close at hand.

Some of my students have written about their childhood and early school days. Here, from the few papers that are still available to me, are some extracts of what they had to say:

Northern Kigezi

'Kigezi is a hilly country. Education, which was introduced by the R.C. and C.M.S. missions, came later in the undeveloped northern parts than in the south.

[1] See below, pp. 217–238.

'In my own neighbourhood of Kinkizi so many people were at one time carried away by malaria, yaws and open ulcers that schools had to close down, and the area earned the name Rejector of Youth. But in 1960 the World Health Organisation came to our rescue. Mr Cullen, the red-bearded Scottish entomologist whom we called Kareju (Small Beard), slew the malaria monster in the Battle of Rwanga 1962. For saving them from the obnoxious malady, the local people revere and idolise him.

'Lack of roads, and wild animals, were another hindrance. As we walked the long distances to and from school, we inspected guards of honour mounted by leopards, lions, elephants and buffaloes. I remember, when I was still in class one, meeting a lion in the day time and a leopard at night. My two small companions gave up going to school. I was sent to another school in central Kigezi where I stayed with an aunt.

'When education was first introduced parents did not want to send their children to school. Under strong pressure from the missionaries, fathers sent the children of their unfavoured wives. Until about 1952 the idea of putting girls to school was an abomination, and out of the question. The few girls who defied the taboo were usually the ugly ones.

'Some of them became teachers. But the mere sight of these frustrated spinsters discouraged parents from exposing their daughters to the same fate.

'Then, when girls began to attend school in larger numbers, some of them were made pregnant—which the Bakiga revile so much that, before the Europeans came, any girl who dared bring that curse upon herself was thrown over a waterfall. I know one of these falls; and my mother very well recalls these victims of sexual appetite.

'But how ideas change! Now it is every parent's ambition to educate as many of his daughters as he can afford to.'

Toro

A student from Toro relates the hardships borne by children and ascribes them to parental ignorance:

'An African parent, unlike the European, considers the adult first and the child last.

189

'He thinks that because an adult deserves respect, he should have priority. So there will be enough money to buy the father's shoes or mother's dress, but none to buy shoes for nine-year-old Nkya; yet in all weathers and during the rains he has to walk four miles or more every day to school.

'Husband and wife sleep on a soft bed with sheets and a warm blanket. Nkya has to make do with grass-filled sacks covered with a mat and a cheap blanket which does not stop the cold from entering his flesh.

'When the children are turned away from school because they haven't paid the school fees, their father tells them to wait till the end of the month because he wants his money for beer. "Meanwhile," he says, "you will work in my garden." For him, beer is indispensable.

'When there is meat, the children will get only the scraps. The excuse is that the child's stomach is young, so it can accommodate anything.

All this is the result of misunderstanding. The practice of having parasitical wives as well as a legal wife means too that the children of the former will tend to be neglected.'

Sebei

Sebei, on the northern slopes of Mount Elgon, is a mountainous area with poor roads and it has been traditionally exposed to a tribal feud with the Bagisu and to cattle-raiding. These factors have not favoured education.

A student from Sebei wrote this outline:

'In 1934 the Church of Uganda opened the first primary school at Sasur. By 1945 it had six classes. The Catholic Church, however, was not going to sit back and watch the Protestants indoctrinate the Sabinjak! The infamous old Church rivalry was imported into Sebei (though, fortunately, it did not cause such tragic events as had occurred in Buganda), and a Catholic mission was soon afterwards opened at Gamatui, a mile to the south of Sasur. This school acquired full primary status in 1947. Then the nuns started a girls' school in the early '40's which is still the only one of its kind in Sebei.

'The Catholic school was successful and popular, for the missionaries put up an attractive church building and they installed an electric dynamo—the "Muzungu's Magic." As one parent said, "I want my son to go to Gamatui to learn how to produce the fire which burns without wood or smoke." As children we would sit out at night watching the magic lights until all of a sudden they all went out at once.

'The two missions were not sensible. They would set up rival schools facing one another, regardless of the number of children present. The Protestant schools would decline, the Catholic ones flourish, for they had more money (from Rome and from the countries of the priests).

'Yet many parents remained reluctant to use schools, and in my village the teachers actually used men to hunt us children down and force us into school. My father knocked one of these men down, and had to pay a fine of ten shillings. This was in 1950.

'Sipi eventually became the chief educational centre. Other districts lagged behind owing to poor roads. In Ngenge, for instance, where the people keep cattle, constant raiding and attacks by the Suk or Karamojong made regular schooling quite impossible.

'There are other grave obstacles to education. One of them is excessive drinking, especially in Sipi and Kaptanya, where the habit has spread even to children. I know of one family (there are many such) which goes to drink early in the morning up to late evening. So children are spoilt. They finish upper primary school at the most, and then lead adult lives.

'Another discouragement to schooling is that children are a valuable source of labour at home. Fathers want their boys to help look after the cattle or to clear bush for crops; girls are expected to work at home or in the plantations. A mother who herself hasn't been to school does not want a daughter with "soft hands who will make a bad wife."

'There are other discouragements to girls. They may get pregnant at school, or in the T.T.C., and are then disgraced. If they continue with education, they will be under pressure from teachers to reject traditional customs such as bride price and female circumcision. So most girls prefer to leave school at Primary Four before they are corrupted by new ideas.

'The question of what attitude to adopt to customs, is a great challenge to boys and girls in Sebei.

'Frankly, many of us are at a loss. Most authorities have condemned female circumcision. Some assert that the clitoris (which is the part that is excised) plays a great part in the enjoyment of sexual intercourse. But Sebei women would assure one that they enjoy sexual intercourse as much after being circumcised as before it.

'Our problem is, should alien customs supersede our own? I myself don't approve of circumcising girls—it is brutal and there is no scientific benefit to it. But it is likely to be long-lived. The Sebei embrace the custom so whole-heartedly that if you dare criticise it in the company of uneducated Sebei, they will get angry and call you a hot-headed, brain-washed traitor!

'Our present task in Sebei is to get more children to go to school and to find teachers for them. At the moment only one Sebei has qualified as a Grade 5 teacher.'

Mengo (Buganda)

Here is a female student's account of growing up in Mengo district:

'Childhood is a time of trial and error. As soon as the child is born he is challenged by the evils of this world. His birth may occur in an evil-smelling home, inside a dirty hut full of dust and cobwebs. Or he may be born out of doors, among the coffee shrubs or banana trees. Of course, this is not the fate of all children. But I am speaking now of the typical child, the village child: for the majority of our people are villagers.

'In the early stages of his growth the child has no difficulty in obtaining food. The mother has a good supply of milk in her breasts. So the child grows well and starts to bloom like a well tended flower. He look healthy, strong, and happy.

'The danger comes when the child is about nine months old and is taken off the breast. The mother is often ignorant of the right food to give her child. She starts filling up his stomach with carbohydrates.

'This makes the child look like a tiny pregnant woman. The stomach swells and bulges on all sides. The hair turns silver and it is thin and ugly to look at. The head looks unusually large, and the eyes—big, full of misery and resentment—project from the skull. The limbs are mosquito-like compared to the rest of the body.

'Children who are suffering from this sort of malnutrition mostly die. Even if the child survives this dangerous phase, his rate of growth, checked by continuous bad feeding, will be very slow.

'Around the age of four or five, the child starts to understand everything. This is the right time for him to begin to learn his duties in the home. Boys have different duties from girls.

'When the boy is five, he starts helping his father. The father may be a farmer working a small *shamba*. The child will share in the work. He may pull out weeds or gather the coffee berries which lie on the ground. Back home, he washes the plates.

'Around twelve, the child is getting grown-up. He can now do muscular work, such as tree-splitting and collecting firewood. Driving the goats to pasture is also his job.

'A girl's work is different. When she is old enough she learns how to peel *matoke*, and how to wrap the plantains in leaves and cook them. In the early morning she goes with her mother to the banana plantation to dig. If she shows any signs of being lazy in this, her mother will scold her, lest she grow up into a good-for-nothing.

'When she is about twelve, an aunt takes the girl into her confidence. It is the aunt's task to prepare the girl for marriage.

'On her genitalia, the girl is shown two small parts that stick out like tendrils. She is told to pull them in order to lengthen them; and when they have reached the right length, to stop. So she has now added to her private parts two long fleshy "skins" projecting from the rest of the body.

'This is a very important thing in the life of a girl in the village. Without this, she cannot make a successful life.

'Schooling is also a difficult time for village children. They mostly go to a day school which is likely to be about three miles away.

'The child gets up early, at about 6 a.m., and sets off on the long journey to school. He often arrives late, and for this he is punished by being caned unmercifully or made to dig in the hot sun.

'If he arrives in time, he will find it difficult to concentrate in class. By 11 a.m. he will be feeling so hungry that his thoughts turn to getting home and having a meal.

'At lunch he will have porridge and beans, which may not be enough to satisfy him. When school is over at last and he is home again, he will be too tired to do his homework. He goes instead to the cupboard and gets out his food, which has probably gone cold. When it is supper time he has no appetite left. So he goes to bed worn out and badly fed.

'The next day is exactly the same. Unless the child has a very strong character, he is likely to develop into a troublesome person both at home and in school.

'The transitional period between childhood and manhood is when the child starts to rebel against his parents. He can no longer do his tasks properly unless he is in the right mood. He gets bad ideas in his head about girls; and the girls develop great interest in men. This is a difficult time both for parents and children.

'From his childhood onwards, the child passes through many difficulties and he learns many things. He will face problems and go on learning until death cheats him of his life.'

Busoga

The hard struggle to survive may start indeed with birth. A student from Busoga writes:

'I was born by the roadside, under a huge *mvule* tree. My father had gone to Mukono Theological College for his religious studies and had left mother alone—"In the care of Almighty God," as he put it—in a remote corner of Busoga. My mother was making her way to hospital on foot. She had already covered a good distance, and had only another mile to go, when she was forced to her knees. With a cry (so I am told) I dropped into this world.

'"That's a boy's cry," said a bystander.

'"He's Kyagwire then," remarked an old man, showing off his knowledge of the local customs.

'"He will live to travel to every corner of this earth," said an old woman who had come up to help my mother.

'Kyagwire, meaning "It Has Fallen," is the name given to a male child born by the wayside; and I would in fact have been named Kyagwire had not my parents been devout Christians. My birth came as a great blessing to them. I was their fourth child but the first son. In Busoga any suspicion that a wife can not produce a boy will soon lead to her being divorced, or to the husband taking a second wife. No wonder my father bicycled one hundred miles from Mukono to see me. "I have come to see the Gift from God", he said proudly on his arrival For long I was familiarly known as Kirabo, meaning "Gift".

'I am told that as a child I was always ill. My mother couldn't tie me on her back (as other women did) while working in the banana plantations because it made me sick. I suffered from gastric influenza. So mother used to lay me on the ground, on a mattress of leaves, and I would lie there for hours "playing with the birds", as my mother put it. This prompted her to call me Francis, after St Francis of Assisi, who loved birds; and this is the name I was properly given when I was baptised by the "Mzungu" priest.'

Seminary education

Finally, what is it like to be an older boy studying at a seminary? Here is an Iteso student's account:

'A condition of being accepted by a seminary was that one's father had been married in church, and was not a polygamist. Not all my relations approved of my going to a seminary. If I turned into a priest, they said, the clan would have no offspring from me. More, my family and relations would get no benefit at all; for it was well known that priests received no salary. One old clan head actually threatened never to enter my father's compound again if I went to the seminary. But my parents decided I should go. And my father bought me a pair of shoes—the first I had ever worn—costing 30 shillings.

' I soon got used to mixing with boys from other tribes at Nagongera Junior Seminary. Some of the older students were bullies. They made us hand over our little stores of groundnuts. The first term I got three letters from home, and they had all been opened by the master in charge of discipline. It was the rule that all letters should be opened by him. We weren't allowed to have pocket money of our own.

'When I got home after the first term, every one said I looked different—because, said one old woman, "I had been living with white men". They imagined boys in the seminary ate European food that was rich in food value. They didn't know that our staple diet was *posho* and cow peas.

'In my second term the water pump broke down and we had to fetch water from a village well. Naturally some of the students took this chance to chase girls. The master in charge of discipline organised a network of informers, and boys caught coming back late at night after their adventures were expelled. We were sorry for them but we could no nothing.

'The third term was a sad one. About a quarter of our schoolmates were expelled. Some had not done well enough in their studies, others were thought to lack moral character. In my final year only six of the original students had survived in my class. Indeed, a great falling out of students is part of life in a seminary.

'I spent six years at Nagongera, and then transferred to Agaba Major Seminary, near Kampala. Life was more enjoyable here. The Fathers treated us as mature persons and we were left on our own. I discovered an interest in music and played the organ. But my stay was short-lived. I began to have doubts about becoming a priest.

'How did this come about? Well. there was the nagging worry about money. I knew my father could never support his family on his small income. My brothers and sisters had to be educated. What could I do, as a priest, to help them materially? No educational authority would accept my prayers in place of school fees. Such was my main concern, and no doubt it started a train of other thoughts in my mind. Like any normal man, I knew I should find it very hard to stay celibate. Supposing I became a priest and broke the vow? Whose failings are the more venial? Those of the priest, who hides (or throws away for ever) his cassock to enjoy women? Or the occasional misdoings of an ex-seminarian? And remember: once a priest, always a priest.

'These matters were on my conscience. I conferred several times with the Rector and the Spiritual Director. At length I left the seminary for the ordinary world, slamming the door on priesthood as a vocation.

'Now four years later, I have had time to reflect on my educational experience. I used to think that government secondary school students were better educated than seminarians. I do not think so now. In point of character and personality development—which is education in its truest sense—the seminaries may do even better. And learning Latin, for instance, gives one an advantage in studying English.

'Still, I have one quarrel with seminaries: the emphasis on obedience is overdone. One has to obey the Fathers without question. If one doesn't, it is a sign that one will disobey one's Bishop! Blind obedience will not get a community anywhere. The authority that listens to its subjects' views will shape workable policies. Students should be given every chance to understand why some things are good, and others bad.

'I conclude with gratitude to the Fathers who taught me; and I commend the work of the missionaries in Africa.'

NOTE

A former student recently sent me this impression of Karamoja:

'When I received an official letter posting me to Karamoja, my heart sank, my happiness was poisoned. Why was I being victimised? During my first week at the Kangole Annexe of Moroto High School I locked myself in my house at 7 p.m. I had been told that to go out at night meant death. I lived in fear. I was shocked to see Karamojong going about naked. Their women wore skins.

'Now, 4 months later, I realise that most of the fantastic stories told about the Karamojong are false. They are gentle people. They won't harm you as long as you don't condemn their social structure or try to interfere with their way of life. And of course, you must leave their women alone or you will be in serious trouble. Yet the girls are seductive. Their naked breasts dance as they walk, as though they were saying, "Please take your turn. Here we are." Their skins glisten with butter. The girls are beautiful.

'Every Sunday evening a crowd of Karamojong gather near the school to dance the *edonga*. Men and women form circles and leap high into the air. I joined in one day, but after four jumps I was out of breath. If one isn't used to it, one can easily pull a muscle.

'I have come to like the Karamojong very much. They can be cruel, warlike, hot-tempered. But you are all right with them if you use tact. Karamoja is quiet and beautiful. I am happy to be far away from noisy Kampala, and from Banda with its juke-boxes and howling drunkards.'
(Agwelakwap-Ogellan)

CHAPTER 20

Three Peoples (2): Indians

The commercial society

Everyone knows that the Indians of East Africa (they are generally referred to as Asians) are gifted, industrious, and extremely tenacious of their own interest.

They have struck quick roots. They have adjusted themselves to climate and to thrifty living. And they have made themselves indispensable, not only as traders and providers of services, but as clerks and professional men, intellectuals and artisans.

This is not to say that the quality of their work and service is particularly high by the standards of Europe. But it is impossible to imagine how East Africa would have made such progress without them. If every Indian in Uganda were an equally skilled African, what an astonishing achievement it would be.

There is, also, another side. The very qualities that have enabled them to survive and prosper also make them unpopular. The Indians (though they are subdivided amongst themselves) remain an exclusive community obstinately imprisoned within caste and religion, race and social custom. Unlike Europeans—with whom it is a matter of choice—they stay apart on principle. Nor are they truly of Uganda (or Kenya). They do not lightly throw away their British passports.[1]

Again, they are generally wrapped up in money making and in the immediate family interest to (it seems to me) an excessive

---

[1] This is less true of the Ismailis than of the others. Following the advice of the Aga Khan, a good many Ismailis have in fact, since Uhuru, opted for local citizenship.

degree. On the one hand, by facilitating the economic develo-
ment of East Africa they have prepared the ground for an
emergent African middle class. On the other, by wielding
economic power and filling skilled positions out of all pro-
portion to their number, they obstruct its opportunities of
growth. So they inevitably arouse deep undercurrents of jealousy
and resentment.

Unless one is oneself a 'tradesman' one tends, no doubt
naturally, to be a little out of sympathy with the class. I
personally find something inhuman in the Indian's untiring preoccupation with money: in the gleam that comes to his eye
when you enter his shop; his lightning calculation of your
means, the aplomb with which he first overcharges and then,
if you object, lowers his price a little nearer the correct one;
in the schemes he concocts with his friends and relations for
bypassing regulations and squeezing the last shilling out of a
situation.

Having said this (and I confess there may be some sour grapes
behind my own rather unjust reactions to people who can
make money by hard work and daring), it can of course be
argued that the Indian's preoccupation with profit is under-
standable. He has generally come to East Africa from a very
poor, rural or slum background in India. Behind him, in the
Gujarat, still looms that chasm of terrifying poverty; ahead the
grinding task of achieving survival and status for himself and
his numerous dependants.

Money grubbing, though, brings with it serious flaws of
character and judgment. Here in East Africa it has undoubtedly
affected the Indian businessman's sensitivity to wider issues—
to his reputation, and to his relationship with Africans—on
which in the long run will depend his survival.

The Indian community makes itself, for one thing, un-
necessarily conspicuous. A wealthy wedding, a visit by the Aga
Khan, a religious occasion are the pretext for costly illumina-
tions, ostentatious promenading and cluttering up of public
places, a five-mile cavalcade of cars to meet the Aga Khan's
plane at Entebbe.

At week-ends in Kampala city centre, Indian car owners
mass bumper to bumper in what looks like a victory parade of

successful shopkeepers and prolific fathers. It is surely provocative to show off like this. The more so, as not only are most Africans very poor, but the Indian in his heart fears the African, and the African knows it.

One must of course tread carefully with this sort of criticism lest one find oneself in the same team as the bullies—the Tsar's Cossacks, Abdul Hamid's Armenian-baiters, Julius Streicher in his brown breeches and jack boots. Because they form a separate, timid, ubiquitous, and yet vulnerable trading community holding disproportionate wealth and influence, the Indians of East Africa are one of history's potentially classic targets for pogrom treatment.

I can't help thinking sometimes of what I used to see of the Jews who once thronged the Pale of Central and Eastern Europe—from Lithuania down to the Black Sea—before the War.

In Warsaw and Bucharest I was astonished to observe how many prosperous Jews remained ostentatious and apparently confident to the last—till German soldiers poured across the frontiers, and they were too late to save themselves; while the mass of Jews, poor, orthodox, hopelessly provincial, crowded in small shops and alleys round the cobbled squares and the synagogues of obscure Galician towns and villages, blindly, helplessly, awaited their doom.

If only they had had the wit, or the opportunity, to forsee the horrors that awaited them: had been less naïve, less self-centred and fatalistic. Bullies trampled on them, and they were submerged. No wonder the Israeli citizen-at-arms has turned his back on that old habit of long suffering, and changed himself into a hard man.

Only five years ago the Lango adventurer Okello, with a few determined followers, smashed within a matter of hours the bogus façade of Arab power in Zanzibar. Thousands of Arabs were then beaten, killed, and dispossessed. Might not this be a warning?

Before the Kenya government's decision in February 1968 to expel unwanted Indians who did not hold Kenya passports, I sometimes discussed with Indians the possibility of violence. My acquaintances were not at all worried. Some of them had already experienced minor boycotting and rioting. It had been, they said, no more than a temporary nuisance. They believed Africans had more pressing concerns than to bait Indians—such as educating themselves, getting white-collar jobs, enforcing national unity. Uganda, anyway, was stiff with police, and with emergency legislation. The government badly wanted to present a favourable image to the world.

'If the worst were to happen,' they would say, 'we have friends and savings abroad, and in a great many cases a British passport.'

Even to hint at the possibility of trouble was taken for unfriendly, malicious talk.

'I've as much right as any African to be here,' a Muslim businessman told me, 'and certainly far more right than you have. Why, my grandfather helped to build the railway from the coast. I pay more taxes than 90 per cent of Africans. I've given my own money to help endow an Indian school which a hundred African children are now attending.'

'Without us', said a Sikh furniture dealer, 'the Africans would be back in the Stone Age. Who would mend and service their cars and radios, doctor them in hospital, buy and sell their cash crops, run the big sugar plantations?'

'Uganda', said another Indian, 'should be grateful to us. Almost everything they have, from sewing machines to motor cars, has been shipped into the country by us. And', he added, 'we are content with very small profits.'

I had the impression that, for all their shrewdness, these shopkeepers were deluding themselves. Perhaps the continued presence of the Europeans was encouraging in them a false sense of security.

Early in 1968, however, the situation deteriorated radically and almost overnight. The Kenya government's decision to expel Indians who were not citizens has been taken to mean that in Uganda too, for a great many of them, their days are numbered. The smaller man, the semi-skilled holders of British passports, arc thought likely to be the first to go.

It is comforting, of course, to know that the squeeze can be effected through legislation and without violence; and it seems inevitable, though it may be unjust, that the Indians will not attract much sympathy in their hour of need.

7*

The Times, in its leader of 2 March 1968, called the British government's hurried defence measures against the threatened rush of Indians from Kenya 'a bad week's work'. 'The Labour Party', it wrote, 'does not any longer profess to believe in the equality of man. It does not even believe in the equality of British citizens. It believes in the equality of white British citizens. This is not a noble ideology.'

The hard, 'realistic' view held by the sort of man who probably doesn't read *The Times* was given, however, in a letter sent to the *Daily Nation* of Nairobi on 26 February 1968 by T. S. Ericson of Jinja.

'Kenya', he wrote, 'has been in a state of independence for nearly five years, and yet in that time Kenya Asians have made no attempt to identify themselves with the changed conditions.

'Instead they have preferred to hang on to their British passports and enjoy the best of both worlds, and if life did not turn out to their liking, emigrate to Britain. Small wonder the Kenya government has decided to make up their minds for them.

'All this talk from Kenya Asians about being "loyal" British subjects is just sheer rubbish. It has merely been brought home to them that they are bad citizens of Kenya and, by the same token, will prove poor citizens of Britain.

'Let me say also that I for one do not welcome the Asian influx to Britain. We are already overcrowded and over-populated and unemployment is rising due to the activities of the present Labour government.

'Let me say now that Britain is a small country and we cannot continue the present rate of influx, unless we wish to face the consequences. Also, any Asian on his way to Britain right now is unwelcome. So please, Mr Prospective Immigrant, bear this in mind.

'Also Britain is, after all, for the British as Kenya is for the Kenyan, and it is damned presumptuous to say otherwise.'

Mr Bahram

Mr Bahram, whom I know quite well, runs a small bar in Kampala. He is a short man, so short that, as he stands behind his bar, all one can see is his round face, the flash of a loose dental plate as he licks it free of food particles, the top of his white shirt, and his receipt pad on which he makes rapid calculations of shillings and cents.

Mr Bahram makes no secret of preferring European and Indian customers to Africans. 'You and I spend more,' he tells me, ' and we don't make trouble. Africans get drunk and don't want to pay.' He polishes a glass. 'Now, sir, a double whisky for you?'

'No,' I say to annoy him, '*kibiriti*, a box of matches.'

Mr Bahram's argument may be a legitimate one. Over a month the European and Indian have more spending power than the sort of African who drops in at his bar on pay day and soon afterwards is broke. But the truth is, Mr Bahram's heart is hard. He will not scruple to take the last five shillings off an African labourer who has already drunk too much; and if the man then falls down on the pavement or gets knocked over by a car, that's not Mr Bahram's worry.

He employs three African girls in his bar. Their job is to attract customers, and to give those who want it 'a nice time' afterwards.

This again is a legitimate arrangement. The point is, though, that he pays them only sixty shillings a month ('but just think of all the free beers they get'), so they are compelled to practise prostitution whether they want to or not. His girls work an eight-hour shift and he gives them nothing to eat—not even one of the old meat balls he keeps under a glass case. About three years ago, when he took over the bar, he asked me for a loan to get some beer in. He now owns three cars. Africans of the lower class are exploitable. Mr Bahram has a hardness of heart.

And yet he is an estimable man. The money he pockets with a cold hand goes to help his dependants: his daughter in London, the newly married son who is expected to father half-a-dozen children within the next decade or so, a brother who is building a house. According to his code he is doing his duty to God, which is to reproduce himself and to cherish his next of kin. Judged in this light he is a good, selfless person and the most dubious of his profits an irreproachable sort of breast milk.

Divisions

Though the Indians are generally alike in their preoccupation with profit from trade and commerce, they are by no means a homogeneous community. They are split by caste and religion which demand separate places of worship, social clubs, and —until denominational schools were recently abolished— education. Intermarriage is rare. It is their internal differences that the outsider tends to overlook when he speaks of an 'Asian community'.

A strict vegetarian Gujarati Hindu disapproves, for instance, of the sophisticated ways of Ismaili Muslims, whose leaders have constantly advised them to move with the times (Ismailis, incidentally, run many of Kampala's bars).

The black-bearded Sikh whose coiled puggaree (when it does not look like an old white head bandage) can bestow dignity on the hairiest and most bucolic face, prefers the company of his own people, drinks double whiskies (but rarely smokes), and is not afraid of hard physical work. You will find him, sleeves rolled up, on building sites all over the country, or driving big German trucks into the Congo. His stolid temperament, his courage, his liking for hard liquor and out-door work, recommend the Sikh to Africans. Of all Indians, they generally like 'Singha-Singha' best.

The Catholic Goans form another compact group. One associates them with stereotyped Portuguese names (de Souza, da Silva, Fernandes and the rest), church-going and professional skills. The women—no doubt because they are considerably emancipated—excel in sport.

Goan men can often be identified by the round, swarthy face, women by their short European dresses, spindly legs and plump behinds. They seem to be torn between nostalgia for their beautiful lost country and admiration for the West. It is possible, sometimes, for Europeans to date their girls. They dislike being referred to as Indians. Yet they are not Portuguese.

Individuals

I have met, of course, many Indians who do not fit into the mercenary pattern.

One, whom it would be hard to forget, was a young woman doctor at Mulago casualty reception station. She was a very small person of astonishing coolness who, night after night in an atmosphere of beer and blood, used to treat the wounds of ragged men.

There is Rohit, a Hindu student who sacrifices everything to study. In his unworldly way he has not yet decided whether to be school master, anthropologist, or lawyer. James Joyce, for a time, pulled him one way. Now Lévi-Strauss pulls him another.

There is the drunken Hindu compositor who carries from bar to bar his crazy, scurrilous manuscript (it is called 'God's Daughter').

There was Naipaul, the Indian writer from Trinidad, who was for some months a guest of the English literature department of Makerere College. He arrived as a celebrity, though not many knew in fact that in a recent book he had castigated society in India for its squalor and selfishness. ('India,' he wrote, 'the world's largest slum'; and of defecation habits, 'Indians defecate everywhere. They defecate, mostly, beside the railway tracks. But they also defecate on the beaches; they defecate on the hills; they defecate on the river banks; they defecate on the streets; they never look for cover'; and, he added, 'they defecate in urinals for men . . . as a result of yogic contortions that can only be conjectured. . . .')

Naipaul, as far as I know, remained a stranger in Kampala, encapsuled, unwilling or unable to communicate with Africans. (I heard him refer to them as *munts*.) Perhaps they were too masculine, not subtle enough, for him. Trifles irritated him: the absence of lamp shades in his little borrowed house on Makerere Hill, the loutish scuffling of labourers and servants outside his window, transistor noises. Naipaul struck me as a sensitive, clever, gently malicious imp.

Then there are the sporting Indians with a passion for cricket and hockey (played with intense inter-communal rivalry that sometimes erupts into an attack on the umpire), the school teachers who have resigned themselves to being poor (they may run a little business on the side), and the up-country *duka-wallahs*, or bush storekeepers, who work for years in discomfort and often at some risk of being violently robbed, in remote, dusty places.

The *dukawallah* tends to be despised by Africans. They say he cheats. Europeans cannot understand the mentality of a man so dedicated to small profits.

It is true that the *dukawallahs* are sharp businessmen, weighing each little packet of damp sugar and counting each drinking straw that is served with the bottles of warm Pepsi-Cola. But like the best missionaries, they have brought essential comforts and services—aspirin, worm powders, cloth that is cut up and sewn on the spot into shirts and shorts, lorries, newspapers, and the mail—to people whose needs would otherwise have been ignored. To the traveller they are a God-send. And their profits take a long time to accumulate.

Africans, then, provide at one end of the scale the political leadership and ideology, the bulk of the civil service; at the other, the crops and copper, the unskilled services, the labour[1] and the brawn: the Indians contribute a good deal of all the rest. Let us recognise that the Indians have brought immense benefits of trade, capital and skills to Uganda, filling a role which the British did not want and to which Africans were unsuited.

But it is a vulnerable role. They have been encouraged to overplay it, and they must soon make room for an African skilled industrial and middle class—even though, for the meantime, it is true that an enterprising African still feels more attracted to a white-collar job, with all its perquisites, than to selling groceries behind a counter.

It is a pity for its overall reputation that so much of the Indian community has been of one type—the mercenary type. One would have welcomed more variety—a fakir or two, dancing girls, some Pathans. . . . Yet all of us have good cause to be privately grateful to an Indian. If one is in trouble—it may be the toothache, or a point of law, or spare parts for one's car—the odds are that an Indian is the man who will help.

Naipaul (in India) was allergic to Indian defecation habits. In the different situation of East Africa I am irritated by their exclusiveness and bored with the money grubbing.

---

[1] Commercial colleges now produce a growing number of clerical staff.

CHAPTER 21

Three Peoples (3):
Europeans

The new society

Kampala's European community is a mixed and—since the decline in British influence—increasingly cosmopolitan bag. It includes Italian artisans and German technicians, UNO experts, the Norwegian Peace Corps, Greek café owners, diplomatists, and a still numerous body of British officials and professional men.

But it has the solidarity of a common culture and standard of living, and of a common experience in a fairly unusual situation. Even the Jugoslav Ambassador has had his new Mercedes Benz audaciously stolen from outside his house. Even the Russians speak a little Swahili and photograph hippopotami.

Most Europeans have readily adapted themselves to life under African government. There is no settler element to create problems of land ownership. The indestructible missionaries with their well preserved bodies and greying hairs stay on; but a good many of the older men who once had some special skill or knowledge to offer—in sewage, accountancy, the administration of education, police work and the like— and whose opinions were moulded in another atmosphere, have gone. They are being replaced, if at all, by a new generation of more docile expatriates on short contracts whose contribution, however, tends to be erratic. In education especially, young British and American teachers come and go like shuttlecocks.

The old professional type of colonial civil servant was, one is told, dedicated to his work.[1] At the least, he felt at home in

[1] See notes on Bradley and Lytton in Annotated Book List. For further opinions on Europeans in Africa see under Hanley.

his exotic tropical world. He often stayed single, or married late. If he had a wife she too was probably devoted to the service.

The new type of expatriate has a very different attitude. Almost from the start he tends to be heavily committed to a girl friend or a young wife who is likely to be only vaguely interested in Africa. He has not much time or inclination to absorb himself in the country and its people. He is migratory, distracted by personal problems, and he has his eye on a 'real' job in England.

Then there are the scholars and specialists who use Uganda as merely an intermediary stage in some field of research. They collect their data, photograph the Murchison Falls—or, if they are very lucky, a circumcision ceremony among the Bagisu—and they go.

The teacher

Young British teachers are everywhere. Their number swells each year. The TEA element among them arrive in batches, by chartered aeroplane, in a curious medley of old clothes—jeans, ski jackets, sweaters.[1] They wear sandals that reveal pale, veined feet.

The sun has a liberating effect on them. They start to bare legs and thighs (what a relief it must be to discard those frowsty English trousers). Many grow beards that sprout from the face like bleached grass. They are unselfconscious, irreverent, and generally friendly to Africans. They are the antithesis of the stage type of stuffy colonial Englishman whose image—if it remains at all—they destroy.

At parties and in the night clubs they jive with the feverish contortions of crested birds that caper before mating. They have zest. It is good—though not entirely good—that they are here, to represent contemporary European youth and to make a brief, cheerful impact. If only some of them did not look as though they had just hitch-hiked across the Sudan!

---

[1] The Teachers for East Africa (TEA) scheme is an innovation in British recruitment for work in East Africa. These people are young graduates of British universities. They are contracted for three years. The first year they study at Makerere College for a diploma in education. The two following years they are expected to teach in secondary schools.

21*a*. Teuso village
near Turkana
escarpment,
Kamion

b. My Teuso
escort, eating

c. Turkana escarpment
view

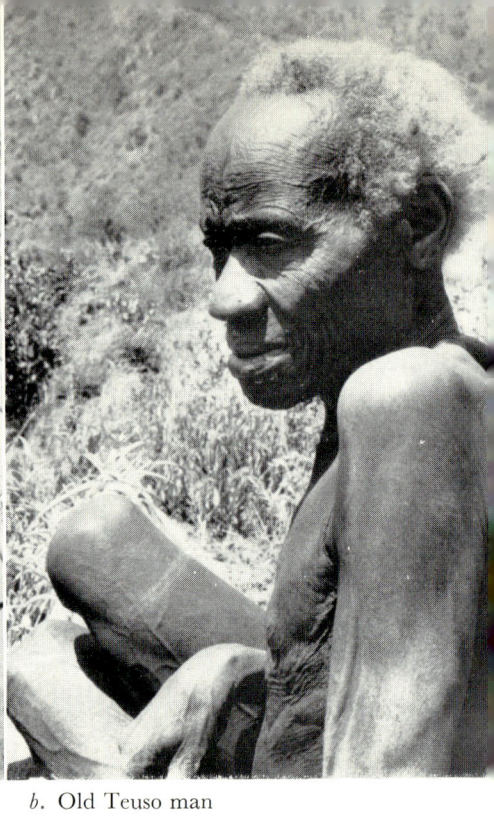

22a. Locham on top of Zulia

b. Old Teuso man

c and d. Teuso girls

a. Galls on thorn bush, Karamoja

b. Aloe, Karamoja

c. Dr Colin Turnbull at Pirre

24a. Teuso escort cleaning up

b. Dodoth cattle owner

c. Teuso outside village fence

d. Teuso escort

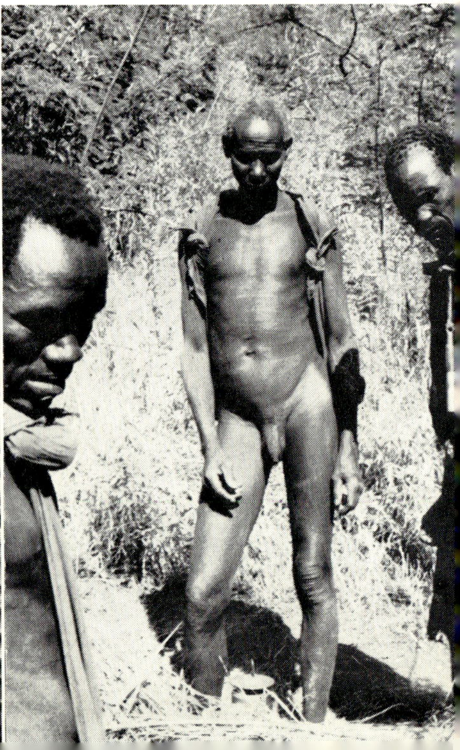

The other day I saw a young Englishman in a crowded café who had two large holes in his trousers, one exposing a knee cap, the other a part of his bottom. He was not on safari, nor had he just fallen off a motor cycle. The trousers had been freshly laundered, so that the gaping holes had a curiously insolent effect. He had his girl with him.

A surge of self-righteousness came over me, and when they left I followed them into the street.

'Excuse me,' I said in the manner of an Oxford proctor, 'but are you aware that your trousers have holes in them?'

'Yes,' he answered.

'And you realise that you are in the middle of Kampala?'

'They're my trousers,' he said resentfully.

'Throw them away.'

'But I wear them like this in London.'

'To hell with London,' I was going to say, but he had already hurried off, taking me for an unpleasant sort of colonial Englishman.

At their best the young British teachers who are plummetted each year into Uganda are an asset. The secondary schools could not be run without them. In their uninhibited way they have made contact with Africans, invaded the dance halls, gone up-country to educate children in remote and sometimes uncomfortable places, helped to break the ice.

At their very worst (and this was far more the case in the early days of 1964–66 than it is today) they are an embarrassment: sloppily dressed, bewildered, and adolescent.[1]

The British still have their cricket and golf, their social clubs and drama societies, their bolt-holes for whisky and gossip—

---

[1] Africans have naturally resented or misunderstood some of their behaviour (feeding dogs, for instance, at the dinner table). A violent demonstration against Europeans made by Makerere College students in the streets of Kampala, March 16, 1968 (Europeans were beaten and their cars damaged) was set off by two TEA students who, at a college meeting to protest against the hanging of two Africans in Salisbury, refused to stand up with all the others in a two-minutes' silence. These street incidents resulted among Europeans in the only note of real bitterness against Africans that I can recall (there had been isolated protests against cases of ill treatment by soldiers during the Emergency of 1966). The mood soon died down. But it has left a doubt in many people's minds: would the police, in case of real trouble, be able to offer proper protection to foreigners?

but with fading echoes of the old in-group life. Behind the suburban hedges emphasis is on respectability cheered by sundowners. A strong odour of domesticity pervades even Makerere College, whose grounds are overrun with the dogs, the children and the nannies of its European staff. Those odd-looking lecturers bearded and semi-clothed like Old Testament prophets who have lost their outer garments, those young-old men who seem always to be in beach-wear, are submissive family fathers.

The tenacious eccentric who has learned something of the local languages may prefer to build his own house in a semi-African neighbourhood outside the town. He will save on rent; but his car may disappear one night. Most of us would rather cluster together in our neat residential suburbs: a colony of commuters with dogs, servants, and rose bushes.

Up-country Europeans have more scope to be truly individualistic, and they have to be more resourceful. To the geologist living in a tented camp under an acacia tree, or to the missionary doctor in Amudat, Kampala must seem a remote place: a voice on the radio, a memory of sophisticated food and smooth pavements.

Neighbours

In Kampala, houses are allocated to government officers on a points basis according to length of service, salary and size of family. If you have enough points—and are lucky—you get a detached bungalow with three bedrooms and its own hedge and servants' quarters. If not, you are put into a flat that is full of doors and sometimes has signs of chickens having been kept in the dhobi room.

I was given a flat on Kololo hill, just below the television mast whose lights twinkle over the city at night like four red eyes. In front, at the bottom of the hill, I could see egrets flying over the golf course; beyond that, the banked terraces of Nakasero, and a part of Mengo skyline. From now on I was committed to the problems of life in suburbia: servants, dogs, drains, thieves and neighbours.

We Kololo residents tend to be birds of passage, with a steady inflow of African civil servants to replace Europeans who move out. This coming and going does not make for close neighbourly relations. Not that they would be particularly welcome. Officials prefer to keep their private lives away from a colleague's probing eye.

The trouble too about neighbours is that, unless we are exceptionally good natured, we first notice what we dislike or find ludicrous in each other. The people next door seem to caricature oneself. They lose their temper with the servants over the same trifles, they are from time to time foolishly outwitted by burglars, they make the same noises when tipsy.

Here, haphazardly thrown together along a small frontage of flats dug into the side of a green hill, we make up a rough cross-section of the sort of people who, as the poor Ugandan says, 'are eating the government's money': teachers, nurses, bank officials, police officers and the like.

I have known only two of my neighbours well. They were lame ducks whose troubles one had to share.

First there was 'Cloth Ears', a government revenue officer who after a decade of fun among the Ethiopians ('finest whores in the world—they *gyrate*!') was due to be retired. He had long since given up going to his office, and was fuddling himself with Cyprus brandy: a mild-mannered alcoholic who shaved, thought no one 'knew', and hid his bottles in a tall brown paper parcel when he brought them home.

He pretended to dislike children ('I hate posterity'). Towards the end he began to fall down and hurt himself. His friends eventually put him on a train and the last they heard of him was that on alighting in Mombasa he had broken a leg. He may have welcomed the accident as a reprieve from that dreaded awakening in Mr Wilson's England.

Then there was the African police officer who arrived one morning from Moroto with his belongings—an old mattress, some bags of charcoal, half-a-dozen chickens and a cock—in a Public Works Department lorry; and with a pretty, new young wife sitting shyly in his blue Cortina car.

The first thing he did was to turn off the electricity, for he was repaying (over four years) the government loan on his car, and his monthly *waragi* bill was a heavy one. He never went anywhere without his transistor set. His wife pounded maize on the floor.

Every week-end he polished his car till it shone like new; and almost every other week-end he dented it. He once came to me and my American neighbour and confessed he was worried.

'Mr Jones,' he said to me, 'you Europeans don't approve of me. I know it.'

We asked him what he meant. 'You see, sir,' he said 'my young wife is not the wife I married in church. You know that, don't you? You think me a bad man.'

'Good God, no,' we replied. 'We envy you.'

It was a shock to him when one night all four wheels were stolen from his car. We went out in our pyjamas to look at it. Wheel-less, the splendid blue Cortina had shrunk pathetically to a toad.

'Mr Jones, sir,' he said to me, 'someone has a grudge against me. This is personal. I know, sir. I am a policeman.'

'Nonsense,' we said. 'You should have fixed a burglar alarm.'

After a few months he sent his young wife away. 'She was useless,' he explained. 'She cannot make a womb.'

Then his first wife, who was middle-aged and jolly, rejoined him with two of his children. For a time he drank his *waragi* at home, and it was a month or more before he dented his car again.

Among the neighbours are generally to be found half-a-dozen unmarried English women in their thirties. They are burglar-prone: the despair of insurance companies. Their cars or their accessories, their radios, record players and cameras are frequently stolen. Only one of them has had the traditional fierce and sex-starved dog as a constant companion. They are courageous, self-contained women—and yet, in African eyes, incomplete.

The type of single European lady towed along by a dog or driving her Fiat alone to Nairobi baffles most Africans. 'A woman,' they say, even a white one with a university education and a car, 'is a womb.' And marriage has some practical advantages for the European woman in East Africa. She may not be particularly fond of her husband, but he can protect her against assault by burglars and be used as escort on safari.

Servants

Government bungalows and flats in Kampala are built to a common pattern. They are made of solid whitewashed brick. They have red-waxed cement floors, numerous small windows protected by bars and mosquito gauze, a bath tub but no shower. They are provided with strong tables and chairs, striped mattresses that hold many secrets, and a dustbin. We are grateful for them. The rent, at under £6 a month, is ridiculously cheap compared with the £60 or more demanded by a private landlord. The servants' quarters for each block of communal flats are sited—in the interests of 'hygiene'—about one hundred yards away. Each flat disposes of two small servants' cells grouped with all the other round a yard. They do not have electricity.

Servants' quarters are always astonishingly overcrowded. Their rightful occupants sublet them to friends, relatives, and hangers-on, and they become small tribal hamlets bursting with pots and pans, children and strangers. It is never possible to know who is living there. Thieves and prostitutes use them as well as *bona fide* employees.

Once, when we were being pestered by car thieves, I asked the police to raid our servants' quarters. The result was that we had to spend the following day at the police station bailing out 'brothers' and 'sisters'.

I used at first to make myself ridiculous by going round the quarters to eject strangers and persuade beer-fuddled cooks to sweep up their rubbish—for the drains were blocked with sludge and bones, and 'we shall all', I said, 'get malaria.'

Within a day or two the hangers-on, the schoolboys who were allowed to sleep on the floor, the unemployed dandies, and the *enguli* (crude alcohol) distiller were back again, and I gave up.

Servants are, of course, underpaid: 140 shillings a month with some sugar and paraffin thrown in. But it is impossible not to envy them a little, cheerfully cooking their stews over a brazier, ironing the white shirts and bright dresses, singing, drinking and quarrelling on Sunday. They introduce, into the prim, private suburbs, the atmosphere of a cheerful and promiscuous village.

The garden

One of the pleasures of suburbia is a garden, even though you may have to share it with spoilt and boisterous dogs.[1] It will have shrubs and trees that attract birds; and mongooses creep round the cocoa-coloured ant-hills at night.

At dawn the bulbuls first break into staccato chorus. Then crimson-breasted shrikes begin their almost simultaneous duet of a fluting whistle and rasp. Plantain eaters chase each other among the cassia trees, and for the rest of the day there is constant bird movement.

Iridiscent sunbirds rustle among the mango leaves and poke tiny curved beaks into the gaudy parasols of the hibiscus. Mousebirds like feathered rats attack the pawpaw fruit, in which they make big juicy wounds. A grey heron stalks along the hedge snapping up grasshoppers. After rain, sooty hadada ibises land on the lawn like wailing witches, with a sea-green glitter of wings.

Towards dusk the kite that whistles in the eucalyptus tree like a breathless referee is mobbed by crows. A little later, as the sun sinks over Mengo, bats come flying over from Wandegeya. Some alight on the pawpaw trees. They squeak in the night, and flutter past one's face.

There is always something in flower. The yellow horns of the thevetia hedge: purple jacaranda, jasmine, cassia, potato tree. Fallen hibiscus blossoms lie in the grass like bloodstains. The air holds the vanilla-scented odour of white moonflowers which open suddenly, wither, and then are blown and scattered about like crumpled paper cornets.

The garden where I had lived for three years on the Black Sea was a rank piece of cliff-top. I associate it with nightingale song, the winter cry of jackals, the red fruit of the strawberry tree, the cannonade of breakers smashing on rock.

My Kololo garden I shall remember for its mango scent, the duet of the crimson-breasted shrikes—and the car thieves, the

---

[1] The difference between European and African owned dogs is that the European generally locks his dog in at night, while the African dog-owner locks his out: so it roams through the night after bitches, knocks over the dustbins, barks at the moon, and keeps everyone awake.

pole-fishers and the burglars who have disturbed, and sometimes entertained, my nights.

An early intruder, whom I found sprawled on my sofa one night, claimed to be drunk; while I was interrogating him he broke wind so horribly that I let him go.

I disturbed another fellow while he was forcing the side window of my car with an iron bar. He had the insolence to say, 'Good morning, sir', before he vanished with a drumming of flat, bare feet.

My most recent visitors were at work on the headlights when I surprised them. They were stripped to the waist, and oiled. As they loped off towards the golf course they looked in the moonlight like two beautiful leopards. They left a sharpened panga behind.

In the long run one cannot win against such agile, persistent raiders. They have an organisation of receivers behind them. And no sleepy householder, in slippers and pyjamas, wants to chase an armed athlete at night through the hibiscus bushes.

PART III

VERSE

VERSE

I have referred (page 188) to my students' natural ability to write verse, which they first revealed in response to a bribe of bottles of beer which I offered for contributions. Here are some examples of their work:

THE BELOVED

Lapobo,
Tall but not too tall,
Short but not too short,
She is of medium size.

Lapobo,
Her teeth are not as ash
Nor the colour of maize flour,
Her teeth are white as fresh milk.
The whiteness of her teeth
When I think of them
Makes food drop from my hand.

Lapobo,
Black but not too black,
Brown but not too brown,
Her skin colour is just between black and brown.

Lapobo,
Her heels have no cracks,
Her palms are smooth and tender to touch,
Her eyes—Ho, they can destroy anybody!

A. R. Cliff-Lubwa (Acholi)

THE BASTARD

An unlucky creation,
His mother a street walker,
His lying father
A champion at producing bastards.

It's not his fault,
Poor innocent bastard,
That in slums he's brought up
By a mother that has no husband—
Though many a husband he sees
Caressing his mother
On a stool or lumpy bed.

Poor bastard,
Dumped on the ground to make room
For his nocturnal fathers
Or on the mat to spend his horrid nights
Among the steaming pots of food
And walking rats.

An unlucky creation,
This bastard,
Before birth heavily and mercilessly tormented
With a rope tied tight round the mother's waist
To strangle the foetus
Or his unformed head
Squeezed with hands rough and murderous.

Down latrines they are thrown,
These bastards,
For the pit's the easiest way
And the mother's a girl again
Ay a virgin, and what a virgin!
Repaired and holy!
O crime! O murder of small flesh
That might have grown
To greatness and wisdom.

An unlucky creation,
This discharge of a street walker,
All know his mother's a whore
His father a cheat,
Everyone knows
The bastard will beget bastards.

Never will he know motherly love
Or feel soft hands
Only the rough fists of old whores
Dried breasts and stinking spittle,
And when his mother's gone
To earn her shilling
In the hot sun he will lie
In his own excrement.

To bars they are brought,
The bastards,
Thrown at the father
Like rotten pawpaws,
And he, to escape abuse and shame,
Runs faster than the kite,
His beer undrunk.

O Sanyu Babies' Home knows their secrets;
At her gate children mew like cats early in the morning
They are wrapped in sacks and rags
Their mothers nowhere to be seen—
The child is gone, the load released,
Sanyu Babies' Home will bear, of course, the cost.

Where could they get the money, the whores,
To feed the brats, when their own meal
Is a cassave stick with salt? Great drunkards
Who vomit on their knees in every bar
And drain old seed
From men they do not know.

                    B. S. Tibenderana (Kigezi)

The Acholi (says the writer) traditionally got most of their meat by hunting game. My poem is meant to express the feelings of disgust with which an old Acholi hunter looks at Murchison Falls Game Park— which he considers an encroachment on his people's old hunting grounds. Anyone caught poaching there by the game guards is gaoled. (By 'Galaya' is meant old tin basins stuck on tree trunks to mark Game Reserve boundaries. The English language is referred to locally as 'Yes-No'.)

THE POACHER'S LAMENT
Schoolboy:
   Sir, what's this 'Galaya' of which men speak?
Poacher:
   The Galaya, boy? You ask me what it is?
   O children of these days
   It is true that you are useless!
   Alas, the white man has killed this land
   That spreads to the Nile and was our hunting ground.

   When Oto gave the word
   People thronged like the black *kalang* ants to a kill
   Listen, O listen to their horns, Tile! Tile! Tile!
   Where do you see such things today?
   Animals were abundant then
   Only cowards did not kill
   Men returned with meat and bloody spears
   That rattled on their shoulders.
   We, with your fathers, we were the champions then
   Our spears never slept cold
   Even the leopard by Tiima stream was afraid
   On the way home women came at our call
   To stagger under our meat
   Their tall necks sagged and shrunk
   Like the penis of a thief when caught
   Our *rudda* horns blared Tile! Tile! Tile!
   Loud over the miles
   And when they heard it women threw away the *malakwang* soup
   They cleaned the pots, they collected wood,
   Opok wood, that is the best for roasting,
   And on such a day my head spurned the pillow.
   Women gyrated. They praised me.
   They brought water for me to wash with
   Aye, water enough for two
   I was given a place near the cooking fire
   And Otim's mother spoilt me
   Yes, when the children slept she fed me with her own hands.
   The mouths of our village were rich, then;
   No one hungered on cow pies.

   Alas, Galaya has swallowed the source of Aswa river.
   Beyond the Galaya is now government land.

They have made wild animals their cattle
Even rats may not be hunted there
They say our animals are beautiful
That white men travel far to see them
They say that if we kill animals
What will be left for our children to see?
Yet the money that the traveller brings,
Who knows the path it takes?
Government eats the whole goodness of it.

If, boy, you had to choose
Between an animal to gape at
And meat in a bowl to eat
Which in your hunger would you take?
You educated youths say you know the world
But can you carry spears on your shoulders?
Think of Ojok, of whom men still speak,
Would he have eaten only millet balls?
What kind of knowledge is yours
Who think that 'Yes-No' and rumba are all?
Yet we grew you on the carcasses we brought home
And so—though one must go shrewdly about the work—
The animals still die. Yes, the old hunter
Can dodge the game rangers who carry senseless guns
That are not licensed to kill people.
Whoever has been killed for hunting game?
They throw out their shoulders
Their guns explode behind you
They order you to stop or die
But you know well what they mean:
Men don't rip each other's testicles.
So with the meat on your back
You tear the forest with your legs:
Truly the game has always been ours
For who can dispute the ownership of the guinea fowl
That is caught in a trap?

                                    Okumu pa'Lukobo (Acholi)

AN OLD MAN WELCOMING RAIN

O Rain! Welcome visits you've brought to lazy men
Chest sickness to lazy women
Reproduction to frogs.

The people with leaking houses
Aren't happy;
Those with good houses
Are happy,
And you hear them beating
On the floor the smoked meat
And breaking firewood with their knees.

O the feeder of orphans is falling like the bull's urine!
It is pouring as if from a giant pot!
Long live the god of rain!

A. R. Cliff-Lubwa (Acholi)

THE EVENING MEAL

The red sun falls behind the thorn trees,
Cattle plod to their caves,
Down to the well tread the women
Chattering and chanting their warriors' songs.
In the well with crooked arms they stoop and draw water
And with one accord up go the gourds upon their strong heads.
Quickly they turn their steps back home.

In a corner of a small tilted hut a tripod awaits the shapeless pot.
Carefully the mother begins her work.
She breathes upon the fire with her mouth
Gaping like the slit in a letter box.
Eyes red and watery she rushes out
And soaks her baby in a rusty basin.

The air is still except for the choked scream and shrill of babies
Sounding like a chatter of small drums.
The house smokes like a train on a hill.
In a corner a boy scrounges food
His eyes glistening like an oyster in a pool.
By the cracked wall a girl chews her fingers.

Soon on carelessly washed plates food presents itself.
Wearily the family leader and father attempts a wash of his hands,
His beard that has not known a razor for ages
Shivers like the tassel on a loose hat.
He grasps food with all his might and skill
And feeds without regard of his age.

There is a cry and a clatter of plates
Children scramble for the last crumbs.
Soon the sound subsides
The family retire to their hard skins
And for a time the hut is restless.
Here a deep grunt, there a high snore,
And all the noises that discordant music knows
Now the only production of the family choir
In sleep.

Vin. Ekwaraun (Teso)

ACHOLI FOLK SONG

See this hunter
This hunter broke my spear,
My spear,
The spear the herdsman gave me.

That herdsman broke my stick,
My stick,
The stick the dancer gave me.

That dancer broke my feather,
My feather,
The feather the kite gave me.

That kite snatched my fish,
My fish,
The fish the river gave me.

That river swallowed my milk,
My milk,
The milk the woman gave me.

That woman ate my berries,
My berries,
The berries the girls gave me.

Those girls fled, they left me,
Their ghosts answered me,
Their airy empty ghosts,
Their ghosts answered me.

C. Okwonga (Acholi)

THE HOLOCAUST

Listen and ye shall hear, said our Lord,
Knock and I will open unto thee,
Look and ye shall see,
Seek and ye shall find.

To Mackay they hearkened and they heard
The word of God, those innocent martyrs
Who in eighteen-eighty-two to the Word listened
With such alacrity and promptitude.

At Mengo chapel they knocked and wide it opened
For them that were ready with open hearts:
For the word of God was large and loud
And Mackay had promulgated it.

Inside the church they turned to look and wonder
And the picture of our Lord they saw
Hanging on a wall with ten mortal gashes.
They wept at what they saw.

Yet more knowledge of God they sought
So to Rubaga they went, those innocents,
Who found Lourdel singing by the gate
Of the chapel that was to be their grave.

On Mwanga their backs they turned
Homage to him they no longer gave
His orders no longer obeyed:
Yes, the word of God must have been strong.

Yet King was King and King indeed
With powers absolute and unequalled.
In sacrificial slaughter men he killed
And wives who had sniggered.
This the martyrs disregarded.

And so to Namugongo they went, those virgins,
With chains round their hands
Their legs with thorns mercilessly decorated
To seek the strong word of our Lord.

Honour to those walkers
Who to their grave went steadily
With whips on their buttocks and barbs in their cheeks:
More than Christ they suffered, those black innocents.

The head of Mulumba at Lugogo was severed
The eyes of Kagwa at Naguru plucked
The hands of Atanazio at Banda were cut
And the feet of Balikuddembe at Kireka dismembered.

Intimidation did not work
For Ambrozio, Luka-Baanabakintu and their group
Marched briskly to the hot faggots, the club, the castrator's knife,
To the Holocaust.

Like rubbish those poor virgins of Namugongo
Whose chastity the King had sought to violate
Into flaming fire were thrown
Yet they were happy, singing praise to our Lord.

S. B. Tibenderana (Kigezi)

END OF THE SEASON

It comes with heat and drooping leaves
With soil cracked and crumbling
With whirlwinds
That scurry leaves, dust and feathers,
Ashes and ordure.

When the scorching rays and the gusts have gone
A cumulus cloud forms
And for a while
Nature is still.

But the small cloud moves. It grows. And look!
It is mantling the earth
The whole earth,
Its dark wings have entombed it
In impenetrable eclipse.

Till a flash cleaves
Thunder booms
And the black world runs amok
In ravaging tornado: thunderous, shaking, swirling,
Raping trees.

As heaven's water-bag splits asunder
Torrents form a sea-carpet,
The wanderer sees it, and on a hill
Crouches in a hole.
His thin spear points to the storm
His hair oozes dye
Bushes drown.

V. Katunzi (Kigezi)

EVENING

Never has the death of a poet
Been tolled by all the world.
God's work on earth, though,
Has its universal funeral in the west,
Recurrent grave of day's almighty soul.

Never was victory so trumpeted
As that of the sun climbing his fiery way
And then in gorgeous colours falling,
Trailing stars.
Life, death, water and aridity
Bow to his morning ray.

With his passing death stirs in the thicket.
In church the bell is rung
In barracks at the last bugle note
Soldiers like ants file;
The busy woman scolds her child
Drunkards like sick dogs retch homewards
The night voice is a harsh guitar.

On a hill among *musizi* trees
Sweet nuns sing litanies,
Priests like lamp-posts in a graveyard
Stoop over the breviary.
There's a piping of crickets in the bush
And bellowing frogs—
All sing the ancient elegy
For the sun that has died in the west.

Hesbon Lubega (Buganda)

The following items are traditional songs which have been rendered from the vernacular into English:

The first item ('Farewell to the Bride') comes from Kigezi. It is (says the writer) sung by women who have escorted a bride to her bridegroom's home. Customarily marriage takes place during a full moon. The moon is thought to be the abode of Mugasya, goddess of marriage. When the moon emerges above the horizon the female escort break into their farewell song. They are ready to leave, for it is held that the image of a person carrying an axe which is always seen in a clear moon is Mugasya warning escorts of brides everywhere to go home and leave the girl to her marriage night. While the women are singing, the bride cries bitterly. They caress her. During the singing they try to face the moon. This song is meant to shape the girl into a brave and enduring woman who will not—after some petty row with her husband or in-laws—childishly run away.

FAREWELL TO THE BRIDE

Burungi! O Burungi! The time of sorrow is come.
Sorrowful are we that we say farewell to you
Daughter of our father
Beautiful handiwork of the goddess of marriage.
Sorrow it is that you are no longer ours
What shame we carry on our heads
That we go back home and leave you
In the traitorous care of a foreigner.[1]

[1] The escorts abuse the bridegroom not because he really is a bad character but to show how deeply upset they are at losing a friend.

Look beyond at the splendid moon
Home of Mugasya, the goddess of marriage,
O Burungi, see the warning look of Mugasya
Urging us to depart
To depart, leaving you to the foreigner,
The traitorous foreigner, who shows fondest love today
But will bind and roast you over the fire tomorrow.

No words, there are no words . . .
A loving foreigner is a chameleon,
Deceptive and inconstant,
A hyena of the day,
A voracious jackal at night,
Now a mad dog,
Now a wild bull,
He will turn against you
And bitterly you will grieve
'Alas, I would I had not married.'

Be brave when the foreigner turns against you,
Be brave, we entreat you, be enduring,
Fasten tight your belt
And pray to Mugasya
'Mugasya, O Mugasya,
Behold we pray to thee our benefactor,
Here is your daughter, your own clay-work.'

Sister of our sisters,
Look, why don't you open the parcel
Your mother gave you,
Why don't you chew the medicine of love and charm
And sprinkle the chewing in your bed?
Be wise: you are a woman now,
The medicine will check your husband's brutality
And bind him fast in chains of tenderness
And love.

G. Tindimwebwa (Kigezi)

*The song that follows ('How Did I Come to Marry into this Home?')
is sung (says the writer) in his part of Bukedi when a bride has stayed
in her husband's home for some time and doesn't like it. By custom
bridesmaids stay with the bride for not less than a month. During this
time the bride should eat only meat or fish. She must not be given green
vegetables. A home is despised if the bridegroom cannot fulfil this
condition. He may be disgraced, even divorced. This song is sung by
the bridesmaids, but in secret lest they be overheard and told to go.*

HOW DID I COME TO MARRY INTO THIS HOME?

I despise, yes, I despise,
The home I have married into,
It is no fit home for me,
O Lord, how did I come to be here!

My father's greed is to blame.
Hungry for quick wealth
He negotiated the bride price
Without consulting me; while my mother
Was confined in the kitchen.
O Lord, how did I come to be here!

No food without toil,
No cloth without cultivation,
No fire without wood,
No drink without water,
And the well five miles away.
O Lord how did I come to be here!

The dwelling is small,
My relations have nowhere to sit,
Its wall is rough,
And I am told to smear it,
The roof leaks all over,
I despise the home I have married into!

Yes, I despair, I despair.
The bed I must sleep in
Full of bed bugs as it is
I share with my husband
Though it fits him alone.
We are two now,
And it is too narrow for two people.
O how did I come to be here!

And I have to provide food
Yet only a single cassave patch there is,
No granary, and so no millet,
Our home suffers famine.
Surely my mother-in-law will fall dead
Begging on the path,
People gossip about her,
Those who know her avoid her,
She is notorious.
O Lord how did I come to be here!

My mother-in-law, a parrot at home,
Is as lazy as a chameleon in the garden.
My father-in-law must have a mountain of food
Served not on a plate
For that would turn it soggy
Nor would the plate carry enough!
It's a rare and merry day when there is meat,
But misery when the dish is green stuff.
O how to satisfy such a home!

My relations are only welcome if they bring gifts—
If not, my husband looks glum,
And they are not attended to, not welcome,
What a home this is!

I am lonely, and my husband's family oppresses me,
I get no support from my husband
Indeed I get beatings instead,
I am scorned, yet much is demanded of me,
They say I am a failure
But I am never allowed to answer back,
Indeed I am reminded of the marriage money
I am threatened with dismissal
With the refunding of bride price.

I think of my lot, and I endure,
But for how long?
Truly my father is to blame.

His greed caused my sorrow
It is for him to solve this trouble,
O father, I cannot stand the beatings any more,
I have grown thin,
I am lost,
What has brought this about?
It is nothing but your greed.

O father, should I divorce?
But no hen would be slaughtered for you,
O no, no hen for you,
Not from these misers for whom food is a child;
If a hen were slaughtered, my father-in-law
Would spare you but the comb.
O father, why did you cause me so much misery?

J. Masiga (Bukedi)

In Lango (writes this contributor) the institution of bride price is very important. A good girl will usually fetch a high bride price, an unsatisfactory girl will get a low one. So the mother gives traditional advice to her daughter before she leaves for her bridegroom's home. She reminds her daughter of everything she has taught her since childhood.

A MOTHER ADVISES HER DAUGHTER

Don't, my daughter, disgrace me,
Remember what I have taught you since childhood
About household duties.
My daughter, don't disgrace me.

My daughter, when you go to your bridegroom,
Remember I taught you to respect elders
And how to serve them.
Control your tongue.
If you speak sharply to your mother-in-law
We shall lose the bride price.

8*

Don't disgrace me, my daughter,
Remember that when your father married me
I served him with obedience and respect.
Your father's father paid much bride price for me,
Your grandparents liked me.
When I was a bride, I was loyal and hard working,
So, my daughter, don't be lazy,
Earn us a big bride price and a good name.

Your work is careless here,
But now, enough of that,
Be quick-witted in whatever you do.

My daughter, don't leave the millet
Where the chickens will eat it up.
If you do, they will call you *Otu-Kene,*
The improvident one.

You must know that mothers-in-law are cunning.
They try to catch new brides
With tricks to test them.
Beware, my daughter, of this,
Or we shall get no bride price.

Your mother-in-law,
Will set traps for you.
She will make you use oil in the food
But she will measure it secretly.

She will put you in charge of the oil,
She will mark well its level in the pot.
And if you taste it for yourself, she will know.

They will call you 'glutton,'
So don't, my daughter, eat of the elders' food,
They will call you 'hyena,' the greedy one.

I know you are fond of meat.
Beware, my daughter, don't touch their meat
Or they will call you *akeo,* the meat swallower.

Another trick. Your mother-in-law
May throw pieces of smoked meat on the floor.
Beware, she will count the pieces
Before she goes to work.

When you sweep clean the house, collect the meat,
Collect all of it, carefully,
And keep it safe for her
Till she comes back. She will count the pieces
And you will be blamed
If any is missing.

Don't my daughter, forget to bring
Your parents-in-law
Water for washing the body:
And water for your husband too.

My daughter, I have taught you all these things,
And now I am reminding you of them.
You will remember,
Go, and fare well, my daughter.

                                        B. Ekwar (Lango)

*A mother-in-law, says the same writer, if she finds fault with the
bride, usually focuses her criticism on the girl's background, using
scornful words.*

A MOTHER CRITICISES
HER DAUGHTER-IN-LAW

My husband,
Our son's bride doesn't please me.
We shall waste our cattle
On that useless girl.

I don't like her.
She cannot cook,
She burns the food
And it is never clean.

How lazy she is!
She trips over calabashes and breaks them,
She pushes things out of the way
With her feet.

235

Truly she is idle.
I don't like her.
Our son has made a bad choice.
Didn't he study the girl's behaviour beforehand?

Perhaps he was only after her beauty.
We expect, of course, to get a beautiful girl
But she must have household ability.

No, I cannot keep quiet,
I don't like her at all.
She is idle. I will give her just one more chance.
That is my word,
She is *eganga*, worthless.

Alas indeed! Whose daughter
Has our son brought home?
Did her mother never teach her?
How can a bride cook with grass!

And the house is as filthy as a rubbish pit.
The rubbish has been collecting
Since I last swept up two days ago.

Look, my husband, how she walks,
As though her body was all fat.
She is swollen and lifeless,
Like a corpse.

She neglects to bring her parents-in-law
The washing water. A-a-i! Eyela-Kwee . . .
What a bride!

Truly our son must get back our cattle.
There's no wife in this one,
She's *eganga*.

You, girl, get back to your home.
You are good for nothing. Your arms
Croak like frogs
When they are given work to do.

Go, go! Let your mother teach you anew.
You will bear idle children.
Go, go! Away from here!

B. Ekwar (Lango)

THE HERDSBOY'S MISERY

Happy are the blacksmith's children,
Happy my brothers
Who spend their time in play
Splashing in cool Hinatye river.

Their mothers embrace them.
They play games in the village courtyard.
In a field, after dark, they tell stories
Of hunting, dancing, and cattle raids.

I—miserable herdsboy—am out of place.
I spend my days in burning heat.
I am enslaved,
Till the guinea fowl cackles at dusk,
To greedy cattle.

My thoughts are always of pasture,
Rich pasture
That makes fat cattle,
Fat cattle for bride wealth.

I am always in fear,
Fear of heat,
Fear of cold and rain storms,
Fear of thorny grass,
Fear, when a sick cow or calf is lost,
Of being starved,
Fear, when the cattle invade a man's farm,
Of being thrashed.

I envy my friends
Who go to school to learn
The white man's words
Which like a hen's claw marks
They scratch on the ground.

237

My friends boast that they can write,
That they speak the white man's language.
They say that herding cattle
Is simpleton's work,
A mark of primitivity,
For modern man lives in a brick house.
I am doomed to follow grass,
To wander after cattle.
Only anthrax, wiping out the herd,
Can save me.

R. Oler-Opyaha (Southern Sudan)

SAYINGS OF THE BAKIGA

The fool tried to trap a hyena with a basket.

He who has been bitten by a snake dreads holes.

Unrequited love is rain wasted in a thick forest.

The flour that is not in your mother's basket is no better than ash.

He who hesitates, spears the tail.

He who is used to killing won't hesitate to bury the living.

He who has never lost a relation will weep for a dog.

It takes really bad luck to abort a hen.

When the bush-pig trampled the cotton plot it said, 'What do I care? It's a rich man's property.'

Hide the stick that has already been used to beat the wife with whom you share your husband.

'When Rwakuburya was asked why he urinated upwards, he replied, 'I learned the trick from a dog.'

V. Katunzi (Kigezi)

PART IV

ANNOTATED BOOK LIST

ANNOTATED BOOK LIST

Bell, Sir Hesketh: *Glimpses of a Governor's Life* (London 1946).
Sir Hesketh Bell, Governor of Uganda 1906–9, arrived in
Entebbe having travelled much of the way from Mombasa on
the 'cow catcher' of a railway engine—'a glorified form of
motoring,' he says.

He had to tackle immediately the frightful scourge of sleeping
sickness which over the past few years was roughly estimated to
have killed more than 200,000 of the 300,000 inhabitants of
Uganda's Victoria lake shore and islands. Describing the
pitiful state of sleeping sickness victims he saw lying about in
bark-cloth rags and on beds of withered leaves, at the White
Fathers' Mission hospital at Kisubi, he says: 'only their doleful
moanings indicated the presence of life . . . a few had gone
raving mad.' Sleeping sickness, he was told, brought on a
craving for meat, so he gave the patients a bullock.

Sir Hesketh Bell rightly decided that the best way of dealing
with the disease was to evacuate everyone from the infected
lake shore and islands. His plan was successfully put into opera-
tion. By 1912 deaths were down to less than one thousand,
and a few years later people were allowed to return home.

The Governor shared the common belief that sleeping
sickness had been introduced to Uganda by Stanley's Congo
expedition (1889). Professor Langlands, however, holds that it
was more probably brought into south Uganda by the remnants
of Emin Pasha's Equatorial troops who were transferred from
Kavalli's, west of Lake Albert, to Toro and Buganda in 1892–
93 (B. W. Langlands, 'Sleeping Sickness in Uganda, 1900–20,'
Occasional Paper No. 1, Dept. of Geography, Makerere Univ.
Coll., 1967).

Langlands estimates that between 250,000 and 300,000
people died of the disease between 1900 and 1920, i.e. one-third
of the inhabitants of the infected zones—mainly the lake shore
of Buganda and Busoga. The effects of the evacuation regulations are still apparent today in numerous deserted lakeside
areas and islands.

During his three-and-a-half years of office (1906–9) Sir Hesketh Bell seems to have shown initiative, foresight and sympathy. He developed cotton and tobacco, initiated the construction of Port Bell and of a branch railway from Jinja to Lake Kioga, built Government House, Entebbe (the golf course was laid out with the help of Sikh soldiers), and imported the first motor car seen in Uganda.

It did not take him long to decide that his policy was going to be 'Uganda for the Africans', or as he put it, 'for the Baganda'.

'I will do all I can', he noted, 'to prevent the introduction of white settlers on any considerable scale. . . . Uganda, unlike British East Africa, is emphatically a black man's country.'

He entertained Churchill on his 1907 visit, and found him 'a difficult fellow to handle, but I can't help liking him'. He relates that at a spectacular and formal welcome staged outside Kampala by the young Kabaka, the Regents and chiefs, Churchill made a nuisance of himself by 'dodging about all the time with his camera'.

Some of his comments on people sound today ingenuous. He refers, of course, to Africans throughout as 'natives'; and to their hair as 'crinkled wool'. His first sight of the Masai with their 'ragged ears and bodies smeared with sheep's fat' appalled him. He was surprised (but not offended) when homely Acholi wives preferred a gift of small white beads to his splendid Brummagem jewellry.

Of the king of Ankole's fat wife he says 'she looked like a great chocolate mound that was going soft and was overflowing in all directions. A huge bag of milk was suspended from what was once her neck.' He begged her not to make the painful effort of rising.

The Baganda he describes as 'surely the most polite people in the world': the Bagisu as 'inveterate cannibals' who ate corpses but were a remarkably bold and healthy race.

The terrible spread of syphilis among the Baganda he associated with the coming of the Indians who built the Mombasa coast railway (an offended reader of the Makerere College copy of the book has written across this passage 'Rubbish! The Baganda have always been notorious syphilis carriers').

He quotes, too, a missionary who was honest enough to admit to an R.A.M.C. inspector that in his opinion the spread of syphilis was largely the fault of Christianity, which by obliging converts to get rid of all their wives but one, had turned the discarded ones into prostitutes.

Sir Hesketh Bell left Kampala to be Governor of Northern Nigeria.

Bradley, Sir Kenneth: *The Diary of a District Officer* (London, 1966);
Brook, Ian: *The One-Eyed Man is King* (London, 1966);
Nicol, Davidson: *Africa—A Subjective View* (London, 1964).

Bradley wrote his diary in 1938 when he was D.C. at Fort Jameson, in what is now Zambia but was then the British Protectorate of Northern Rhodesia. It is an endearing record of an attitude and an era which it has become fashionable to revile. A good deal of the diary was jotted down in camp, by lantern light. It is filled with affectionate descriptions of villagers and landscape.

The Colonial Service in those days appealed to a varied bunch of Englishmen, often to the sound type of graduate who looked forward to opportunities for sport, adventure, and, when the last sundowner was over, to a pension. 'The day of the expert', wrote Bradley in a later book (*Once a District Officer*, 1966), 'had not dawned . . . a service of amateur humanists was admirably suited to the administration of unsophisticated peoples.' 'None of us', he admits in the preface to the fourth edition of his diary (1966), 'dreamed that self-government would come so quickly. . . . In so far as we D.C.s thought about ultimate independence at all, we did so in terms of two or three generations, and we were content to use the newly introduced system of Indirect Rule.'

The author did not aim at miracles. But he had, he says, 'an unbridled passion for making people dig latrines.' Digging family latrines, he explains, was the answer to African nomadism—the constant shifting of a village as soon as it became insanitary. Once a village was settled, it soon learned to provide itself with amenities and to use crop rotation.

'In the end', he says at the end of his diary, 'I shall perhaps console myself with the small concrete achievements (the new court house, dispensary, and school), and they, what with the white ants and the Axis, do not seem to have any great significance ... but it is going on all over Africa. And it's worth doing.'

Those were the quiet backwaters of Africa before the new politics, the world of David Caute, took over. People today may say that Bradley and his like did not have the wit to foresee it all; that they were preoccupied with small bumbling achievements. But the official who rids a district of deadly mosquitoes, who builds a dam or a bore-hole, is remembered in the villages for a long time. Who would deny him 'the proud proprietorial smile'?

A different sort of memoir, that breaks with the old tradition of benevolent attitudes and self-imposed discretion, is *The One-Eyed Man is King* whose author ended up as a Senior District Officer in post-war Nigeria. Brook is frank about booze, sex ('the pubic mound seems to be less prominent in African women than in Europeans, the cuneal division more concealed'), and irreverent towards government ('... our eternal nagging auntiness. We were always at Africans to blow their noses, use Fly Tox, send their children to school and construct latrines—we bored them'). At the end, 'the British Empire', he writes, 'collapsed like a wet fart.'

Davidson Nicol, Principal of Fourah Bay College, the University College of Sierra Leone, has given an African's opinion of the old British Colonial Service (*Africa—A Subjective View*): 'On the positive side it paid more attention to the African masses than the African élite would have done. Although paternalistic, it brought more law, order and progress to the hinterland than we would have done or been able to do at the time. The British of the older type had more in common with illiterate Africans than with educated ones. ... On the negative side, the Colonial Service was riddled from top to bottom with racial discrimination, and it regarded the educated African more as a challenge to its authority than as an ally. A great opportunity was lost to train the latter for leadership and they were put in a position where they were either hostile or servile.'

Burton, Sir Richard: *The Lake Regions of Central Africa* (London, 1860).

'Travellers,' wrote Burton, 'like poets, are mostly an angry race.' The account of his journey with Speke in search of the Nile source is a mass of observation and comment, dogmatic and curiously learned, often querulous. In discussing at length the character of the East African peoples, Burton starts with an unexpected assertion. The African in these regions, he says, 'is superior in comforts, better dressed, fed, and lodged, and less worked than the unhappy ryot of British India. His condition, where the slave trade is slack, may indeed be compared advantageously with that of the peasantry in some of the richest of European countries.'

The native's days and nights, he goes on to say, are torpid, sensual, and idle. Food is his constant thought and dream, with drinking bouts, quarrelling and an occasional hunt to relieve the tedium. 'He drinks till he can no longer stand, lies down to sleep, and awakes to drink again.' His main characteristic is selfishness. 'He looks upon a benefit as the weakness of his benefactor. . . . In these temperate and abundant lands Nature has cursed mankind with the abundance of her gifts . . . he is contented, improvement has no hold upon him.'

'A stranger must be stared at. . . . We felt like baited bears,' says Burton in exasperation at one stage. 'The starers thrust forth their necks like hissing geese to vary the prospect.'

And again, 'Fond of music, his love of tune has invented nothing but whistling and the whistle. . . . His religion is a rude and sensual superstition. . . . Marriage is a mere affair of buying and selling.'

Burton shows not so much lack of sympathy for Africans as active dislike, treating them (says Moorehead) 'as delinquent children with marked criminal tendencies.' He speaks of their 'apparent incapacity for improvement.' He admits, nevertheless, that 'much of this moral degradation must be attributed to the working through centuries of the slave trade. . . . Robbed and spoiled by their oppressors, this wretched people,' he concludes, 'call themselves "The Meat," and the slave dealers "The Knife".'

At his worst Burton is a clever Victorian gentleman poking contemptuously among the nasty ant-hill life of 'debased and beer-sodden savages.' The Africans on whom he focused his sun-inflamed eyes had no one to express their own views of the eccentricities, the bad temper and ingratitude, the frequent helplessness and physical prostrations of the two explorers themselves.

Speke's more good natured and more pedestrian account of his subsequent journey to the Nile with Grant (*Journal of the Discovery of the Source of the Nile*, 1863) stresses too the curse of slavery, of wars, and of laziness. But he did not consider the native hopeless ('To say a negro in incapable of instruction,' he declares, 'is a mere absurdity'). What was needed, Speke thought, was a dose of the white man's government, 'like ours in India—they would be saved; but without it, I fear, there is very little chance.' Of the slave trade, he thought that if the white man did not put an end to it, 'it would wipe these grandchildren of Noah off the face of the earth.' Speke showed slyness and some humour and understanding in his relationship with Africans. He tried hard to communicate with them, if only out of boredom or to further his own ends. Among the Baganda especially he found much to admire.

On the personal aspect of the expedition to Lake Tanganyika Burton has much to say of illness. For long periods they were both blind; they had frequently to be carried in a hammock. On reaching the lake, Burton says, 'I lay for a fortnight upon the earth, too blind to read or write, too weak to ride, and too ill to converse. . . . My companion suffered from a painful ophthalmia, and from a curious distortion of face, which made him chew sideways, like a ruminant.' Burton's legs, as the result of malaria, were for a long time swollen and useless. When his mouth ulcerated he had to live on slops for seventeen days. Then on the return march, at Hanga, Speke fell seriously ill with the *Kichyoma-chyoma*, or 'Little Irons'. He began to utter a barking noise; and he was so alarmed that when the spasm passed he called for pen and paper and wrote an incoherent letter of farewell to his family.

As to the relationship between the two men, Speke already bore a grudge against Burton for his behaviour during an ambush at Berbera (1855). Speke, fancying that Burton had impugned his courage, had rushed forward alone into a mob of Somalis and been wounded eleven times. 'A touching lesson,' remarked Burton later, 'how difficult it is to kill a man in sound health!'

Burton ridiculed (apparently with good reason) Speke's first impulsive claim to have found (after a bare glimpse of the Nyanza Lake) the true source of the Nile. They agreed not to quarrel over the matter or to mention it further. But by the time they turned back for home, they had had enough of one another. They parted at Aden. Before Speke went on ahead to England he promised Burton he would say nothing about the expedition till Burton returned. Speke broke his word, announced his 'discovery', and soon went back to Africa to confirm it. Oddly, when he stood at last at Ripon Falls, his new companion Captain Grant was not with him. By agreement with Speke he was many miles away, marching downstream to the north!

Cook, Sir Albert R.: *Uganda Memories* (Kampala: The Uganda Society, 1945).

Dr Cook arrived in Kampala with a party of c.m.s. missionaries in 1897. The walk from Mombasa (850 miles) took them three months. He died in 1951, at the age of eighty-one, at his home in Makindye (Kampala) after fifty-four years of service as a medical missionary in Uganda. He seems to have been one of the finest men ever to have come to East Africa.

Dr Cook's memoirs record the development of modern Uganda from a country where, when he first saw it, European dress was unknown, white men travelled by bicycle or rickshaw and often died of blackwater fever, sleeping sickness and syphilis were rampant, cowries were used as currency, there were only five Indians in Jinja, and in the whole of Uganda only three Africans who spoke English.

There was, in those early days, serious ignorance of tropical diseases. Here is Dr Cook's summary of the situation: 'The mosquito theory of malaria had not been promulgated, though Ross had started on his researches in India which only a couple of years later were to clear up this long-concealed mystery. Mosquito nets at night were used merely to avoid the annoyance of bites. The London School of Medicine for Tropical Diseases did not start till some years later, and Manson's standard textbooks on Tropical Diseases had not yet been written. Much knowledge, now the ABC of the subject, had to be laboriously learnt by us in actual experience. The origin of one of the serious forms of anaemia (anklyostomiasis) so prevalent in women in Uganda, was not discovered until, when conducting a post-mortem on a fatal case, I found the hook-worm in the bowels. Though seeing spirilla in fever cases, we confused them with flagellated malarial parasites, and only identified them as the cause of tick fever in 1903. The different forms of dysentery—amoebic and bacillary—were only clearly distinguished in 1898–1900.'

'Most of the medical ailments are met with,' he concluded after many years in Uganda 'together with a rich and varied assortment of tropical diseases not met with in temperate climates. There are some curious exceptions; though smallpox, measles, whooping cough and chicken pox are common, scarlet fever has never been noted and diphtheria only a few times. Cholera and yellow fever have fortunately not appeared. . . . Rickets is unknown among the children, perhaps owing to their full exposure to sunlight from an early age and the universal habit of breast-feeding for eighteen months or longer. Appendicitis is astonishingly rare in natives. . . . Cancer and sarcoma though both met with are far more uncommon than in England, while tuberculosis of the lungs, though a little more common, falls into the same category. . . .'

Dr Cook and his wife were tireless travellers. Here is a typical extract from his diary: 'February 20th, 1909. Soroti. Nine miles over roads which were really capital for cycling brought us to this densely populated district. The Teso turned up in large force for medicine, and I saw nearly 400 cases in the two days. . . . There were over forty lepers, with fingers and toes dropping off, some blind, alas! . . . Many had huge ulcers, with lumps of cow dung clapped on by way of medicine. There were babies with malarial spleens. Enormous hydroceles, which in many cases reached the size of a child's head, or even bigger, were common. On Saturday we operated on thirty-one of these, on Sunday afternoon on forty-seven. . . . Wherever we go with our operating case and loads of medicine we find these crowds of needy ones, hungry for help, and crying out in that universal language of mankind for sympathy and healing.'

The Bagisu on Elgon, he noted during a journey in 1914, 'were still cannibals—though the practice was rapidly dying out'.

Of sleeping sickness, which ravaged the country during the first decade of the present century, he says 'This dreadful epidemic wrung the withers of all those at that time in Uganda. The mortality was frightful.' 'On one occasion', he writes, 'I was passing through Jinja. The government was desirous of ascertaining the mortality of sleeping sickness throughout the affected areas. In Busoga at that time the teaching or art of arithmetic had not gone very far, so the chiefs were bidden to bring in to the District Commissioner a twig for the death of every one known to have succumbed to this disease in his district. We met a train of men carrying in bundles of twigs in this manner. The first day the twigs totalled eleven thousand and the sad little procession continued for several days longer. . . . I was asked to preach at a Sunday service in the sleeping sickness camp at Buvu. It was a moving sight for any preacher. There were four hundred and fifty in the congregation, all doomed to die, for at that time no certain remedy had been discovered.'

Of syphilis he wrote in 1920: 'For more than twenty years careful records have been kept at Mengo hospital. These show that two out of every three Baganda mothers have had syphilis at one time or another, i.e. 66 per cent of the female population. (In England, in our seaport towns, the rate is 10 per cent for men and 5 per cent for women.) The ante-natal mortality, that is, the number of miscarriages or dead premature births, is 67 per cent in pregnant women suffering from syphilis.' (See note on page 273.)

Dr Cook was actively engaged in the fighting during the mutiny of Sudanese soldiers in 1897. He dressed Jackson's lung wound at Luba's Fort, where Thruston, Wilson and Scott were taken hostage and murdered, and Fielding, Pilkington and Macdonald were killed, during operations to relieve the fort.

The first white baby to be born in Buganda (Richard Leakey) was born in his house on Namirembe (1901). Twenty-five years later the recent Kabaka, Mutesa II, was born in Dr Cook's home. 'A fine healthy infant,' he says, who was baptised in the Anglican cathedral with 'a truly royal profusion of names—Edward Frederick William David Walugembe Mutebi Lwangula Mutesa II.'

Dr Cook married an English nurse, Miss Katherine Timpson, who had originally accompanied him on the walk from Mombasa in 1897. She helped him for many years in his medical work. When he died, in 1951, there was a great funeral congregation of Baganda, and his grave was lined with royal bark-cloth—a unique honour for a white man.

Dawson, E. C.: *James Hannington* (London, 1887).

Hannington was appointed Bishop of Eastern Equatorial Africa in 1884. In June 1885 he set off for Uganda from Mombasa. He took the northern route (recently followed by Joseph Thomson as far as Busoga) in preference to the normal southern route, arguing that the former was healthier and more direct. He also hoped to open up the countries of the Masai and Wakavirondo to the Gospel.

Hannington's choice of route, though, was wrong-headed and fatally mistaken. According to Mackay the Baganda had a long-standing fear that the approach of white men from the east through Uganda's 'back door' would lead to conquest. Further, they had been alarmed by recent news of German annexations at the coast.

Hannington had expected that his chief threat would be from the Masai. But beyond demanding excessive gifts of cloth, beads and iron wire, pilfering, and smearing his goods with the red earth and oil with which they daubed their bodies, the Masai (described by Hannington's biographer as 'like a troop of lithe and beautiful, but half-tamed leopards') made no trouble. They stroked the bishop's beard and said, '*Lumuru Kito* (a very great old man!).'

On October 12th the bishop ('sunburnt, shaggy, but glowing with health') left his main body of porters at Mumia's (Kwa Sundu) and went forward with fifty men into Busoga. The Kabaka meanwhile had sent orders for him to be stopped. He arrived at Lubwa's in Busoga on October 21st; and there, on a hill which he had climbed to view the Nile, he was suddenly seized and dragged struggling violently into a dirty hut where he was put under guard.

There he lay, in pain and fever, for several days, knowing that his life was in peril—'Fearfully shaken,' he wrote in his diary, 'scarce power to hold up small Bible. Shall I live through it?' The chief brought his wives to stare at him 'in cruel curiosity'.

On October 29th the bishop noted in his minute writing, 'A hyena howled near me last night, smelling a sick man, but I hope it is not to have me yet.'

It was his last entry, for word had come from the Kabaka to kill him. He was taken to a place outside the village, stripped of his clothes and, with most of his porters, speared to death. Before the death stroke he is said to have drawn himself up and bade the killers tell the King that he was about to die for the Baganda and that he had purchased the road to Buganda with his life.

Jackson relates how at Mumia's in 1890 he recovered Bishop Hannington's remains. A small boy who said he had been the bishop's guide gave them to him wrapped in banana leaves. The parcel contained the bishop's skull without the lower jaw, his boot-soles, a hot-water bottle, and a basin-lid. Jackson had the remains buried secretly in a tin box inside his camp. Bishop Tucker later recovered and reinterred them outside the Anglican church on Namirembe hill, Kampala. Mwanga himself, to show public repentance, attended the burial service.

Canon Roscoe met Chief Lubwa about seven years after the bishop's death, and made a friend of him. He says that Lubwa was no ruffianly murderer; he simply did his duty to his king. 'It was not such a shocking deed for him and his people to kill an intruder like Hannington: indeed he felt he was rendering his country a service'. (*Twenty-Five Years in East Africa*, 1921.)

Faupel, J. F.: *African Holocaust* (London, 1965);
Roscoe, J.: *Twenty-Five Years in East Africa* (London, 1921).

Mackay wrote as a Protestant with a strong dislike of 'Romish priests'. The writings of the priests are likewise partisan. Thus Father Faupel portrays Mackay as a prickly, bigoted Calvinist —though courageous and of upright character. He pays his tribute to the Protestant martyrs of 1886 but considers them outsiders. ('The Catholic Church has no mandate to judge and bestow honours upon those who have not died doing battle within her own ranks.')

Father Faupel seems too passionately concerned with totting up the number of Catholic as distinct from Protestant victims of Mwanga. After extensive research he finds that thirteen Catholics and thirteen Protestants were put to death in the holocaust of Namugongo hill—a tie. Of the total number that died in the persecution he says that the names of twenty-two Catholics are known for certain and those of twenty-three Protestants with considerable probability—the latter win by a neck. He records in great detail the manner in which the victims were put to death—by castration, dismemberment (using hatchets, clubs, and razor-sharp slivers of cane), and fire. The exact manner of death qualifies the degree of martyrdom.

Father Lourdel he describes as 'a man of powerful frame and iron will determined to do great things for Christ'. In reference to Bishop Tucker's assertion that the White Fathers had the deliberate purpose of sabotaging the Protestant effort, he argues that the Catholic Mission to Buganda was the continuation of a long-standing enterprise for evangelising Central Africa, and that had it not been for Stanley's appeal, 'Catholic missionaries would almost certainly have been in Buganda well in advance of any Protestant body.'

Father Faupel stresses that a decisive factor in the story of the persecution was Mwanga's homosexuality (a habit not native to the Baganda, which the Arabs are alleged to have taught them). It was, says Father Faupel, the constant refusal of Mwanga's Christian pages 'to practise with him the works of Sodom' that finally provoked Mwanga to commit wholesale murder. Among the Christian converts, it was his pages who bore the brunt of his fury.

The modern sequel to these events is that on October 18th 1964 the twenty-two Catholic martyrs of Uganda were proclaimed saints by Pope Paul VI in St Peter's basilica, Rome.

Referring to the frequent practice of execution, Father Faupel says the Baganda had thirteen such sites. Many of the executions were large-scale ritual murders, others of ordinary criminals. Death by burning was held to be the least degrading form of capital punishment. Pages, women and others at the Kabaka's court were frequently killed for minor breaches of etiquette (sneezing, giggling, inadvertently touching the Kabaka's rug), which horrified early Western visitors.

Speke relates that nearly every day he saw two or three palace women being dragged through the grounds to execution, crying out '*Hai Mimanga!* O my lord! *Kbakka!* My king! *Hai N'yawo!* My mother!' and yet, 'There was not a soul', he says, 'who dared lift a hand to save any of them, though many might be heard privately commenting on their beauty.'

Speke's companion, Grant, who was housed next to a place of torture, agrees that 'the shrieks of poor people, night and day, were quite heart-rending.'

Canon Roscoe (*Twenty-Five Years in East Africa*) emphasises the religious significance of the mass executions in Buganda, which he prefers to call human sacrifices to deified kings or to gods. At the death of a king, a number of his office bearers and slaves were appointed to die in order to continue their duties to him in the ghost world. They did not, says Canon Roscoe, complain of their fate. (Mutesa, incidentally, when he died, left orders that there should be no ceremonial bloodshed.)

Other human sacrifices, writes Roscoe, were made by order of the priest of the temple of the war god to avert calamity. On such occasions the Kabaka would send his secret police (they wore a rope twisted round their heads like a turban) to ambush and capture the appointed victims. They too, claims Roscoe, went calmly to their death, believing they would pass over to the gods as followers and retainers.

Canon Roscoe ends with an odd comment. The practice of human sacrifice for religious purposes contributed, he believes,

to the national good, as victims were commonly chosen among
the mentally and physically unfit, 'leaving the clever and more
shrewd subjects to propagate the nation'.

Greene, Graham: *Journey Without Maps* (London, 1936); *A
Burnt-Out Case* (London, 1960); *In Search of a Character*
(London, 1961).

In his first, very early book about Africa (*Journey Without Maps*),
the account of a long foot-march he made with carriers through
Liberia, Graham Greene already shows his sensitivity to
squalor, discomfort, and the shortcomings of Europeans in the
tropics. He dwells on ordure, smells and rats: on yaws, dust,
illness. He is offended with the Europeans for their inertia,
their contempt for Africans, the seedy, squalid settlements they
had built ('Everything ugly in Freetown was European . . . if
there was anything beautiful in the place it was native'). He
often felt ill and sad. Even the forest through which day after
day he trudged or was carried in a hammock seemed to him
ugly and dead: 'No one had ever transferred to *this* forest any
human emotion at all . . . it had never been lived in.' It was the
moments of relief—a bath and a whisky—that he enjoyed. But
even when (after dosing himself heavily with Epsom) he went
out in the dark to relieve himself, he feared he might crouch
upon a snake.

   Graham Greene accepts that there were powerful reasons for
all the ugliness and suffering. He has also a number of sympathetic things to say of the Africans he met. 'Their laughter and
happiness', he writes, 'seemed the most courageous things in
nature . . . love existed here without the trappings of civilisation.' Among them he met with only 'gentleness, kindness, and
honesty'.

   The coast white, he knew, would sneer at such delusions.
'"You can have a boy for ten years," they'd say, "and he'll do
you at the end of it," and laying down their empty glasses they'd
go out into the glaring street and down to the store to see whom
they could "do" in the proper understood commercial way that
morning. "No affection," they'd say, "after fifteen years. Not
a scrap of real affection," expecting always to get from these

people more than what they had paid for. They had paid for service and they expected love thrown in.'

When Graham Greene returned to West Africa in a convoy in 1942, he wrote on sighting Freetown once more: 'It was like seeing a place you've dreamed of. Even the sweet hot smell from the land . . . was strangely familiar. It will always be to me the smell of Africa, and Africa will always be the Africa of the Victorian atlas, the blank unexplored continent in the shape of the human heart.'

Later, in *A Burnt-Out Case*, deliberately and legitimately for his purpose, he recreates a myth of Darkest Africa. There is scarcely a healthy African in it. Almost all are hideously maimed by leprosy. The crippled servant Deo Gratias raises a stump and howls. A catechist who had lost nose, fingers, and toes looks as though he had been 'lopped, scraped, and tidied by a knife'. The small boy has 'sad frog-like eyes'. His wasted body is 'like a cage over which a dark cloth has been flung at night to keep a bird asleep, and like a bird his breath moved under the cloth'. The child is going to die, but not in peace; for the mother is cutting his breast to put her native medicine in.

Of the forest in this sick, sweltering Congo he says, 'it had never been humanised like the woods of Europe . . . with cottages of marzipan.' The continuous clatter of insects reminded him of 'some monstrous factory where thousands of sewing machines were being driven against time.'

Heat, frustration, ennui. Graham Greene's Congo diary (*In Search of a Character*) shows how studiously he collected the raw material for his version of 'Darkest Africa' in *A Burnt-Out Case*; how he noted down the macabre details of crippled bodies ('the man with elephantiasis, testicles the size of a football . . . the woman without legs who has born a child'); how he looked for, and sometimes found, naive and facetious priests, or unpleasant types of *colon*.

So in the novel the Belgian missionaries who live, on the forest's edge, among the yaws and the copulating, leprous couples are wrong-headed, almost authentic simpletons. The local white people have 'high vexed colonial voices', and go in for malicious gossip. Rycker, who smells of stale margarine,

255

lies in bed with his young wife like an old sack. In his journal, Graham Greene had noted 'the stringy wet sweaty hair of white women'.

Earlier, the author recorded 'The laughter of the Africans: where in Europe does one hear so much laughter?' And then, inevitably, he adds, 'but the reverse is true: the deep sense of despair . . .'. He found some African women beautiful—'the most beautiful *backs* of any race' (my students cheered when they read this). But even they, he suspected, had a worm inside them. They were probably rotten with gonorrhoea.

So Africa, for the novelist, still has its sinister side. There are the tropical diseases: the buzz of the mosquito, the bilharzia parasite lurking in a pool. There are the vultures and wild animals, and the violence: the drunks lying across the gutter, the painted tarts of shanty town with mouths like wounds. On the other hand, much of Africa is becoming suburbanised and respectable: a happy hunting ground for the Peace Corps and for tourists from Denmark.

When Dr Jung was in camp on a spur of Mount Elgon he remarked primly (*Memories, Dreams, Reflections*, 1963), 'I enjoyed the "divine peace" of a still primeval country. . . . Thousands of miles lay between me and Europe, mother of all demons. . . . My liberated psychic-forces poured blissfully back to the primeval expanses.' But a little later he was told that a neighbouring village devoured its dead; and when the local people organised a dance for him, the dancers got so wild that Dr Jung grew afraid. He had to swear at them in Swiss-German that it was enough and they should go home to bed.

Hanley, Gerald: *Drinkers of Darkness* (London, 1955);
Hinde, Thomas: *A Place Like Home* (London, 1962);
Oyono, Ferdinand: *Houseboy* (London, 1960);
Mphahlele, Ezekiel: *In Corner B* (Nairobi, 1967);
Van der Post, Laurens: *Venture to the Interior* (London, 1952).

Thomas Hinde (*A Place Like Home*) gives the indoor type of European—Nairobi commercials, sanitary inspectors, bank people and their wives—such a hammering that, for all their unpleasantness, one begins to wish they had someone to speak up for them. 'Settlers for a year or two,' he calls them, 'with no place in the country and not much interest in it except as a faintly disagreeable curiosity they happened to land in.' They have escaped from one sort of suburbia, in England, to another of their own creation: cemented bungalows that stand in the moonlight like small grey boxes on the flat land of Nairobi; gossip and servant problems; fear of burglars and—for out here with their sundowners and servants these people are at least somebody—fear of losing their jobs.

Writing in *The Cage* of a social welfare gathering of prosperous commercial wives, he says of them 'We aren't thinking how to help the Africans, but how to make ourselves look as if we're helping them.' How absurd, anyway, that people should hope they would want 'the monotonous, painless life of Northern Europe'. Perhaps the whole thing was a great joke; and that what Africans really wanted was a 'corrupt, violent, unfair, but exciting and colourful country'.

Gerald Hanley, in *Drinkers of Darkness*, describes the pre-Uhuru, tough, outdoor sort—the adventurers, he calls them, the unmanageable, those with secrets to hide: the sort whose qualifications would read 'ex-officer, able to handle men'. Up-country in Kenya a group of them are using underpaid native labour to clear land. Out of the fug of alcohol and maudlin talk some crude ideas emerge.

There are the white man's ambivalent feelings towards blacks. Tamlin, the manager, half regrets the whipping he has just awarded an insolent labourer ('twenty on the arse'), 'for they forgave everything, these Africans, bringing the familiar pang of guilt to him as always when he had been hard to them, and sometimes he was afraid it would conquer him, but he was saved from this when he witnessed some scene of callousness among them, or saw them hacking an animal to death, as though it were wood.'

Africa meant nothing to these grumbling Europeans in the bush, 'it was only a place in which to earn. . . . So they fretted about the days to come when Africa became a man, not wanting them—fond of them when simple like children, but afraid of the days to come.' On sex, O'Riordan, who reads books, says,

'The presence of the white women denied the biological fact
that white men, to justify their presence and their message,
should take their wives from the dark ones. . . . The "colonial
problem" had been solved privately in bed from Lagos to
Singapore for a hundred years, but this was denied in the clubs
where white men could "get away from the black faces".' To
have a black woman, however, required a sort of guts, or at any
rate indifference to public opinion. Plume, though he often
thought he wanted an African woman, 'had not the courage for
intimacy with Africans, even the men made him nervous . . .
their mad dancing . . . their fierce animal joy.'

When the native labour goes on strike, Tamlin was anxious
to act, and 'like all white men in a time of African crisis, torn
between justice and clemency, and fury and injured pride, for
the whole thing rested on African acceptance of the white man's
superiority—in all things.'

'We're always afraid', says Major Mallows, 'that if we give
a wog something before he asks for it, and even when he asks,
we'll spoil him. . . .' 'That's true,' Tamlin said, 'give them a
shirt and they'd want a dress suit.'

The employer-servant relationship often crops up in writings
about Africa. It is a situation fruitful of misunderstandings.
The African servant knows our habits—but not our thoughts
—too well. We know too little of him, of his shadowy, elusive
background.

There are those hopeless interrogations (the white man's
passion for truth). 'Give them a lie,' is one housegirl's advice to
another in Mphahlele's 'Mrs Plum' (*In Corner B*, 1967), 'and it
will do. For they seldom believe you whatever you say. And
how can a black person work for white people and be afraid
to tell them lies? They are always asking the questions, you
are always the one to give the answers.'

Doris Lessing ('A Home for the Highland Cattle', *African
Stories*, 1964) mocks at the servant dilemma in a vulgar white
suburb in Rhodesia. A newly arrived English woman had
scruples, at first, about employing servants. ('There was something absurd in a system which allowed a healthy young man

to spend his life in her kitchen, so that she might do nothing. Besides, it was more trouble than it was worth'); and the servants' quarters with their rows of dirty dustbins and the unmarried pregnancies horrified her. When she gives her houseboy a ration of vegetables, her white neighbours complain. All the servants in the building were now demanding vegetables. 'They aren't used to it. Their stomachs aren't like ours. They don't need vegetables. You're just putting ideas into their heads.'

Inevitably she spoils her houseboy with kindness. He steals her property, and lands up in gaol.

Mphahlele goes to the limit in 'Mrs Plum'. He has a scene in Johannesburg where an African house girl peeping into her white mistress's bedroom sees her being mounted by a pet dog. Her mistress is a good woman who in a woolly, liberal way 'loves Africans'; but not quite enough to stop her from quibbling over the servants' miserable wages and holidays. She loves her dogs more. 'Dogs with names,' says the house girl, 'men without. . . .'

Ferdinand Oyono (*Houseboy*) gives the African servants' view of Frenchmen in the Cameroons. Their eyes miss nothing. They know that the Commandant—'his legs have great muscles like the legs of a pedlar'—is uncircumcised ('A great chief like the Commandant uncircumcised', the houseboy Toumin tells himself on discovering this fact. 'I knew I should never be frightened of the Commandant again').

Toumin's knowledge of his white employers' private lives is his undoing. Once he has seen the used contraceptives of his mistress's adultery ('When Madame saw me turning the little bags over and over with the end of the broom she sprang on me and tried to push them back under the bed with her foot. . . . "Get out," she screamed, "Get out!"'') his days are numbered. The cook makes a joke of it ('These whites with their craze for putting clothes on everything, even their . . .'), but the joke turns sour. The police are told to eliminate Toumin, and he dies (stinking of putrefaction) of a lung wound caused by a rifle butt.

Oyono's Europeans are all vile, except Father Gilbert— 'he taught me to read and write,' says Toumin, 'nothing can be

9*   259

more precious than that, even if I have to go badly dressed.'
Father Gilbert's successor liked to make sinners undress in his
office and then beat them with a cane. 'The eyes that live in
the native location', says Toumin, 'strip the whites naked. The
whites, on the other hand, go about blind.' The cook survives
('I am the cook. The white man does not see me except with
his stomach'), but not the houseboy who, as a village child, had
wanted to get close to the white man with hair like the beard
on a maize cob.

Van der Post (*Venture to the Interior*) writing of the British in
East and Central Africa, says their towns were unworthy of the
country around them. Blantyre was small, ugly, commercial.
'The lawns impinged on borders which grew European flowers
of a sickly and outraged appearance.' Most of the Europeans
had 'set, sallow, lifeless, disillusioned faces. . . . I had the impression that they all longed for nightfall so that darkness and
drink would help them to imagine themselves to be somewhere
else.' Nairobi was 'completely without fantasy, emotion,
character, or colour of any kind'. Kenya Europeans struck him
as dominated by a useless nostalgia. They were eccentric,
agitated, angry, living apparently in a permanent state of
resentment against various facts and circumstances of their daily
lives. Van der Post wonders what effects living among Africans
has on the European. Perhaps, in the case of Kenyans, it partly
accounted for the violence of their emotions, their 'love of eating
and drinking, feasting and hunting, of collective excitement and
of the unorthodox in dress . . .'.

Negley Farson thought that Africa produces 'some of the
most unpleasant white men you will meet anywhere on earth',
Graham Greene spoke of 'the squalor and the unhappiness and
the involuntary injustices of tired men'. 'The less intelligent
the white man,' wrote André Gide (*Voyage au Congo*, 1927), 'the
more stupid he thinks the black.' Gide refers often to the
meanness of 'les blancs' and to their contempt for the native.
The white employer who calls his servant 'sale nègre' and
'triple idiot' will get the sort of servant he deserves. Of European
administration and attitudes, he says 'quel art diabolique,

quelle persévérance dans l'incompréhension, quelle politique de haïne et de mauvais vouloir il a fallu pour obtenir de quoi justifier les brutalités, les exactions et les sévices'.

Writing of European children, Van der Post refers to the 'little white master of everything except himself' (a Rhodesian schoolboy), and Robert Collis (*A Doctor in Nigeria*, 1960) said 'African children in hospital made far less fuss than children in Europe. Maybe they have much more security in their subconscious than ours, all being breast fed for many months, sometimes years, and all carried on their mothers' backs till they are 2-3 years old ... maybe they have better nerves ... white children by comparison look insipid, horribly pale and sweaty. We usually find them spoilt and not very lovable.'

It would be easy, by deliberate selection, to extend indefinitely the indictment. White women with servants, and white men enjoying privileges, in tropical Africa, are a sitting duck for the writer. How do we account for a situation that can produce this sort of picture?

Profit and privilege based on cheap labour are bound to spoil Bwana. There is the unnatural social relationship between Europeans and the dark-faced people among whom they live— and the ambivalent feelings (of guilt, superiority, callousness) that spring from it. There are heat and glare, and the small daily frustrations that sour a man's temper ('the great thing is to slow yourself up and not get mad,' says Collis); the conflict of motives—is one in Africa to make money or to do a little good?

All this seems to produce people who are a little off balance, a caricature of their true European selves. It is the caricature that a writer dwells on. The white man's position in black Africa is in any case under fire. Writers have been after him for some time, and they are articulate.

Jabavu, Noni: *Drawn in Colour* (London, 1960).

Noni Jabavu, an educated Xhosa woman from South Africa, with an English husband, looked forward to finding much in common with the Baganda, to one of whom, a barrister, her sister was married in Kampala.

On acquaintance she found the Baganda so different that she could not accept them; and she began to get hysterically indignant over trifles. 'You interlacustrine savage,' she screams one day at a man who was wheeling his bicycle across her bed of seedlings. Her sister too had failed to adjust herself to her Buganda marriage. There was a divorce, and the two Xhosa women went back home.

Among the many small irritants that accumulated within her a sense of almost total frustration she instances: the closed wooden shutters of Baganda houses (they gave her a sore throat), and the 'tasteless' Indian-made furniture; the claustrophobic atmosphere within the banana gardens; women in gorgeous robes squatting next to decaying garbage heaps; the senseless protein deficiency of children's diet which gave many of them 'pinkish hair, rather wet noses and prominent stomachs'; the different body smell of the Baganda (though her sister pointed out that 'people smell basically because of what they eat'—in this case it was the green *matoke* plantain); their 'flat feet, reserved, unfriendly, unsmiling faces' (can this be really true?) and their blackness.

Mrs Jabavu disliked the use of men as house servants, instead of women, and the 'pomp and obsequiousness' that surrounded the Kabaka. She couldn't help looking down on people who 'tilled the soil, cultivators only fit', in the old Xhosa tradition, 'to be raided and pillaged by us'. (The cattle-owning Wahima class of neighbouring Ankole, on the other hand, naturally attracted her.) Above all she disapproved of Baganda morals—the attitude to marriage, for instance, which she says 'allowed a man to enjoy concubines (having the other ladies, as they put it'), the (to her) 'incestuous relationships and contempt for virginity'. She was horrified to learn that one reason why her sister did not appeal to her husband was that as a young girl her clitoris had not been manipulated to make it 'grow long and hang down—a special attraction'. 'Wear waist beads at night;' a Muganda woman advised her sister, 'the men like it.'

Mrs Jabavu seems to have looked at things with the cold and almost Puritanical eye of an English *mem-sahib*. Hygiene, diet, morals—these were the very things to attract that unfriendly Anglicised stare. But she does admit to having felt ashamed of her peevishness, her 'cerebrating'. 'What I was suffering from', she says, 'was not a sort of race prejudice, black though the Baganda were compared to my own people, but their disparate social observances and manners, the attitude to incest....' Towards the end she realised she was suffering from 'expatriate *malaise*.... But now that I had my dose it was probably more acute than in fellow outsiders for I had not originally thought myself a foreigner. My disillusionment was profound.'

One ought not to generalise from one family's personal failure to adjust itself to the life and manners of another people. Clearly, though, the inter-tribal differences in Africa are enormous. How much, for instance, within the confines of Uganda alone, has a Dodoth cattle owner in common with a Christian *shamba* farmer from Busoga?

Jackson, Sir Frederick: *Early Days in East Africa* (London, 1930).

As a young man Jackson had as a neighbour Rider Haggard. It was Haggard who suggested that Jackson ought to visit the novelist's brother, who was then Vice-Consul at Lamu—thus beginning an adventurous career in Africa which culminated in Jackson's appointment in 1911 as Governor of Uganda.

Jackson found the Lamu area in 1884–5 still full of slaves, including wretched children 'dragging about the streets a great pole fastened by a ring to their necks'. The strange dugong, which sailors sometimes took to be a mermaid, was plentiful (Jackson says that when a fisherman caught a female 'he had to swear on the Koran before the market master that he had not had carnal intercourse with it').

Jackson subsequently made many foot expeditions to the interior. As the B.I.E.A. Company's agent he walked from Mombasa to Kampala—he turned aside on the way to climb Elgon; Jackson's Summit is named after him; the tree groundsel reminded him of a 'Jersey walking-stick cabbage'.

Naivasha in those days was Masai country (the Rift valley was commonly referred to as Masailand), and more flies were to be found there, says Jackson, 'than there ever were in any other part of the world'. He describes the Kedong massacre of 1895 when, in retaliation for their having molested some of their girls in a *manyatta*, Masai slaughtered 98 Swahilis and 456 Kikuyu of a passing caravan.

Porters in those days carried loads of up to 75 lb., in addition to their personal belongings, for hundreds of miles (the regulation load was later fixed at 65 lb.). It was the building of the Uganda railway from Mombasa that reduced the need for portering—which was in any case getting too costly for commercial enterprise. Jackson was one of the first Englishmen to criticise the type of Indian immigrant. The Indian coolie railway camps, he says, were 'crowded with prostitutes, small boys, and other accessories to the bestial vices so commonly practised by Orientals'. The many time-expired coolies who took to roaming about as petty traders he describes as 'low-class pioneer parasites'.

When he revisited Lamu in 1903 he found the area already semi-deserted and reverting to bush—the combined result of the local abolition of slavery (1896) and of the attractions of employment on the Uganda railway. The mosquitoes were still a pest ('a single brush from shoulder to wrist would leave the arm wet and shining with blood').

Jackson was well known as naturalist and sportsman. Rider Haggard used some of his experiences in *Allan Quatermain* and other romances of Africa. Jackson's hartebeest is named after him.

Lebon, J. H. G.: *An Introduction to Human Geography* (London, 1966);
Chaudhuri, Nirad C.: *Autobiography of an Unknown Indian* (London, 1951).

Lebon restates the fact that 'among negroes, the pigment, a substance called melanin, which is found in minute granules at the base of the epidermis, is especially abundant. . . . Experiments have proved its efficacy in protecting deeper and more vulnerable tissues [against strong sunlight]. . . . Ancient beliefs that heat and sunshine produce black skins are thus largely confirmed by modern science.'

264

Julian Huxley, during his visit to East Africa (1929), was struck by the rightness and the beauty of black skin in its natural setting, and by the pallor of white men. 'Why', he asked himself in *Africa View*, 'does a good physique look better when the skin over the muscles is black than when it is white?' There are many Europeans, of course, who feel that their natural skin colour, in the bright light and the outdoor life of East Africa, is unattractive. Doris Lessing (*Going Home*) has written sneeringly of Europeans sunbathing in Rhodesia— 'carefully accumulating pigment under their precious white skins'. Among Africans a white skin may be associated with leprosy, an albino, or succulent meat. Achebe has this passage (*Things Fall Apart*):

'The world is large,' said Okwonko, 'I have even heard that in some tribes a man's children belong to his wife and her family.'

'That cannot be,' said Machi. 'You might as well say that the woman lies on top of the man when they are making the children.'

'It is like the story of the white men who, they say, are white like this piece of chalk,' said Obierika . . . 'And those white men, they say, have no toes.'

'And have you never seen them?' asked Machi.

'Have you?' asked Obierika.

'One of them passes here frequently,' said Machi. 'His name is Amadi.'

Those who knew Amadi laughed. He was a leper, and the polite name for leprosy was "the white skin".'

Doris Lessing has said of colour prejudice that it is simply an 'atrophy of the imagination which prevents us from seeing ourselves in every different creature that breathes under the sun', and again, 'Colour feeling is basically money feeling. . . . Could it be that many people who imagine they have colour prejudice are merely suffering from fear of the Joneses?' No doubt many will have observed in Kampala that small white children who go to racially mixed schools and have Indian and African playmates do not appear to be colour conscious, and are certainly not upset by the difference. It is not until later that they pick up prejudices from older children or from parents (which is why they ought to be taught early at home to treat African servants with kindness and respect).

To the eighth Army soldier who landed in Italy from Africa, the 'wog' line (which for him had commenced in Baghdad, or Cairo, or Alexandria) continued to stretch as far as the Po. 'Wogs' had been Arabs and Egyptians. They were now the defeated Italians, associated with cowardice, venereal disease, and messy food. Yet once the fighting was over hundreds of Allied soldiers took Italian wives, many of them from the squalid neighbourhood of their base camps in the Naples area. Italian males remained 'wogs', but not Italian girls!

Nirad Chaudhuri points out (*The Autobiography of an Unknown Indian*) that 'colour prejudice is the common—and should I also say?—the original sin of all the peoples of European origin. The Hindus only systematised and practised it *first*, as the *first* people of European origins confronted with the threat to a fair complexion from the dark.' 'The life of a dark marriageable girl in Bengal', he goes on, 'used to be one of unending private and public humiliation. . . . The mother-in-law would give a scream if the bride on her arrival was found to be dark.'

Alas, remarks Naipaul on all this, climate has played a cruel joke on Hindus. 'The first white people to come into contact with a black race, and the first and most persistent practitioners of apartheid, they have themselves, over the centuries, under a punishing sun, grown dark.'

Lytton, the Earl of: *The Desert and the Green* (London, 1957).

The Earl of Lytton, as a twenty-three-year old officer with the King's African Rifles, was sent in 1923 to an up-country post in the Samburu country near Lake Rudolf.

Unlike Sir Kenneth Bradley he did not make villages dig latrines, or build schools. His job was to uphold the King's Peace with a platoon of askaris, and to order, if he thought it necessary, ten strokes of the *kiboko* (a damp cloth was first placed over the buttocks). Some tribes, he says, disliked the *kiboko* more than others. The Turkana 'did not even twist a toe'.

Lytton's book contains some healthy protest against official-dom, the wrong sort of white settler, the deceptions that underlay land alienation, and the folly, in some instances, of preserving game at the expense of the food supply—and the safety—of local people.

Before he left for his first up-country post, his c.o. gave him some memorable parting advice:

'You must take care of your comfort; those who live hard on the frontier die young. I am not pleased with what I hear of Lodwar, where they seem to ignore all human comforts. Take with you at least one case of champagne for occasions when someone visits you, and you can have two tots of whisky a night; I do not recommend more as a general rule, but you certainly must not do with less—it is something to look forward to in the evenings. When on safari take a comfortable tent, and do not be satisfied with huddling under a wait-a-bit thorn. Get the best cook you can find, and take a canvas bath; do not camp in places where you cannot get a bath. Some officers like dressing for their supper when they are at headquarters; I leave that to you, but do not walk about in a loin-cloth like a native!'

'The first principle of your administration', the c.o. concluded, 'is the King's Peace. . . . Thou shalt not kill! I expect you have heard it said that coming to Africa affords an opportunity for active service and that every regular soldier should go to the scene of active operations whenever he can. These notions are as they may be, but out here it is the officials who are warlike and the soldiers who prevent wars. Foolish officials go and get murdered and then their colleagues demand a punitive expedition to avenge them; officials get murdered because they do not know what the natives are thinking about, and the remedy is to know the native. You need not become a blood brother of the Samburu, but you must know them. Do not stick in your headquarters all the time doing your office work; get out on safari in the district and see people!'

Mackay of Uganda, by his sister (London, 1893).

The first c.m.s. missionaries reached Uganda in 1877. Mackay followed in 1878, a few months ahead of the French White Fathers trained at Algiers and sent by the Notre Dame d'Afrique society with, complained Bishop Tucker, 'the one fell purpose of opposing Protestantism rather than heathenism'.

There were now, together with the Muslim Arabs, three rival claimants to Kabaka Mutesa's soul. Mackay describes the frequent disputes they had in the presence of Mutesa, his chiefs and courtiers. At their first public clash Father Lourdel called him a liar. Mutesa and his chiefs were bewildered. 'Every white man', they said, 'has a different religion.' The Muslims for their part mocked at the assertion of Christ's divinity and at Christian 'picture worship'.

Mackay seems to have more than held his own. He could argue logically, and he was practical and industrious. He printed alphabets, reading sheets and vernacular versions of the Scriptures, taught classes of 'readers' whom he prepared for baptism, built and operated a smithy where he made and repaired articles in exchange for food (plantains and goats).

But his earlier hopes of turning Mutesa into a sincere Christian were shaken when the Kabaka insisted on receiving the head witch-doctor with much ceremony at court. There was a quarrel and the *katikiro* told Mackay bluntly that what they really wanted was not men to teach religion but how to make guns and powder—'guns innumerable as grass.'

Mackay's journal goes on now to indict Mutesa for his 'inhuman cruelty' of which, Mackay says, he had been ignorant at first. Murder at caprice as well as human sacrifice was practised. On the occasion of a *kiwendo*, or mass butchery, relates Mackay, Mutesa's executioners had orders to seize and execute anyone passing along the highway or the paths approaching the capital. Victims were knocked on the head. For other crimes noses and lips were cut out. Mutesa, concludes Mackay, was a 'murderous maniac . . . a heathen out and out'.

The next entry in Mackay's journal gives a cheerful account of the report which Saabadu, one of Mutesa's envoys to England, gave of his journey.

'England', Saabadu told Mutesa, 'is a very great country . . . oh my master, we have not got a country at all. The state of one chief in England is as large as all Uganda and Bunyoro and Busoga together. . . .'

'Do you hear that,' Mutesa said to the chiefs, 'we have no country at all.'

Mutesa, however, had the last laugh. He rewarded Saabadu

with some cattle, bark cloth, and two wives. The *katikiro* gave him another two women. This, says Mackay, was Mutesa's way of telling the man, 'Yes, you have seen wonderful things in England, but you did not get a lot of wives in England, as you get here. You will enjoy yourself better here than in England.'

Mutesa died in 1884 and was replaced by his son Mwanga. During Mutesa's lifetime the missionaries were at least safe from violence, frequently in favour, and allowed to get on with their work. One of Mwanga's first actions was to order the murder of Bishop Hannington who was on his way from the coast.

Mwanga then began to persecute and burn native Christians. After the holocaust of 1886 the mission temporarily broke up. Mackay was ordered to leave and took refuge at Usambiro on the south-western shore of Lake Victoria. Just before he died, after a short illness, of blackwater fever (1890), Mackay was visited by Stanley, who describes him as 'a gentleman of small stature, with a rich brown beard and brown hair . . . and a grey Tyrolese hat'.

'And so you are Mr Mackay? Mwanga did not get you then, this time? What experiences you must have had with that man! But you look so well, one would say you had been to England lately.'

'Oh, no; this is my twelfth year. . . .' (It was, in fact, his fourteenth.)

Patterson, Lt.-Col. J. H.: *The Man-Eaters of Tsavo* (London, 1907).

Colonel Patterson was sent from England in 1898 to take charge of constructing the Uganda railway which had by then reached Tsavo, about 132 miles from Mombasa.

Shortly afterwards two man-eating lions came to the neighbourhood and for nine months so terrorised the Indian coolie camps that at length all railway work was brought to a standstill for about three weeks. The lions used to snatch their victims from a tent and (like huge cats with mice in their mouths) drag them out through the thorn fences. It was frightful, says the author, to hear the huge beasts growling and purring and crunching up the bones in the night. The Indian coolies imagined that *Saitan* (the Devil) was tormenting them.

Colonel Patterson at last shot one man-eater from a rickety shelter erected in the bush, the other, which he had already hit from a hide-out, on the ground. Their fame had spread. The Prime Minister Lord Salisbury referred to them in the House of Lords as having 'conceived a most unfortunate taste for our porters'. The two lions had eaten twenty-eight Indian coolies in addition to 'scores of unfortunate African natives of whom no official record was kept'.

The author tells of a third man-eating lion which later gave trouble at Kimaa station 250 miles from Mombasa, 'a most daring brute, quite indifferent as to whether he carried off a station master, the signalman, or the pointsman'.

It was from Kimaa that a terrified Indian railway clerk sent his famous telegram to the Traffic Manager, 'Lion fighting with station. Send urgent succour.' And it was here that the lion dragged Mr Ryall, Superintendent of the Police, through a railway carriage window and ate him a quarter of a mile away.

The construction of the Uganda railway employed 20,000 Indian coolies and attracted a large number of merchants and contractors. It marked the beginning of a large-scale Indian migration to the interior of East Africa and across the Congo border. The railway continues to convey a large number of Indian passengers. The journey by road to the coast, though it now runs for most of the way over tarmac, is still exhausting.

Portal, Sir Gerald: *The British Mission to Uganda in 1893* (London, 1894).

Britain's connection with Uganda, recently and tenuously established by the B.I.E.A. Company through its representative Lugard, who had persuaded Mwanga to accept the Company's protection for two years, was in the balance when the British government sent Portal there in 1893 to advise on the country's future.

A fortnight after arriving at Kampala fort, Portal raised the

British flag and thus ended the Company's responsibilities. He then, on May 29, 1893, negotiated a treaty under which Mwanga accepted British protection, and soon after returned home. Britain made formal announcement of a Protectorate over Buganda on June 19, 1894.

Portal's account of his mission has interesting notes on the organisation and routine of an early foot caravan. His expedition left Zanzibar on January 1, 1893 and reached Kampala, exactly on schedule, on March 17, having done the 820-mile journey in seventy-five days. It was a large caravan—800 men including 9 European officers, 200 soldiers and 400 porters recruited in Zanzibar, 'slowly winding', says Portal, 'in single file along the narrow path like a brilliant and gigantic serpent'.

A porter carried a headload of 70 lb. or more deadweight. Each officer had ten porters to carry his gear and boxes of cocoa, jam, oatmeal and lime juice. The expedition started shakily as the porters were still suffering from their final debauch in Zanzibar. But Portal soon came to admire their strength and tenacity, and says of them, on reaching Kampala, 'These half-savage Zanzibaris had performed a feat which could certainly not be equalled by even a picked battalion of beef-fed, cloth-clad Englishmen, and which would probably prove to be beyond the powers of any race of people existing in the world except the despised, crushed, and enslaved East African.'

Earlier, Portal had been astonished to see ivory porters at Kikuyu Fort dance and sing with huge tusks (up to 140 lb.) on their shoulders—'the muscles standing out in great solid lumps, glistening in the sun.' Like other Englishmen, he was impressed by the bearing of the Masai he met at Naivasha—'a great curse', he says, 'to the whole of British East Africa . . . but of superior race, intellect, and physical development.'

Portal was heart-broken when his brother Raymond, whom he had sent on a mission to Toro, sickened there of malaria and staggered back to Kampala to die. Portal himself died of typhoid fever a few weeks after returning to England.

Speke, J. H.: *Journal of the Discovery of the Source of the Nile* (London, 1863).

Speke has a long account of his protracted stay at the Kabaka's court and of his efforts to get permission to march on through Buganda to the source of the Nile.

Kabaka Mutesa regarded Speke as a rich prize. He would thoroughly fleece him before letting him go. Speke had to win the Kabaka's respect, keep him in good humour, and bribe him with a nicely judged flow of presents.

The first confrontation between the two men was a test of dignity and of Speke's nerve. Speke angrily refused to await the Kabaka's pleasure sitting on the ground in the sun like any common Arab trader. He had come, he insisted, as a prince. So he sat on his iron stool and opened his umbrella.

The Kabaka simply stared at him. Not a word was exchanged until the Kabaka asked at length if Speke had seen him. 'Yes, for full one hour,' replied Speke.

The opening scene was over. A little later the Kabaka reappeared and Speke gave him a gold ring from his finger. 'This,' he said, 'being the king of metals, gold, is in every respect appropriate to your illustrious race.'

The Kabaka subsequently played a cat-and-mouse game with Speke—cordial one day, refusing to see him the next, and fleecing him little by little of cloth, beads, guns and ammunition.

Speke meanwhile—to his shame—taught the Kabaka how to shoot at cows and sitting marabou storks. He ingratiated himself with the Queen Mother ('her royal corpulence') who was amused by his flattery and drank *pombe* with him; and after a good deal of nagging he got himself respectably lodged inside the palace.

Speke's difficulty, as he put it, was 'how to manage these haughty, capricious blacks'. The intricacies of court etiquette and the Kabaka's rapidly changing moods bewildered him. After much argument he managed to negotiate food for his men (who at first had been let loose on the plantain groves, which led to brawls). He took two girls to keep him company (but soon got rid of them), he hung on to his compass, which the Kabaka coveted, and he patiently waited for Grant to rejoin him.

Speke eventually got what he wanted. With a parting gift of sixty cows, fourteen goats, ten loads of butter, coffee, tobacco, and one hundred sheets of bark cloth, he and Grant were given leave to march towards the Nile at Urondogani and then northwards into Bunyoro. The Kabaka and his women turned out to see them off. The last Speke saw of them was the Kabaka walking with gigantic strides up a hill with a pretty girl crying 'Bana! Bana!' trotting after him.

NOTE

Sleeping sickness has not been entirely eradicated from Uganda. According to the *Uganda Atlas of Disease Distribution* (Makerere Univ. Coll., 1968), since 1960 the two main foci of disease have been Busoga and Bukedi Districts, and the West Nile District. In its note on bilharzia, this publication states: 'Observations on yacht club members, swimmers, and sporting fishermen at Jinja, Kampala, and Entebbe showed over 15% infected." Vector host snails appear to be absent from Lake Nabugabo (Masaka), but Lake Bunyoni (Kigezi) is infected, A further note states that gonorrhoea is now the most prevalent venereal disease in Uganda. A recent investigation (1963) estimated that 'half of Ganda women are made sterile from gonorrhoea by the age of 30'! In a survey (1961) of 1,000 consecutive VD patients attending Mulago Hospital, Kampala, only 41 cases of syphilis, all primary, were found. Finally, Ministry of Health returns show that there are over 30,000 cases of leprosy under treatment at present. It is thought that the number of disabled lepers in Uganda is about 70,000.

INDEX